SYNCONOMY

Also by Joseph A. DiVanna:

Redefining Financial Services: The New Renaissance in Value Propositions
Thinking Beyond Technology: Creating New Value in Business

SYNCONOMY

Adding value in a world of continuously connected business

Joseph A. DiVanna

First published 2003 by
PALGRAVE MACMILLAN
Houndmills, Basingstoke, Hampshire RG21 6XS and
175 Fifth Avenue, New York, N.Y. 10010
Companies and representatives throughout the world

PALGRAVE MACMILLAN is the global academic imprint of the Palgrave Macmillan division of St. Martin's Press, LLC and of Palgrave Macmillan Ltd. Macmillan® is a registered trademark in the United States, United Kingdom and other countries. Palgrave is a registered trademark in the European Union and other countries.

ISBN 1–4039–1115–0

This book is printed on paper suitable for recycling and made from fully managed and sustained forest sources.

A catalogue record for this book is available from the British Library.

A catalog record for this book is available from the Library of Congress.

Editing and origination by Aardvark Editorial, Mendham, Suffolk

10 9 8 7 6 5 4 3 2 1
12 11 10 09 08 07 06 05 04 03

Printed and bound in Great Britain by
Creative Print & Design (Wales), Ebbw Vale

To my Brazilian in-laws, Vania and Marco de Noronha, whose kind support has made many new things possible in my life, including writing.

To my adopted grandmother, Natalia, who endeavours patiently to teach me classical Brazilian cooking through a barrier of language.

And once again to my wife Isabel, without whose help writing would be impossible.

CONTENTS

LIST OF FIGURES AND TABLES

Figures

Tables

In my book *Redefining Financial Services*, I discussed a concept which I called 'synconomy'. In the context of financial services, 'synconomy' was used to describe the business condition emerging from the convergence of globalization, disintermediation and the continual advance of technology on the processes of business.[1] This triumvirate of forces, mostly beyond the control of any individual corporation, alters not only the performance of industrial business entities, but also institutes a fundamental change in how corporate performance is measured. The socio-economic and technological environment that is a synconomy is not, however, limited to financial services; it is the very nature of business in the twenty-first century.

If given a more formal definition, 'synconomy' can be described as the condition in which business processes interoperating between geographically dispersed corporate business partners are directly influenced by culture, collaborative actions, co-opetition and the generation of value which can be attributed to the synergistic relationship between internal business processes and macro-level economic networks. The capabilities and productive output of these combined organizations and their underlying business processes are greater than the sum of its parts. It can be said that in a synconomy, the actions of these combined assets develop, over time, the capability to act independently of the external forces which traditionally shape corporate behaviour. Simply, synconomy exists when companies operate synergistically in a network of value to generate a value proposition or output greater than the one which can be achieved by the sum of the individual organizations.

Although synconomy could be considered a relativity new business phenomenon, in fact its origins are deeply rooted in the behaviour exhibited by business over the centuries, which today is accelerated to new levels particularly because of technological innovations. During the dot-com phenomena, Porter steadfastly professed that the goals of business have consistently been the same: to generate sustained profits. As Porter

and Skapinker put it: 'In our quest to see how the Internet is different, we
have failed to see how the Internet is the same.'[2] Keeping this in mind, to
understand synconomy is to look at the technology as a change in the
means of production, distribution and methods of commerce, and not as
the establishment of a fundamentally new economy. In this sense, the
economics of the world and the activities of business may have grown
more complex as time has passed, but the observation of past economic
systems still provides valuable insights into our modern business behaviour. What is different about business in the twenty-first century is that
every firm has the means to conduct business in all parts of the world, to
forge relationships with business partners, customers and suppliers on an
unprecedented scale. Most importantly, businesses, regardless of their size,
can now alter their value propositions to either reflect changes in their
markets or specialize to fill an emerging market need at a speed barely
imaginable by the previous generation of business. Technology has given
the opportunity to engage customers globally, form new relationships and
interact with the economic activities of every nation state, ultimately
forming transnational business entities which are collections of specialized
competencies operating synergistically in a network of value.

The manifold implications of a synergistic relationship between
internal business processes and global economic systems mean that they
cannot all be covered within the confines of a single book. Furthermore, it
would be naive to think that the premise of corporations interoperating
within a connected global technological framework can be fully explored
and its outcome predicted now, during the birth of this phenomenon. The
intent of this book is twofold: first, to explore the nature of the global
factors influencing today's businesses, leading them to develop new
competitive strategies and, second, to stimulate discussion within the
business and academic communities which will lead to increased levels of
research along the lines of business in the new transnational environment.
In both cases, these issues must be understood by business executives and
professionals at all levels in order to put them in the context of an established global business agenda. The influence of local or regional socioeconomic factors on global business has to be addressed by organizations in
order to meet the challenges presented by a connected global economy.
Changing consumer demands, political motivations, economic uncertainty
and social factors are exerting greater competitive pressures on organizations, rendering business models and value propositions transparent or of
little perceived value to customers. The media hype of the 1990s generated by the extolled benefits of the Internet has made terms such as 'intermediary' or 'traditional middleman' synonymous with 'no value added'.

Corporations must now rethink how they add value within their respective industries and, more importantly, how they deliver customer value in a global business environment. That said, the biggest influencing factor on business today is the process of change itself, the speed at which change occurs and the pace at which the factors influencing and accelerating global business change, such as the advance of technology, the rising influence of culture and consumer behaviour. As Eisenberg states:

> In the past, change was predictable, incremental, and evolutionary. In other words, it was linear. In modern times, however, change is the opposite: it's 'nonlinear'. It's unpredictable, rapid, and revolutionary. Therefore, it's considerably more challenging.[3]

The objective of this book is to provide organizations with insights into a variety of issues which companies must now consider in order to remain competitive in the changing, globally connected economy. Enthusiastically, it is proposed that achieving new competitive levels can be accomplished by developing an understanding of the synergistic relationship between a corporation's value proposition (represented by the internal business processes it employs to deliver the firm's output) and the macro-level whole system (represented by the global economic industry in which it operates). Sensing external market factors and interpreting the trends using a multicultural lens enables firms to correlate the direct influence of these forces on internal business process change. Simply, individuals must learn to interpret external global factors and put them into a context which is meaningful to a firm's value proposition.

Chapter 1 explores the new corporate globality made possible by the relentless advance of computer and telecommunications technologies. Indeed, to many organizations, technology has become not simply a mechanism to conduct business, but a business in its own right. Technology's use and application by globally minded people contributes to three factors that will shape business activity in the next decade: a re-examination of a firm's value proposition; the structure of an organization; and the level of economic collaboration between geographically distant corporations, peoples and nation states. Chapter 1 asks: what has changed and why are firms suddenly global?

In Chapter 2, the reader is invited to consider the relativity of a firm's value proposition to generate viable products in a global economy. What is perceived as valuable by one culture (or group of consumers) may be less valuable or valueless to another. In a synconomy, the generation of value is no longer the activity of a single autonomous business, but the orchest-

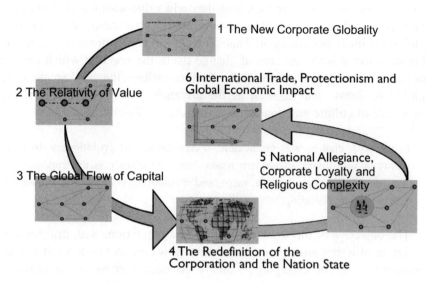

1 The New Corporate Globality

6 International Trade, Protectionism and Global Economic Impact

2 The Relativity of Value

5 National Allegiance, Corporate Loyalty and Religious Complexity

3 The Global Flow of Capital

4 The Redefinition of the Corporation and the Nation State

Figure 0.1 The structure of the book

ration of partnerships, alliances and affiliations which provide resources whose combined capabilities are greater than the individual parts. In the global environment, the distance between the disparate centres of competency can be reduced by advances in technology such as video teleconferencing and collaborative applications. Although these technologies have been available for a number of years, organizations have yet to realize the full potential of these mechanisms to alter profitability in a networked world. Furthermore, the bundled capabilities – or new competencies – made possible by new technology require a fundamental rethinking of leadership and organizational design. Chapter 2 asks: is what we make valuable to the whole world, and if so, how can we engage partners and technology to achieve our goals?

Chapter 3 reveals that the factors influencing changes in global business activity also facilitate a transformation in the structure of organizations. The evolution and subsequent adaptation of hierarchical corporate structures are altering a firm's approach to business process execution. A fundamental change in a firm's organizational structure, coupled with significant alterations in the underlying way in which a firm adds value, raises the argument that firms must consider measuring the performance of corporate activities differently. That is not to say that all previous organizational measurement methods are invalid; it is merely to state that a set of new measurements must be considered to report accurately corporate performance in the changing business environment. Today, the measurement of corporate performance is the return on shareholders' investments and, more importantly, how organizations use investment capital to sustain a long-term growth agenda. In a truly global business environment, the sources of capital investment will be worldwide like technology, thus crossing international boundaries just as easily as today's consumers are able to transfer money between accounts within a single institution. This will require significant restructuring in international regulations controlling how capital flows to companies, the role which government plays in facilitating commerce, how firms are financed in a dynamically flowing capital marketplace, and how organizations will report performance against objectives and compliance with international regulations. This chapter asks: will changes in the world of finance alter a firm's behaviour and how companies are measured?

The central theme of Chapter 4 is the growing discourse on the emergence of corporate nation states. Not intending to be a prediction of a fundamental redefinition of geopolitical social structure, the issues of nationhood, citizenship and disintermediation are addressed and examined in the context of a corporate value proposition. The aim is to explore the relationship between organizations, employees, customers, and their influence on the generation of corporate value propositions. The behaviours of individuals, corporations and nation states – each representing consumer buying habits, company spending cycles and economic policies – have a tremendous influence on how a firm develops products, approaches the market and, ultimately, produces and sells its output. All the aforementioned items must be assessed, prioritized and linked into a cohesive strategy which companies can use to make a profit during the next evolution of the nation state. Although some may argue that corporations are beginning to behave like nation states, there is a fundamental distinction, one which does not always make itself evident, between a company's economic activity and societal development and change. Chapter 4 asks: why would a company want to be a nation?

Chapter 5 makes synconomy personal by delving into how synergistic relationships will influence a firm, impact individuals and act as catalysts for change within an organization. People, or 'human capital', rather than technology, will determine the rate at which a business adapts to the new synergistic business conditions in order to operate effectively within an interconnected networked world. Human capital starts with individuals, thereby increasing the need for people to assess their self-worth, goals and behaviour as the firm changes its posture from local or international to transnational. Ultimately, the point is that a firm's greatest asset, its

employees, should be represented in a corporation's balance sheet.
Chapter 5 asks: how do individuals adapt to the new state of business, and
how will a synconomy affect them personally?

International trade, protectionism as well as other economic influences
and their impact make the basis for discussion in Chapter 6. The rhetoric
of politicians frequently centres on world peace and yet the actions of
governments typically reinforce nationalism, protectionism, special
interest groups and the promotion of self-interest. Corporations operating
globally must now be ever-vigilant of regulations, taxation, social attitudes
and economic policies in order to develop strategies which will enable
them to compete more effectively in global as well as local markets.
Chapter 6 asks the question: how do we synergistically bring together
geographically dispersed resources to deliver value?

The conclusion outlines how synergistic relationships will influence an
organization's ability to execute its core business activities and ultimately
establish a global strategic agenda. Developing a comprehensive strategy
to compete in a global market appears overly complex if all the direct and
indirect factors are assessed and considered. However, strategic thinking
becomes much easier when these issues are placed into what can be called
a 'topography of value'.

As stated earlier, one of the intentions of this book is to stimulate a
dialogue on how organizations engage in global commerce, measure their
effectiveness and, more importantly, deliver value. It is in this same light
in which John Maynard Keynes stated that ideas, issues and observation
are not a comprehensive guide, but merely 'a collection of material rather
than a finished work',[4] that this early work on the nature of business in the
first years of the new century is submitted. Correspondence from professionals, academics and other parties interested in this line of discussion is
welcome and the interested reader is invited to contribute to this debate on
the Internet at www.synconomy.com.

JOSEPH A. DIVANNA II

Notes

1   J. DiVanna, *Redefining Financial Services: The New Renaissance in Value Propositions*,
    Basingstoke: Palgrave Macmillan, 2002, pp. 18–122.

2   M. Porter and M. Skapinker, 'Death of the Net Threat', *Financial Times*, 21 March 2001, p. 18.

3   H. Eisenberg, 'Reengineering and Dumbsizing', *Quality Progress*, May 1997.

4   J. M. Keynes, *A Treatise on Money* (1930). *The Collected Writings of J. M. Keynes*, Vol. V,
    London: Macmillan – now Palgrave Macmillan, 1971, p. xviii.

ACKNOWLEDGEMENTS

Like all writers, I owe a tremendous debt to countless individuals in the business and academic communities whose lives touched mine and, more importantly, whose ideas influenced the formulation of my perspectives on business. First, I must acknowledge once again the dedication of my wife Isabel, whose perseverance in reading and re-reading this text has been instrumental in reducing the industry jargon. I would like to take this opportunity to express my most sincere thanks to organizations such as Visa International, IBM Corporation, Misys International Banking Systems, Parametric Technology Corporation, Hewlett-Packard and UBS in Zurich and all those who have contributed to my perspectives on how businesses should operate in the new century. I am grateful also for the numerous conversations I have had with many individuals who attended my lectures and participated in the ongoing dialogue of how business is changing.

Once again, I wish to acknowledge Richard Buckminster Fuller, one of the biggest influences in my life, whose gift of inquisitiveness forever changed my ability to accept what is already known. The discussions on leadership and the role of autonomic technology were the product of lively debates with Boxley Llewellyn and Roy Frangione of IBM Corporation, who were kind enough to include me in their thought leadership process. I would also like to thank David Thomas of the Careers Research and Advisory Council (CRAC), Cambridge, England, for his thoughts on leadership and the role of lifelong learning in business. Janice Nagourney, of Thought Leaders International in Paris, deserves special thanks for always finding new organizations for me to share my views on technology, business and leadership. I would also like to convey a special recognition to my longtime thought partner, Jay Rogers of the Valence Group, Boston, for his insight on the changing nature of organizational structures and their influence on corporate agility.

I am forever grateful to my publishing editor Stephen Rutt at Palgrave Macmillan for his willingness to take the ideas found in my lectures and formulate them into this text. My unending thanks to Jacky Kippenberger,

Sanphy Thomas and Fionnuala Kennedy, also at Palgrave Macmillan, for their time and patience in assisting the promotion of all my books.

To my contemporaries in business, I once again offer this text as a mechanism to stimulate conversation and debate on the challenges facing corporations in the continuously changing environment that is becoming the foundation for the new order of business. To my academic colleagues in business and management sciences, I wish to offer my most sincere thanks for the numerous conversations and exchanges of ideas that have been coalesced into this text. I have made every effort to include thanks to everyone and offer apologies to any who inadvertently may have been overlooked. To my colleagues in medieval history, I once again beg forgiveness for making liberal generalities in the interpretation of historical facts when comparing the past to the socioeconomic business discourse of the present day. The intent is and has always been to learn from the past by exposing the learning of past behaviour to the often-blinkered perspective of today's busy business executive. Historical references are meant to stimulate corporate readers who may not have had the time to experience the rich insights that the past has to offer.

Additionally, my most special thanks to Professor Patrick Bateson, Provost of King's College, Cambridge and the fellows of King's College for permitting me to continue my research into the practices, techniques and behaviours of the medieval masons which continually sheds new light on the behaviours of business in the twenty-first century.

I wish to express my most heartfelt thanks to the people of the United Arab Emirates and the Republic of China for their unparalleled hospitality during my visits. I would like to convey in advance my most sincere apologies if I have misunderstood any of their values, beliefs, objectives and other cultural distinctions in formulating my interpretation of both regions.

Introduction

In his keynote speech at the Labour Party's annual conference in Blackpool on 1 October 2002, Tony Blair articulated the essence of business in the emerging synconomy:

> The paradox of the modern world is this: We've never been more interdependent in our needs; and we've never been more individualist in our outlook. Globalization and technology open up vast new opportunities but also cause massive insecurity.[1]

Prime Minister Blair identifies the four key factors which businesses today must address: mitigating the risk of interdependence in a connected network of value; how to reduce costs continually when customers demand higher levels of personalization; harvesting opportunities presented by technological progress; and becoming more confident during increasingly ambiguous economic business cycles. Striking a balance between these often diametrically opposed forces requires corporate management teams to develop a greater understanding of the factors controlling the momentum of these forces and, more importantly, of how to capitalize on the phenomenon of continuous change.

The first issue that organizations must acknowledge is that few businesses today can meet the challenges of global competition by operating as a solely independent entity. Businesses are, as Michael Porter defined, part of a value chain of discrete activities.[2] Alternatively, as Hines described, businesses can be part of a set of activities that are linked functionally, forming a value stream in which the functions of design, customer specification, production and distribution are the product of bi-directional sharing between firms.[3] Despite these two perspectives on the nature of business since the 1980s, one must acknowledge that in the evolving state of business, companies are adapting to operate in a more integrated and synergistic way, and therefore these current definitions need to be readdressed.

Businesses in a synconomy fall into a third category: they can be defined as nodes in a network of value-generating, co-dependent, functional business relationships capable of executing a single element of a business process or a process in its entirety. The result of socioeconomic and technological progress is that firms must now actively engage other organizations to fulfil the expectations of their customers on the delivery of their goods and services, irrespective of international geography. Corporations working together is not in itself a new phenomenon, neither is it a product of modernity. However, the higher degrees of interdependent interactions in the execution of core business activities such as partnering and, in some cases, outsourcing of business processes in their entirety require a more dynamic need for control and monitoring of individual process activities. New levels of technological achievement must be employed as a mechanism to measure business processes, assess the relevance of information and monitor the conditions of the relationship between interoperating firms. A higher rate of interoperability demands a comprehensive look at the relationship between data, information and the business processes to which they are linked. The understanding of these interdependencies is essential in order for management teams to develop short-term performance goals and long-term corporate objectives.

Mitigating Risk

Management teams must develop a holistic approach in assessing the value of an internal/external business relationship in order to manage the risk effectively. This is especially true when the relationship centres on shifting the resources needed to fulfil and execute a core business process outside the traditional organizational structure, which is often the case in an outsourcing agreement. Mitigating the risk that may be associated with externalizing a business process becomes even more complex when shifting resources occurs across international boundaries or in a culturally diverse workforce. There are significant risks to interdependent firms when product demand cycles rise and fall because of or during fluctuations in local economies. The higher degree of interoperability makes it critical for business processes to compensate dynamically for these peaks and troughs as a component of a standard operating plan, rather than a reactive reply to changes in cyclical demand. The strategy must be based on providing proactive responses established on information that is projected by the interlinked organization's ability to sense changes in market activity. Strategic business plans often centred on a growth agenda must now build contingency scenarios for periodic reductions in product demand. In a connected, synergistic business relationship, understanding the cyclicality of demand is paramount for effective risk mitigation and long-term viability because the changing nature of business cycles affects not only the firm, but also all the associated partners. As corporate operating units and companies transform into smaller networked collections of specialized core competencies, their strength becomes their agility in adapting to changing market conditions, their weakness being their inability to absorb economic shocks relative to their larger corporate counterparts. These two factors influence not only a firm's ability to compete during economic cycles which may occur at different times in different parts of the world; but, more importantly, the changing composition of business entities alters the nature of economic cyclicality, making business cycles larger in their impact or volume, but perhaps shorter in length.[4]

Balancing the Cost of Service

One of the traditional roles of management has been to direct resources to continually and systematically reduce costs, ultimately resulting in a set of core business activities which are traditionally organized into a process to reach a maximum level of optimization over time. This process of optimization is made more complex as organizations begin to derive greater direct process value by outsourcing, collaborating, partnering and engaging with external entities at all levels to fulfil key process activities. Furthermore, the complexity is magnified as indirect process support activities, such as information technology, human resources and other traditional administrative functions, are also moved to external service providers. In this case, managers must view the firm from a macro-business process level whilst attempting to balance the cost of service by making gross high-level adjustments to the work flow. When management teams manipulate the business at the macro-process level, they simply have fewer pieces of the puzzle to adjust, giving them greater adaptive speed when marching to a growth agenda. Conversely, fewer pieces make individual process and micro-process cost optimizations more difficult in times of lower business volumes or economic downturns, because many of the elements which control the activities are no longer under the direct control of a firm and must be adjusted via the extended business relationship. In extreme cases, when organizations elect to push core functions outside the traditional structure, they sometimes hinder their ability to make rapid changes to balance cyclical customer demands because they also push the brainpower associated with the activities of the process out of the corporation by dumb-sizing the organization. Unless the aggregate process knowledge of the firm is less than that of the outsourcing provider or partner, in many cases organizations are at risk because their ability to react to changes in market conditions and control costs will be inhibited by the relationship between the firm and the provider. To minimize this risk, management teams must demand higher levels of communications between all parts of each business process activity. Senior managers need to play an active role in specifying the dimensions of the intra-business and extra-business relationships in order to protect the intellectual property of the firm and conscientiously manage the collective competence of an organization. Ultimately, with the advent of interoperating, co-mingled business processes, firms must develop operating partnerships in which the specificity of activities, cost controls and shared brainpower are exchanged seamlessly between organizations. Unfortunately, controlling costs is a continual challenge, made more complex by the level of interoperability and rising customer demands for the higher personalization of products and services. Management teams now have to assess the relevance of each process activity with its ability to adjust to changes in the product offering. This new level of complexity is not only the result of the all-pervasiveness of technology, but also the increased pace at which business is globalizing. Technology does offer significant ways of providing a solution to this problem by reducing the risk of miscommunication.

Harvesting Technology

Technology's value is not something that can be attained simply by buying hardware and software components; infrastructure and advanced technologies must be applied to a specific business process to reduce costs, increase organizational performance, achieve greater customer service levels or gain access to new markets. Technology's benefits must be harvested by deliberate and calculated interventions by management, not by the simple act of implementation. Since its inception, the promise of technology has always been to make life better, business simpler, work easier and reduce cost. In the technological surge of the 1980s and 90s, organizations were often caught up in the media hype of specific technologies such as client–server computing, the Internet, mobile computing, biometric recognition and other technologies aimed at discrete functions, and embarked on implementation without assessing the long-term implications of the technological execution and performance. One could argue that firms which followed each technology trend ultimately reduced or annulled the perceived long-term benefits, with each establishment of a new legacy system making integration increasingly difficult. Many firms that embraced the migration of technology architectures from mainframe computing to client–server computing found themselves at a disadvantage when the Internet combined with search engine technologies emerged as a viable cost-effective mechanism to mine data stored in large mainframe databases which they had just eliminated. Regardless of technology architecture preference, it is safe to say that the Internet caught most firms off guard and without a clear understanding of how it fitted into the value equation.

The Internet's sudden perceived technological disruption to the traditional mechanism of business was so profound that firms raced to implement technology and adopt new business models and unfortunately took risks that were more hazardous than if they had done nothing at all. At the dawn of the twenty-first century, the technology surge and the associated media hype of a profoundly new economy subsided, and businesses around the world started suffering from a technology-induced economic hangover. As a result, firms have reduced technology spending and are now scrutinizing every technology purchase, focusing chiefly on cost reduction. One could argue that during an economic downturn is the ideal time to invest in technology and, more importantly, a very opportune moment to reassess the business and its technological future simply because no one else is doing it. Technology vendors eager to make sales are now more willing to structure deals that were unimaginable in the not so distant past. This counterintuitive philosophy is predicated on the belief that new technology advances stem from a disruption in the cyclical business continuum, as observed by Christensen.[5]

The ultimate impact and application of Christensen's 'disruptive technologies' occurs not in their initial introduction into the market, but after the initial hype has waned and their true value is discovered. This is often the result of technology used in conjunction with other legacy technologies or those which have been altered as a result of the more disruptive technology. For example, Internet technology – which is simply a very comprehensive communication pathway – ushered in a frenzy of eCommerce capabilities whose benefits were overestimated by the media and other prognosticators and have yet to realize their full potential. The Internet also introduced the less discussed capabilities of collaborative commerce in which firms work jointly to design, develop, manufacture and distribute products that result from partnership design processes such as Parametric Technology's Windchill product.[6]

If one subscribes to the belief that the nature of product demand is cyclical, with technology following a similar cycle of innovation and disruption, one can then postulate that the technology-led economic downturn in the early years of the twenty-first century is the progenitor of the next generation of business activities in an interoperative network of value. Moreover, it therefore seems logical that investment in technology during the trough of the economic cycle is prudent for management teams in order to ensure long-term viability. Unfortunately, many corporations during the post-dot-com era have significantly curtailed additional spending in technology, especially on infrastructure, presenting an opportunity for less technological regions to advance towards technological parity, as evident in China and eastern Europe.

Economic Ambiguity

At times, the uncertainty of customer demand in concert with general rises and falls in the greater economic cycles make it difficult for management teams to assess the best use of capital to meet the firm's short-term objectives and long-term needs. However, it is in times of economic uncertainty that organizations find the resolve to reinvent their corporations, redesign product offerings and assess their overall business models. Apparently, after finding themselves following old adages such as 'don't mess with success' and 'if it isn't broken, don't fix it', they realized that profitability often requires abandoning the status quo and using change as a mechanism for business revitalization, as observed by James Champy.[7] Companies undeniably tend to come across faults faster in times of failure, and search for someone to blame, instead of simply reassessing their business models. Managing traditional resources, such as people, materials, processes, time and risk, is now compounded by new elements of interconnected process/partner risk, cost of co-mingled services, harvesting technology and economic ambiguity. The new business climate requires that an organization must be able to operate in synergy with other organizations. Business operations in a synconomy absorb changes in demand more easily through coordinated business activities, because their ability to expand and contract is directly proportional to the type and number of external business relationships. It is this co-dependent synergy of business processes and their ramifications for a firm's long-term viability that is at the heart of a synconomy.

The ambiguity of economic demand, coupled with the shift from linear to non-linear business change which Eisenberg identified, is what prompts organizations to adopt a synergistic approach to the markets in which they operate. Synconomy is the state in which organizations operating in a free-market economy act synergistically to deliver greater value to both customers and shareholders than they could do independently. The new global reach of the economy requires that corporations engage both partners and competitors in providing goods and services to a transnational audience. Companies operating within a synergic network of value must consider the rising need to be interdependent with external resources, suppliers, competitors and customers. Yet this cooperative, co-mingled and networked state presents organizations with the conundrum of balancing the dichotomy between competition and collaboration. Firms developing truly competitive value propositions are learning that competition in the new business environment is not a matter of merely opening Internet websites or establishing foreign agents to bring a product to an international market. Long-term viability requires embracing a comprehensive, holistic approach to managing the execution and performance of disparate, globally focused activities.

Management gurus, academics and business practitioners have provided a plethora of ways in which to measure how an organization performs against a set of business objectives. Corporations large and small have adopted, adapted and implemented many of these measurements, often leading to a condition of overmeasuring or simply assessing the wrong things. This is because, as the nature of business changes, the measurements must change to provide adequate information to control the process. It can be argued that a perplexing problem of the new globalized environment is that traditional performance measurements are no longer valid as a way of predicting long-term viability. A corporation's performance must be weighed against measurements that are relative to the external forces that influence the markets in which they operate. This book does not attempt to prescribe the definitive answer to performance measurement; it merely examines ideas from a wide variety of disparate sources and alternative mechanisms that businesses engaged in developing a competitive, global commerce strategy should consider. The intrinsic value of a company resides not only in the production of the products it sells or the services it performs, but in the aggregated value of the process which it uses to harness internal resources (such as materials and personnel) with the external relationships of partnerships, associations and affiliations that it can leverage to deliver discernible value to its customers.

According to Blaine's observations, there is a direct connection between the structure of a corporation, the environment in which it operates and the overall performance of the organization.[8] Blaine argues that changes in environmental factors lead to corresponding changes in the structure that an organization uses to fulfil its business processes. An organization responds to changes exhorted by external forces primarily because of an impact (positive or negative) on its ability to deliver within an acceptable range of profit/cost objectives. The evaluation of external factors and continual reassessment of internal restrictions are reflected in the resulting behaviour of a corporation. Moschandreas identifies an essential position for a management team to take on synthesizing all relevant external information:

> But while all firms are likely to be affected to a certain extent by each other's actions, it is infeasible or extremely costly for a decision maker to consider the possible links and interaction of a large number of competitors. Decision makers are more likely to confine their attention to those firms whose behaviour they believe to have a significant influence on the result of their own actions. It is reasonable therefore to assume that the extent to which firms take each other's actions into consideration depends on the extent to which products are considered as substitutes for each other by their consumers or producers.[9]

Corporations competing in a global marketplace must be able not only to assess these external factors, but – more importantly – weigh their relative value and prioritize their influence on a firm's performance. A firm's ability to perform in a global environment is directly proportional to two key variables: the optimization of their business processes; and the organizational structure which is employed to execute the activities of the processes. Stabell and Fjeldstad establish a framework of organizational topography which codifies corporate business models into three distinct types of organizational structures: value chain; value shop; and value network.[10] The variations in business models illustrate that there is a direct relationship between the structure of an organization and its inherent ability to perform primary business processes, as well as the approach the organization takes in adapting to changing market conditions. This correlation between organizational structure and performance puts into context the effect of internal and external factors on an organization's ability to perform.

Corporate performance is thus relative to a firm's ability to harness resources wherever they are located, optimize its business processes, and counter a new competitive challenge, or both. Worldwide, business activity is moving at an ever-increasing speed as a direct result of continual technological innovations and consumers' desires for international goods. A firm's ability to compete in the changing global environment is no longer simply a matter of rapidly reacting to changes in consumer demand; corporations must now develop and master the ability to interpret information on global and regional economic conditions in order to develop proactive strategic actions. This shift from reactive tactical thinking to proactive strategic thinking raises the question: why does one organization fail and another appear to be successful even though both were equipped with the same technology and similar business models?

Although history is not an accurate predictor of the future performance of a corporation or the market in which it operates, a historical perspective is necessary to consider the cyclicality of the demand for goods and services and, ultimately, the value proposition that a firm brings to the market. Looking into the past is beneficial to corporations because it helps them to establish benchmarks against which the organization can be measured and, more importantly, provides valuable insights into what not to do again. For centuries, economists, academics and historians have reminded us that the rise and fall of business activity is part of the larger cycle of global business. Yet, as people within a corporation and as individuals, we often ignore this market cyclicality, such as investing in the wrong stock at the wrong time.

Business Cycles

During times of economic prosperity, when the cycle of business is reaching its peak, business management teams concentrate on continuous growth as executives marshal their resources, making growth the main focus of how the firm will provide a return on investment to its shareholders. When markets make corrections and the level of business activity approaches its cyclical trough, thus creating an economic drought, individual investors and consumers tend to be psychologically devastated, and management teams shift from growth to maniacal cost savings. Ironically, management teams and investors are faced with the same suite of questions and hard decisions at each extreme of the business economic cycle, forgetting its cyclical nature. For management teams, the perceived value in their products coupled with the business cycle determines where resources are committed to achieve their goals and produce a return on investment. For investors, the business cycle influences what firms should invest to receive the maximum return on funds. In both cases, the process of investment follows the market observation which John Maynard Keynes made in the early part of the twentieth century:

> The conventional valuation which is established as the outcome of the mass psychology of a large number of ignorant individuals is liable to change

violently as the result of a sudden fluctuation of opinion due to factors which do not really make much difference to the prospective yield, since there will be no strong roots of conviction to hold it steady.[11]

Keynes' observations seem to describe the behaviour of investors during the dot-com phenomena, where stock valuations rose and fell without any apparent link to a firm's actual ability to generate a return on capital employed. Therefore one could argue that an investor's ability to perceive prospective yields is directly proportional to the accuracy and fidelity of the information related to the operations of a firm (found typically in financial statements), coupled with the ability to place corporate performance in the context of overall market behaviour by weighing factors such as consumer attitude and behaviour, product appeal, brand reach and other cyclical economic factors. This analytical arbitrage is indeed a process of assessing a dynamic set of interrelated, complex variables. To the average investor, this means an amount of investment research work much greater than the prospective reward. One could surmise that the popularity of managed funds resides in the fact that the great majority of contemporary investors are basically indolent, that is, the pressures of modern society limit the amount of time available to research each and every investment decision. The by-product of modernity's behaviour for the typical investor is to outsource the activity of investment research to fund managers and other financial agents, who theoretically perform the same level of discerning rigour one would use in making an investment. This behaviour can be observed and quantified purely by the sheer number of mutual funds offered in America compared to the total number of individual corporate equities listed on the stock market. However, a fund manager or investor's ability to assess the performance of a company is directly proportional to the information presented by the firm, the information's accuracy, its timeliness and relevance to the economies in which it operates. It can be said that today's contemporary measurements for corporate performance do not accurately reflect a corporation's ability to capitalize on its assets because they are devoid of two fundamental components: a definable measurement of human capital or corporate brainpower, and an accurate measurement as to the extent of a company's interoperative business processes and their associated throughput. Corporate brainpower has been clearly identified as an asset of modern business, yet its value and relevance to the firm's performance is not reflected qualitatively or quantitatively on company balance sheets. Additionally, as companies develop value propositions that are based on externalizing more and more corporate functions, the risk, management and measurement of these processes are also not represented on either side of the balance sheet. These increasingly externalized components of value coupled with the structure of an organization are an integral part of assessing a firm's ability to combat competitive pressures. The very structure of an organization often enables its competitiveness or its ability to adapt to changes in the business climate. As noted earlier, Stabell and Fjeldstad identified that firms organize around three distinct configurations for value generation: a value chain; value shop; and value network.[12] In summary, the composition of the network of value and its dynamic interdependent relationships with market activity, rapidly changing customer behaviour, a supplier's ability to meet ever-shortening delivery cycles, and a partner's ability to execute specific actions comprise the central area of study labelled a synergistic-economic relationship, which is called 'synconomy'.

Synergy

In this sense, it can also be seen that a synergistic relationship exists between the cycle of investment, or available investment capital which ebbs and flows, and the larger cycle of global economic activity. The flow of investment capital is governed by investor attitude, which in turn results in a rise or fall in total industry output, leaving individual corporations either awash with investment capital, seen during the dot-com era, with an overinflated stock price or struggling to secure new sources of investment funds. That is to say, the advancing and receding investment phenomena can be attributed directly to a shift in the behaviour of individuals and fund managers moving from an attitude of traditional long-term investors to next-quarter focused speculators. This interdependent, cross-purposed, dynamic capital arbitrage demonstrates a cyclical demand curve upon which firms rely in order to fund growth activities. Simply, firms must develop an understanding of the synconomy, the synergistic behaviour of capital markets, consumer behaviour, supply and demand cycles and the international flow of goods, which are all vital elements for corporations to survive in the new connected global economy. Firms must learn to leverage their synergistic relationships in order to optimize their business processes, extend the reach of their products and, most importantly, meet the challenges of the next generation of competition.

Synconomy can be best understood by analysing the market forces that have a direct influence on the profitability of a firm. Market forces fall into two categories, those that a company creates by its own means, such

as product demand resulting from advertising, and those which are
beyond an organization's ability to control, for example a product
suddenly shunned by customers due to association with a greater dissatisfaction, such as a fad or change in fashion or cultural rejection. For
example, the downturn in the stock market's high-tech sector reduced the
demand for personal computers, resulting in a drastic cutback in the need
for semiconductors. Most semiconductor manufacturers are operationally
efficient, with costs reflecting production at optimum volumes; a drop in
volume is perceived differently from a reduction in potential growth,
which has no bearing on the company's current ability to generate profit.
In a classic value chain, the ripple effect of supply and demand can be
attributed to two sources: a specific event that triggers a change in product
volume, or cyclical changes in demand. Nevertheless, in a network of
value, a company must consider these factors in order to maintain long-
term profitability. The synergistic relationship between two business entities
ties and the markets in which they operate must be understood, measured
and monitored in order for senior managers to develop strategic actions
which will be pre-emptive in times of decline and anticipatory during
times of growth. Buckminster Fuller's observation of the unpredictable
behaviour of the whole system dissociated from the output of any particular component is at the heart of the corporate dilemma in an economic
climate demanding synergistic relationships:

> Synergy means behaviour of integral, aggregate, whole systems unpredicted by
> behaviours of any of their components or subassemblies of their components
> take separately from the whole.[13]

Organizations must therefore develop an understanding of their overall
interconnected process and their desired results as well as an in-depth
knowledge of the individual components within a process and their
discrete output. The reason why firms need to understand this relationship
is not to predict when rises and falls in demand will occur, but rather to
develop proactive interventions which are based on anticipating scenarios.
The relationship between the behaviours of business processes (which are
the essential components of a value proposition) must be combined with
the external forces that often influence the performance, transaction
volumes, profitability and labour rates. A firm's ability to optimize business conditions thus brings to the foreground a new paradigm in thinking
about how corporations are strategically directed and how performance is
subsequently measured. Given that, the actions of investors have profound
implications for a company's ability to raise capital; investors must be

approached in their behaviour as case studies. In the case of an investor, he or she depends on the fund manager to assess the economic playing field and invest in businesses that are most likely to profit from the activities in the current state of the business cycle. Fund managers in turn depend on market analysts who research the market and find out which corporations have the best value propositions for shareholders and customers to maximize their profits during the peaks of cyclical business production and minimize losses in economic troughs. The mainstay of market analysts is simply access to information that is credible, reliable and represents the true activities of a corporation and its business activities. In other words, the fidelity of the information that reports corporate performance must be placed within a greater context of the cyclicality of the market and the relative performance of other firms operating within the same market conditions.

However, market conditions are not solely responsible for a firm's ability to compete in adverse economic cycles or during a heavy demand time; market forces create opportunities to which a firm must react in order to capitalize on the resources at its command. What makes one firm excel over another in a synconomy is either a clear value proposition to customers, an exceptional low-cost operating structure, the brainpower of the employees, or a sudden unprecedented rise in demand caused by a change in consumer attitude or media exposure. Put simply, as Porter has argued, the drivers of business and its goals have not changed. What has changed is the transnational context in which we place these objectives and influencing factors in order to compete in collaborative global commerce.

Synconomy and the synergistic behaviour of corporations are not simply about being connected to the Internet. The argument here is that technology is the wild card which in some organizations enables synergistic behaviour, whilst in others it hinders their ability to adapt to the new environment. In a global business environment, merely using technology to participate in an interconnected economy does not guarantee profitability, as we have seen in the retreat of the dot-com companies. A higher level of interconnection between internal and external business processes demands a change in corporate behaviour. Profitability is the result of managers and individuals adopting a behaviour that optimizes processes and strategically invests and leverages a firm's two main assets: technology and people. With the advent of the Internet and electronic commerce, the technology industry declared that business was entering into a fundamentally new era of economic activity labelled 'the new economy'. The dot-com collapse is evidence of the fact that the notion of the new economy is groundless and the fundamentals of economic activity

remain the same; although technology has increased the volume of transactions possible within a given time, the number of partners who can
process transactions efficiently and the depth of information on processing
the transaction by new or established business relationships. The true
value of technologies such as the Internet and other advanced mechanisms
to facilitate commerce lies in the fact that they enable a firm to act prof-
itably, perform services at a higher level of quality and capitalize on
opportunities quickly. What is different when we compare today's
economy to that of the 1970s is that because of the arrival of new technologies, global business activities are no longer reserved for large multinational firms.

Profitability in a synergistic environment is a product of the timeless
formula attained when there is a balance between cost and revenues. This
relationship does not change in a synconomy, nor do the fundamentals of
managing a business operating within a synergistic environment.
However, as Nordström and Ridderstråle correctly point out, corporations
in the 1980s and 90s were often sidetracked by the concept of synergy,
when they used it simply as a mechanism to build larger and larger companies.[14] Corporations do not need to dilute their collective brainpower by
trying to be all things to all customers. Firms can develop synergistic
behaviour by focusing on a single product or group of existing products
and, after optimizing their internal business processes, develop external
relationships with suppliers, outsourcers and distributors which provide a
service or competency in a network of value. Synergistic behaviour is not
simply coupling together products that consumers might want or products
that share common purchasing behaviours. Corporate synergistic behaviour looks for products and services that are interdependent and or share
requirements for a common infrastructure. For example, a bank has 20,000
Internet banking customers paying a single utility company for their water
bill. The opportunity for synergy resides in the fact that the bank can
extend its service to customers and act as a buying group to get customers
the best price for water, also acting as the outsourcer for the water
company's accounts receivable. When the focus of a firm shifts to an
external extension of business capabilities, this realignment of purpose
demands a proactive change from the traditional internally focused measurement criteria to a dynamic assessment of the performance of newly
established, externally focused relationships.

These new dynamic relationship measurements must take into account
several key characteristics of business in the twenty-first century global
environment, such as the relationship of a firm in a network of linked businesses, the value of human capital employed and the interdependency of

internal business processes to their outsourced external partners. Synconomy is at the heart of this redefinition of corporate measurement, and synergistic behaviour can be best understood when placed within the context of the cyclicality of business volume.

Dynamic Business Cyclicality

It is during the transition between the zenith and nadir in economic business cycles that companies operating within an international marketplace (or organizations with aspirations of global trade revenues) must consider the factors reshaping the business environment: technology, social realignment, geopolitical redefinition and local/global conflict. In this new dynamic and globally focused environment, corporations must focus on growing, perfecting and optimizing long-term business activities which offer synergies with existing internal operations as well as external partners. Companies need to adopt a forward-looking posture especially during times when corporations and their intra-operative partnerships experience a steady rise of business activity. More importantly, maintaining the ability to act and think strategically to fulfil long-term objectives is critical amidst a precipitous downturn in business volumes. One could argue that an organization which jettisons strategic long-term initiatives in favour of short-term tactical manoeuvres sets a dangerous precedent for shareholders, who will come to expect continual tactical returns in favour of long-term viability. In other words, when things are seemingly under control and numbers are looking good, organizations tend to adopt a philosophy of 'do not rock the boat', and when business conditions take a turn for the worst, firms shift their attention and focus on immediate short-term problems. Some organizations simply state that they do not have time to think of the future and are suddenly surprised when it arrives. In the most drastic of cases, companies often experience this realization the morning after they file for bankruptcy protection.

The process of business change is possibly the only consistent tool that management teams have to control the flow of business, drive profitability and sustain a viable business entity over time. Business change became a more formalized process in the 1990s, when management consultants, academics and, to some extent, industry practitioners began to discuss change as a controllable process and labelled it 'change management'. With the introduction and newly developed understanding of change as a process for corporate intervention, the act of change became a valuable tool for management to exercise when business reached either end of an economic cycle. However, the result of change management that is a refocused or realigned collection of business processes, people and financial resources is itself a depreciating asset. Once the change has been put into place, businesses then relax, having just passed through an often-emotional experience, and forget that change is a continuous process not an event. Business change is unavoidable; it is part of the natural cyclical process of business. Management teams need to adopt a process that continually introduces change as a mechanism to nurture business activities.

Embracing Change

Many firms embrace a change agenda by reorganizing the hierarchical structure of the organization and simply reshuffling people, without addressing changes to the underlying business process, the value proposition of the products or investments required in alterations in infrastructure. In the confusion of the reorganization, reactive businesses hope that the problems will solve themselves. To a synergistic business change is the means to temper the flow of intra-process activity and engage the mechanisms of measurement which monitor business activity.

However, change is not an exclusive mechanism shaping corporate behaviour; technology and, more importantly, society's attitude towards technology are factors that wield a tremendous influence on corporate behaviour. Many technology projects have been thwarted simply because the organization did not want to do the project or because it was perceived as unimportant. During the 1990s, technology overflowed from its corporate confines into everyone's daily life. Over time, the influence of today's technology appears to be leading towards a redefinition of geopolitical and economic boundaries. In effect, the redefinition of nation states, or at least the economic aspects of nationhood such as taxation, tariffs, trade agreements and other mechanisms which facilitate commerce, will change and dramatically affect how business will interact with global economic activities. Naisbitt identified the characteristics of a fundamental shift in the structural composition of the modern nation state as a proportional relationship between the rate, frequency and level of interaction of people within a geography and the optimum number of people who can be self-governed as a viable, financially sound entity.[15] Naisbitt observed that there is an optimum level of population – approximately five to ten million people – who can be serviced by a socioeconomic infrastructure provided by a governing body. If recognized by citizens, this will eventually lead to a realignment of today's geopolitical borders to reflect a closer adherence to a social services ratio. In many cases, countries will become smaller, more optimized in the cost of delivering services and possibly evolved towards a shared infrastructure which will act as a cohesive mechanism for international commerce. This population to services ratio is strikingly similar to the objectives of corporations trying to optimize the process of business. Carrying Naisbitt's logic to its ultimate conclusion, it can be surmised that the ever-rising demand for social programmes vying for available tax revenues follows the same cyclical demand curve but slightly askew of the investor capital cycle. In fact, these two representations of co-mingled economic activity act and react to each other synergistically. This change in the infrastructure (nations) that is the underpinning to economic and business activity, increasingly represented by digital technologies such as eCommerce, electronic payments and eCurrencies, should be a growing factor in today's corporate strategic planning.

This inherent change in the basic structure of nation states – or at least the mechanism that interconnects international commerce – must be placed into a strategic context when businesses endeavour to develop value propositions in a networked economy. This is important for business because the methodology for reducing labour costs by seeking a lower wage geographical workforce will evaporate over time. Time has shown that a well-educated, skilled and ready workforce will demand that wages rise relative to their western counterparts. If, for a moment, one acknowledges that over the next 50 years there will be a dramatic redefinition of nationhood on an economic level, businesses engaged in a network of value which spans international borders must factor this phenomenon into their corporate intelligence. Akin to the economic shift that occurred when Machiavelli developed his observations on the birth of nation states, businesses now must embrace this next step in the evolutionary process of commerce and, more specifically, rethink the structure, mission and value propositions of their organizations operating within a global marketplace. Machiavelli realized that governments must take into account a combination of factors represented by people, cultures and beliefs as new social structures take shape. This is also true in the formation of a corporate culture within multinational corporations and organizations that are participating in networks of value spanning geopolitical boundaries. In Machiavelli's words:

Prudent men are in the habit of saying, neither by chance nor without reason, that anyone wishing to see what is to be must consider what has been: all the things of this world in every era have their counterparts in ancient times. This

occurs since these actions are carried out by men who have and have always
had the same passions, which, of necessity, must give rise to the same results. It
is true that their actions are more effective at one time in this province than in
that, and at another [time] in that [province] rather than this one, according to
the form of the education from which these peoples have derived their way of
living. Understanding future affairs through past ones is also facilitated by
observing how a nation over a lengthy period of time keeps the same customs,
being either continuously avaricious or continuously deceitful, or having some
other similar vice or virtue.[16]

Machiavelli's observations should strike a chord with today's business
executives having just experienced the dot-com boom–bust cycle. The
behaviours of the market, investors and individuals within businesses all
followed an unmistakable pattern that one can see clearly in historical
market behaviour. Unfortunately, it is difficult to assess rationally these
conditions while they are happening, and even harder to institute business
objectives that are counterintuitive to a current business trend. For
example, a prudent business activity during the rapid growth of the
Internet would have been to redirect a percentage of corporate profits and
establish a reserve to hedge against an unforeseen downturn in the
economy. However, investors whose main concern is short-term profits
would have vilified management teams that might have adopted this type
of benevolent business behaviour.

Businesses have yet to realize the ramifications of extended business
processes that are tightly coupled with partners, affiliates and associates on
a global scale. This co-dependent, intermixed transactional relationship
alters the value of a firm positively because it increases the depth and
breadth of a firm's capabilities, and negatively because a downturn in
business activity becomes magnified throughout the network of relationships. This phenomenon is a product of new technological capabilities
coupled with the corporate desire to engage in commerce on a global
scale. However, business professionals often do not understand the
dynamics of this phenomenon. One could argue that organizations must
define the new operating state of business in a connected economy and,
more importantly, ascertain the risks associated with conducting business
in these conditions, while defining the new measurements required to
monitor a firm's ability to compete. The interoperational nature of newly
formed, customer-centric, globally aware business process will be
discussed in an international context. Competition is becoming global, and
so should a firm's capabilities, competencies, products and services, as we
shall see in Chapter 1.

Notes

1 T. Blair, 'Keynote Address', Labour Party Conference, 1 October 2002, source: www. itv.com/news.

2 M. Porter, *Competitive Advantage*, New York: Free Press, 1985, pp. 11–15.

3 P. Hines, R. Lamming, D. Jones, P. Cousins and N. Rich, *Value Stream Management: Strategy and Excellence in the Supply Chain*, Harlow: Pearson Education, 2000, p. 5.

4 G. Junne, 'The end of the dinosaurs? Do technologies lead to the decline of multinations', in M. Talalay, C. Farrands and R. Tooze (eds), *Technology, Culture and Competitiveness: Change and the World Political Economy*, London: Routledge, 1997, pp. 64–8.

5 See C. Christensen, *The Innovator's Dilemma: How Disruptive Technologies can Destroy Established Market*, Cambridge: Harvard University Press, 1997. See also J. DiVanna, *Thinking Beyond Technology*, Basingstoke: Palgrave Macmillan, 2002.

6 Parametric Technology Corporation, Windchill product, available at www.ptc.com, October 2002.

7 J. Champy, *X-Engineering the Corporation. Reinvent your Business in the Digital Age*, London: Hodder & Stoughton, 2002, p. 160.

8 M. J. Blaine, *Co-operation in International Business*, Aldershot: Avebury, 1994, p. 9.

9 M. Moschandreas, *Business Economics*, London: Routledge, 1994, p. 12.

10 C. Stabell and Ø. Fjeldstad 'On value chains and other value configurations', Working Paper 1995/20, Sandvika, Norway: Norwegian School of Management, 1995. See also C. Stabell and Ø. Fjeldstad 'Configuring value for competitive advantage: On chains, shops and networks', *Strategic Management Journal*, **19**(5) (1998), p. 413.

11 J. M. Keynes, *The General Theory of Employment, Interest and Money*, London: Macmillan – now Palgrave Macmillan, 1946, p. 154.

12 Stabell and Fjeldstad, 'Configuring value for competitive advantage', p. 414.

13 R. Buckminster Fuller, *Synergistics: Explorations in the Geometry of Thinking*, New York: Macmillan, 1975, p. 3.

14 K. Nordström and J. Ridderstråle, *Funky Business: Talent Makes Capital Dance*, London: Pearson Education, 2000, p. 133.

15 J. Naisbitt, *Global Paradox*, London: Nicholas Brealey, 1994, pp. 9–52.

16 N. Machiavelli, *Discourses on Livy*, Oxford: Oxford University Press, 1997, Book III, Chapter 43, pp. 351–2.

CHAPTER 1

The New Corporate Globality

American business conference audiences often ask about the nature of global competition and why local and regional firms should care about globalization, culture and other issues beyond their borders. Small to medium-sized businesses in all parts of the world have yet to realize that with the latest advances in technology, all firms are now global, if not by concrete factors such as the sudden entry of a new competitor, then by the implicit realities of consumer buying habits and pricing pressures. The Internet and the latest generation of communications technologies have opened a new chapter in business, ushering in an era in which customers and competitors can come from any region of the world.[1] In order to develop an understanding of this new corporate globality, one must define the factors of interoperability, culture, collaboration, co-opetition and the generation of value that are attributed to the synergistic relationship between internal business processes and macro-level economic networks.

Few companies have been willing to abandon their traditional buyer–supplier and distributor–dealer relationships in favour of a more technologically enhanced process offered by the Internet to sell directly to a customer relationship. Even during the dot-com frenzy, the majority of companies did not want to risk disrupting the existing distribution relationships simply to sell directly to customers, nor was their infrastructure prepared to handle direct consumer transactions. The heralded benefits of technology that seemed inescapable during the dot-com boom have waned, lulling many firms into a false sense of competitive security. One can find a host of business cases supporting the position of technology as a viable alternative to traditional buying–selling channels and an equal number of cases extolling the virtues of maintaining the traditional relationships. This raises the question of who is right and who is wrong, or, more specifically, when is the right time to adopt technology and change

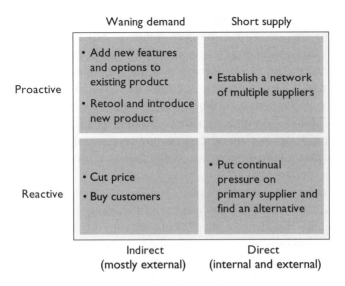

Figure 1.1 Direct and indirect factors

the status quo? Frequently, organizations that made the transition to conduct business on the Internet have not gained higher business volumes or substantially lower costs. The inability of an organization to reap the benefits associated with using the Internet as a medium for business may be a symptom of two distinct problems: the lack of an in-depth understanding of external factors; and the lack of aptitude to realize savings within the internal cost structure. Understanding the external factors affecting the total output of a firm is a complex and difficult task, one that is best approached by breaking down the factors influencing a firm, such as changes in consumer attitude, product obsolescence, new technology or higher levels of customer expectations set by a competitor. Each set of external factors must be further delineated into the responses, either reactive or proactive, that can be taken by a firm, as illustrated in Figure 1.1.

One could argue that the more reactive a firm is to direct and indirect factors, the more likely its core business processes will not be optimized. That is, a company which is continually reacting to changes in the business environment and problems emanating from direct and indirect factors clearly has underlying business processes that are not within an acceptable level of process operating tolerances (such as profitability, levels of quality and timeliness). Therefore, when individuals within the firm feel as though they are continually 'putting out fires', this is a symptom of a more fundamental problem, that of process design. When a business suffers from this condition while trying to engage in global commerce, the condition is exacerbated to the point that product delivery experiences shortfalls, customer service satisfaction levels drop and gross margins decrease. Many firms have turned to outsourcing as a quick fix to this condition, and today realize that, unless a process is known and understood, outsourcing only alleviates the immediate symptom, it does not cure the problem. In a synconomy, a poorly designed business process is magnified as firms develop a greater number of process-related relationships with external entities. Each time the firm proposes to externalize a process, the process and its interconnection points should be re-examined, clearly understood and their performance measured.

Business processes are both the heart of a firm during its growth and the Achilles heel once the business reaches maturity. In the early start-up of a firm, the core business processes are indeed the sole activity of the company. Newly designed business processes are typically simple, with few steps and focused on a single outcome. Over time, these business processes grow more complex as an organization becomes larger, adding layers of management, and business conditions change. As more activities within a business become institutionalized into formal business processes, the rigidity of the processes themselves initially act to galvanize a firm's ability, because it concentrates resources on specific tasks that reflect the business conditions at that time. Eventually, the organization reaches a point at which the structure of the business processes, coupled with the hierarchical command and control bureaucracy, become a mechanism hindering the organization's ability to adapt to any sudden change in the business environment. This condition can be avoided if the organization integrates two key factors into its strategic thinking. Firstly, by empowering individuals closest to the process to make dynamic adjustments within a broad set of guidelines, and secondly, by formal periodic re-examination of the firm's value proposition, followed by an adjustment of the business processes to reflect the new business conditions. The frequency of this value proposition to business process realignment is directly proportional to the rate of change within the industry in which the firm operates. Organizations must assess their capabilities, competencies and skills with the products and services they sell in order to remain competitive. Businesses invariably make a key mistake when they do not ask themselves a fundamental question: customers recognize that our product is valuable, but do the things which we do (business processes) to add increased value to the product have value in their own right?

Organizations fall short of achieving their objectives when they confuse organizational *capability* (that is, the ability required for a specific task in a business process) with business *competency*, which is the condition of being adequately qualified to execute a business function. Although these two characteristics of business sound similar, it is necessary to understand the difference between them. Most organizations have the capability of performing almost any business function. However, few are competent at prolonged profitable execution. This is often put to the test during times of economic downturn. In a synconomy, organizations must be able to turn capabilities into competencies rapidly or engage with competent partners collaboratively to meet new business challenges. One way to think about these two characteristics is that capabilities are the skills and knowledge of individuals which give a firm the ability to do the work, while competency combines skills, knowledge and experience to capitalize on an opportunity.

The difference between capability and competency may seem relatively small on the surface, but the implications of this distinction to businesses operating in a synconomy can be the difference between profit and loss. In order to achieve the level of competency to operate in synergy with other global business entities, organizations must shift from firm-centric capability thinking to network, participant-sensing capabilities. To illustrate this principle, we can examine the difference between two types of sonar technology used in naval warfare. Surface ships use an active sonar which sends out a sonic pulse that travels through the water, hits an object and sends back a returning echo. The time between the pulse and the echo gives the distance or range of the object and the location of the object is ascertained from the direction of the returning echo. Destroyers, helicopters and other listening devices are combined to provide a battle group with a competency for strategic antisubmarine warfare in which active sonar 'seeks out' the enemy to engage it in battle. Under the ocean, there are submarines, whose mission is to move undetected, and which use passive sonar to listen for the sounds made by objects moving through the water or on its surface. Submarines use passive sonar as a means to determine where objects are, recording the direction of the sound, measuring the intensity and assessing the time between sounds. The combination of technologies that analyse sound, its origins and movements give the submarine the capability to take strategic actions in order to move through the ocean undetected. One thing is clear: for businesses operating in a synconomy, like their naval counterparts, technology plays a pivotal role in transforming a firm from a capable producer to a competent global competitor.

For corporations engaged in synergistic, international business activities and collaborative commerce, the integration of business process activity can only be accomplished with a predictable, leveraged, technological

infrastructure. Hammer and Champy observed a direct link between technology and corporate activities in the early 1990s:

> Information technology increasingly enables companies to operate as though
> their individual units were fully autonomous, while the organization still enjoys
> the economies of scale that centralization creates.[2]

How corporations use technology to engage in global commerce is not
a mystery: they link business processes in a bi-directional information
dialogue, employing technology as an ever-improving conduit. The immediate problem with the increased level of interactivity between firms as
found in a value chain or network of value is brought about by two
factors: the advance of technology; and the fact that firms often underesti-
mate the true value of information, as Evans and Wurster point out:

> When we think about a value chain, we tend to visualize a linear flow of phys-
> ical activities. But the value chain also includes all the information that flows
> within a company and between a company and its suppliers, its distributors,
> and its existing or potential customers. Supplier relationships, brand identity,
> process coordination, customer loyalty, employee loyalty and switching cost all
> depend on various kinds of information.[3]

Organizations operating in a synergistic network of value must have a
clear understanding of the role which information plays, its value to the
business processes it serves and the intelligence which it brings to an
organization, such as customer behaviour, product utilization, brand effectiveness and other factors which are used to make vital decisions. If we
subscribe to the concept that information is a valued commodity or
currency in the new global commerce, then its relative and intrinsic values
must be used by a firm to negotiate with partners, collaborate on product
designs, consolidate resources and many other inter-partner activities.
Information and the interactions that technologies such as the Internet and
eCommerce enable transform a firm from a corporate-centric entity that is
part of a linear value chain to an omnidirectional sensing node in a
network of value. Organizations collaborating in a synconomy must be
able to co-exist as partners and competitors in order to serve the changing
needs of global customers and capitalize quickly on new opportunities.
According to Moschandreas's sharp observation, the co-existence of firms
and markets is attributed to two fundamental reasons:

1) Depending on the nature of business, replacing market transacting by internal transacting may involve no cost saving or the cost saving may not be of sufficient magnitude to compensate for internal organizational cost. In the absence of net cost benefits transactions will be carried on under the price mechanism (through market exchanges). Examples are provided by the existence of self-employment.

2) The existence of decreasing returns to the entrepreneurial function will imply that cost savings may decline as the firm expands. The firm will keep expanding up to the point where the marginal cost of an extra transaction carried on in the firm is equal to the marginal cost of the same transaction carried on in the market or by another firm. Increasing organizational cost limits the size of the firm so that several firms may co-exist and inter-firm trading (market transacting) takes place.[4]

However, although Moschandreas identified these two conditions rather well, a third condition warrants consideration, as firms externalize transactions by enabling customers to perform tasks such as placing orders, checking order status and other activities that are traditionally internal transactions. In effect, firms today are outsourcing these transactions to their customers at little or no cost. When corporations self-organize into an international network of value around a specific product or customer value proposition, the depth of the interrelationships is governed by the types of transaction that are processed by the interlinked firms. For Moschandreas, there is a direct correlation between market efficiencies and transaction types that can be delineated by the attributes of the transactions such as transaction uncertainty and/or complexity, transaction frequency and repetition, the number of transactors needed to complete the transaction and asset specificity.[5] Moschandreas defines 'asset specificity' in three categories: human asset specificity; physical asset specificity; and site specificity, which influence corporate behaviour in a network of value. These three attributes are essential ingredients to direct market differentiation because their specialities often dictate the extent to which firms recognize their value proposition. As firms engage in synergistic global activity, they attain varying levels of capability by leveraging technology with human capital and physical assets, often producing a greater interactivity within the firm and to external partners. However, competency is the result of combining technology with these assets within a network of partners, which anticipates a continual reassessment of capabilities relative to the needs of other participants in the network of value, as we shall see in the next section.

Interconnected Global Business Processes

The world of business continually changes, adapts and evolves, based on corresponding changes in political, social, technological and economic factors. The transformation of business during the closing years of the twentieth century was not revolutionary, but merely part of a long-running evolution in corporate economic activity. Often attributed to the advance of technology or fundamental progress in consumer behaviour, the rising global reach of business or maturity of business capability is not restricted to firms operating in the United States or Europe, being rather a product of companies in all geographic areas seeking new clientele. In previous generations of business, someone had an idea, found a source of financing and subsequently started a firm which was typically organized hierarchically with a specific product or service at the core of its operations. In this classic corporate model, social, cultural and economic circumstances and customer behaviour were part of the environment in which the firm operated. These environmental forces shaped the structure of a firm, the business processes it used to create its value proposition, the people it hired and, in a large way, dictated the skills which individuals needed to perform their work. In today's environment, however, an organization can leverage technology to define its own operating environment, giving it the ability to pick and choose geographies to which it can offer its products and services. The new factors that senior managers must now consider are the depth of each activity they wish to execute in the geography they select. This spanning of the physical geopolitical structures of the world creates a new dilemma for businesses operating in a synconomy, that of spreading one's resources so thin that they become diluted. To avoid this dilution factor, business once again must develop strong international partnerships which, once mature, enable them to extend themselves continually into additional geographies.

Business processes are now extended beyond the traditional boundaries of the firm to external entities that also extend their processes even farther by outsourcing and other associative means. During the second half of the twentieth century, a global company was simply one with customers in various geographies and/or an organization with sales offices located in foreign countries, sometimes supported by satellite operating facilities. In contrast, today's corporations are engaged in a newly defined economic globality in which customer demand must be met regardless of geography and the process of business must be clearly understood in order to perform within profit objectives. Business

processes which were traditionally contained within the firm are being
outsourced, or performed by partnerships and affiliates, creating a technologically networked business activity, nodes or cells of corporate
competence, as Champy described:

> What the world's harsh new economic conditions teach us, above all, is that
> every part of business is now connected at some level to every other part. All
> are interdependent. No part can thrive in isolation. Like the human body, the
> whole is healthy only if the parts are healthy.[6]

Champy rightly identifies that, as companies search for partnerships,
alliances and outsourcing deals, the level of interdependent complexity
between business processes increases. Previously, corporations carried out
business process resource planning to balance resources as transaction
volumes increased and/or decreased. The new interoperative business
processes require organizations to take a much more holistic view of business processes and their interdependencies, incorporating dynamic factors
such as raw material shortages, rapid rises and falls in demand and
varying levels of quality across international borders. Therefore, companies need to look at how their business processes act synergistically with
all firms interacting or providing levels of service which are directly or
indirectly a part of the primary and secondary business process activities.
In this sense, what are synergistic relationships and, more importantly,
how are they measured?

Traditional business and its associated measurements centred on
processes which were often viewed as sequential, with many handovers
between processes. Each handover resulted in slowing down the overall
throughput. In many cases, companies actively engaged technology
simply to automate the traditional view of business and process. For
example, in the 1980s, a small steelworks tried to implement a materials
resource planning (MRP) system to monitor the fabrication process,
measure the process's output and optimize the organization's throughput.
The implementation was burdened with problems because it merely tried
to automate the process, assuming that the process itself was structurally
sound. An isolated handover example illustrates the basic problem: in the
mill, there were two buildings; large plates of steel often weighing several
tons had to be moved from one building to the other to complete the fabrication work; a heavy-duty forklift device was used to move the plates.
The plates were taken to the shipping bay of the first building where their
movement was recorded, and then moved to the second building 30
metres away, where they were inspected and they arrived in the receiving

Network relationships

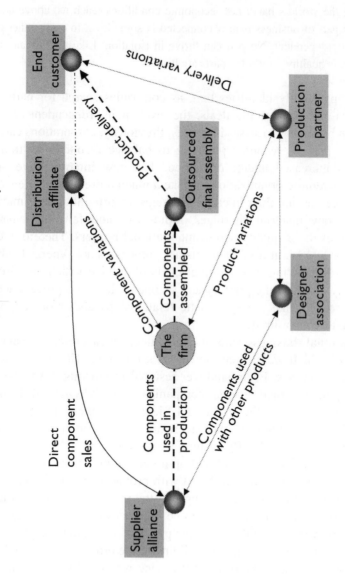

Figure 1.2 A network of value

department, where employees of the second building recorded the delivery. In each case, a computer transaction documenting the transfer took place. During phase two of the MRP modernization project, consultants determined that the process could be more efficient if a rail line was put in place connecting the two buildings. In the new process, a steel plate reached its last production activity in the first building and was automatically routed to the shipping department and the second building's receiving department and then to the appropriate work centre. Since it was virtually impossible for the multi-ton steel plate to escape from a permanently fixed rail line and the person performing the last process activity in the first building knew which work centre in the second building was going to perform the next activity, the shipping and receiving functions were two unnecessary process steps with three non-value-added handovers. Unfortunately, although the technology was capable of supporting the old process, it introduced a new capability which was quickly dismissed because it challenged the incumbent organizational compartmentalization of tasks.

This example demonstrates how using technology to simply mimic the past process definitions and organizational structures only results in marginal improvements. As organizations now enter into synergistic relationships with external entities, greater attention to the detailed working elements of each process is essential to optimize processes which cross intra-company, inter-company and international boundaries. The problem of the steelworks would be compounded if the activities in building two were outsourced to a fabricator who still performed the activity in the same building, now owned by an external company. There is a direct relationship between synergistic business process interaction, the relationship between the parties engaged in the activity and their underlying organizational structures. It is precisely the argument here that we can overlay this synergy onto a structure of relationships that is similar to a network, in which each corporation is a node and each business process is a conduit in which business activities pass, add value and finally are distributed to a corresponding node, as depicted in Figure 1.2.

Participating in a Networked Economy

In a synconomy, technology, data, information and transactions all play a vital role in the synchronization of business, commerce and international trade. Participating in a synergistic network of commerce is built on leveraging technology to facilitate an implied and expressed trust. An implied trust is something that is taken for granted; it is an often unwritten assurance that a transaction will take place although no single business entity is making a claim to do so, such as when an eMail is transmitted. An eMail may pass through many servers owned by many companies on its way to its final destination without any one firm expressly corresponding to the sender with a guarantee of delivery. On the other hand, an expressed trust is a more formalized guarantee specifying the level of fidelity or truthfulness of a transaction, such as when you make a credit card transaction on the Internet using a secure server technology or digital certificate.

Technology has now advanced to the point where it is fundamentally changing not only the role of the intermediary in a network of value, but the social contract of trust, the exchange of value between two parties. The Internet, coupled with eCommerce technologies such as digital certificates, gives organizations the ability to project an expressed trust to a trading partner. Traditionally, financial institutions acted as intermediaries between international companies, offering products such as letters of credit and other guaranteed commerce-related products. These intermediary products provided an expressed trust because they guaranteed, with some degree of confidence, the fidelity and validity of a commercial transaction. One of the roles of the Internet is to act as a mechanism to facilitate international commerce, thus destabilizing the role of financial institutions, resulting in a perceived higher degree of trust in the mechanism of exchange, not the service of the intermediary. The industry initially interpreted this capability as the end of physical intermediaries and labelled the phenomenon 'disintermediation'. As a direct result of the drastic retreat of the dot-com companies, the role of the intermediary has been reprieved because intermediaries are capable of brokering an expressed trust and are competent in providing an implied trust.[7]

Digital commerce technologies, with an expressed level of trust in their certification of value, raise the question of whether traditional intermediaries still add value in the emerging global economy. One could argue that, in the future, as these technologies are incorporated into day-to-day business activities, they will, over time, bring about the condition where a technological expressed trust may circumvent the need for an implied trust. Therefore, it can be said that the value of the intermediary rests in the establishment, development and facilitation of commercial activity, and not in the brokering of individual transactions.

The fidelity (or truthfulness) of each transaction is an essential element needed to conduct synergistic economic behaviour. Corporations can standardize on technological protocols which enable them to achieve a level of conductivity between one organization's business processes and a corresponding business process in a partner organization. This level of technological accomplishment does little for businesses unless the information and transactions which pass between the two firms have value in one of four ways:

1. as data needed by the process

2. as information required to control the process

3. as knowledge forecasting changes to the process or the volume of the process itself

4. as information about the process that can be used in conjunction with another process.

Although the standardization of data has improved dramatically in the past 20 years, many computer systems still have not reached a level of interoperability between software applications in order to circumvent some level of translation when exchanging data with external business entities. High-quality data is needed by the core and non-core business process to achieve bi-directional dialogue for international commerce. Data such as items shipped, reorder points, quality inspection levels, design tolerance adhesion and so on is necessary to inform the work activities on the state or condition of a process, or the transaction between processes. For example, a transaction is generated about the receipt and condition of material upon arrival; accompanying this transaction are instructions on what is to be done and who is next in the chain to do something. Detailed data providing information about the transactions and informing the process of internal activities is synthesized into information. Information comprises various pieces of data that can be manipulated and used to take action within or external to a process, such as lead times, sales volume projections and other elements which help to manage the process or provide information on the condition of each subprocess. Finally, data and information are brought together to become half of the corporate knowledge equation, in the form of databases and computer software components designed to aggregate, postulate and equate data and information against predesigned business process operating parameters. The second half of the corporate knowledge equation is that of the experience and skills of the people involved in the execution of the process. Most corporate databases and other repositories of information, if viewed as component parts of a corporate intelligence, appear as a jumble of data, not a mechanism on which to base an entire modern economy. Sorting out the definition, use, actions and composition of knowledge and, more importantly, how the organization uses this abundance of information is paramount for firms participating in a synconomy.

As organizations become more like nodes on a network of value, creating activities, the flow of information to and from each node on a network has a relative and intrinsic value. To achieve value, the accuracy, validity and fidelity of data and information are critical to establishing and reaffirming trust between global trading partners, customers and suppliers. Therefore, like the physical currency of the international monetary system, whose many currencies are backed by the full faith and credit of each issuing government, information which has been heralded as the new currency for business must reach a high level of fidelity and be backed by the integrity of each issuing company.

Technology controls the speed of information and the ability to process data, information and knowledge. Therefore, it is essential that firms should maintain a technological parity with each adjacent node in the network. If a company is operating at one technological level and its partner upgrades to another, suddenly data may no longer be 100 per cent compatible. Therefore, in many cases, when negotiating a strategic partnership or outsourcing agreement, technological parity must be part of the complete relationship. Without technological parity, synergy becomes much more complex.

The complexity of having multiple synergistic relationships with a myriad of partners, affiliates and associations can be made even more challenging when the product which a company is developing or manufacturing requires a high degree of customization. Pine and Gilmore observe that in a global economy, as more firms create similar goods and services, the more they risk being commoditized and confined into a pricing war unless they can offer customers a way to customize their product to fill a particular need.[8] To optimize the ratio of cost to sales price, corporations must learn to mass customize products efficiently. Pine and Gilmore rightly identify that firms must endeavour to modularize goods and services. This modularization, often associated with discrete business sub-processes, is vital because it allows the organization tighter control of the direct and indirect forces acting on the modular component, thus making it easier to outsource it strategically with an external partner.

The ability to modularize business process components reduces the complexity of applying technology directly to a module of business. However, at the same time, it increases the amount of effort needed to integrate components together or into an infrastructure's architectural framework. Here again, since technology is the linchpin, a clear understanding of how it is applied to the process is a prerequisite for synergistic interaction between firms acting as nodes in a network of value.

Since the late 1970s, there has been rising discourse on the general benefit of technology and its inherent effect on how corporations engage customers, employees and productivity. The impact on the structure of organizations, the processes they used to add value and the ways in which they engage in global business activities will continue to adapt as successive waves of technological advance. The latest adaptation of business has brought corporations to the realization that they must collaborate to compete in a global marketplace, this being especially true in western Europe and the US, where the sudden awareness was heightened during the 1990s by the Internet. Roche points out that the advance of technology continues to reinforce the underlying trends of employment away from manufacturing into information/knowledge services jobs:

> The 'information technology revolution' of the late 1970s and 1980s has accelerated these trends. It involves the widespread use in both the manufacturing and services of the science-based high technologies of computerization, robotics, and new communications technology. Arguably, the development, convergence and synergy of these technologies in the late twentieth century represent something of a world-historical importance, on par with the nineteenth-century industrialization in Western Europe and the USA.[9]

How technology is linked to the creation of value and is a key component in the development of product value is discussed in Chapter 2. At this point, it is important to understand that if products have an intrinsic value and customers perceive that value, regardless of the technology used to create the product or contained within the product, then the question is, what makes our product valuable to a global marketplace? This is discussed in the next section.

Global Value Propositions

Products in an interconnected global marketplace where companies currently dwell have reached a level of operating synergy that enables the easy, convenient and fairly priced exchange of goods and services. However, global companies must now clearly differentiate their products or face a rapid commoditization by other global competitors. Products, in an international context, must still fit the classical definition of horizontal differentiation – appealing to a specific demographic subgroup – and vertical differentiation – appealing to all customers, delineated by cost.[10] To corporations operating under a collection of global synergistic relationships, product differentiation must also encompass another set of variables – global or primary appeal and local or cultural adaptations, which are also discussed in Chapter 2.

To compete effectively in a global marketplace, products must be differentiated in some way from other competitors and network partners. In a synconomy, the differentiation must not only be a clear distinction to customers but it will also need to be reviewed periodically to maintain position against competitors who will copy various aspects of its attributes and properties. In many cases – perhaps some day in all cases – organizations will need to establish a comprehensive global value proposition for their products, services and organizations. This value proposition will reflect the utilization and incorporation of technology into products themselves and in their creation, coupled with an ever-changing set of design specifications based on shifting multicultural appeal and demand. How value is liberated from a firm's business processes, wherever they reside, in order to satisfy the demands of a global audience is the subject of this section.

A global value proposition has two fundamental relationships operating in synergy which must maintain a balance of resources in order for a firm to remain competitive: the efficiencies of global cost optimization versus local appeal or a highly segmented product design. As the independent think-tank the Conference Board points out, the changes in the new world order of business result in firms no longer having a clear understanding of how they add value to the markets they serve:

> Customer loyalty and retention have taken on a whole new meaning in the new economy. Never in the history of commerce have customers had as much power as they have today. The information that is now available to them, plus the speed at which their decisions can turn into completed transactions, have so dramatically changed the dynamic of business in both consumer and commercial sectors that companies are scrambling to understand what this now requires of them.[11]

In order to meet the challenges of global competition, firms must engage in a fundamental philosophical examination of their value proposition and answer the question: are we just selling products or are we creating customer value? One could imagine that these two business results are essentially the same, but in reality they are not. Each carries a straightforward business model optimally designed around a central philosophical attitude towards the customer. Although both are seemingly customer focused, each requires a fundamentally different approach to the process of customer fulfilment. An example of an organization which subscribes to the 'product-selling' approach is McDonalds, which has set the customer's expectations on the dining experience by portraying a consistent brand image and in effect pre-sells the product service experience to the customer. However, although this approach appeals to a variety of market segments, it cannot appeal to all. The elements of value in the product-selling business model are:

- product consistency

- concentration on the quality of raw materials

- standardization of the customer experience

- competitive pricing

- global/local market appeal.

However, this product-selling model is limited in its ability to fulfil individual customer requirements. In many cases, the rigidity of the standardized processes makes rapid adaptation to a customer request more difficult. This is because the processes are often designed for an optimal throughput and the set-up and tear-down costs make it less profitable to cater to individual customer needs. This can be easily demonstrated by trying to order a breakfast item at a fast-food restaurant in the late morning. The store obviously has the ingredients to fulfil the request in the kitchen, but the cost of interrupting the current process to handle the exception makes it uneconomic. The product-selling model sets your expectation, and customers inherently know how to apply it to their lifestyles. That said, product consistency and consistent delivery are the cornerstone of the product-selling value proposition. Although sometimes the customer is treated as a commodity and may be disappointed during the delivery of products, such as standing in a queue, wrong orders, sold-out products or quality at the time of receipt, their loyalty is assured for the most part because of the clear and deliberate value proposition: fast food is cheap. Conversely, in an ever-increasing, cross-cultural world, customers are not always satisfied with the sameness of products and opt for products reflecting their specific tastes or providing them with an experience beyond their daily routine. This is also demonstrated by McDonald's ability to deliver regionalized products such as the veggie burger in the UK, lobster sandwich in Maine, McPizza, crumpets and croissants on the breakfast menus in England and France respectively, and other locally focused specialty meals.

In the 'creating customer value' model, however, developing an awareness of local and regional cultural preferences must be combined with an understanding of market segmentation, in order to focus a product's attributes on a specific customer need. A corporation, such as Dell Computer, which enables customers to tailor a computer to meet his or her needs, can see this process of customization in action as consumers' desires for computers change. A company such as Wal-Mart has discovered that taking a centralized, highly efficient, product-selling model and applying it in various countries creates problems which demand adaptations to the fundamental structure of the model. For example, Wal-Mart's German operation, made several initial miscalculations when it introduced the US model of centralized control of distribution. German suppliers were unable to meet the rigours of Wal-Mart's central control model, resulting in regular stock outages and erratic supply.[12] Benoit noted that coupled with the confusion caused by the introduction of the US distribution model, Wal-Mart created an additional layer of challenges when it misjudged the human element by placing US employees in the top management roles in German stores. The sudden exodus of German employees was exacerbated when Wal-Mart insisted that each German store manager would be subject to American oversight on an individual basis.

The failure of US companies to incorporate cultural aspects in their forays into foreign markets is a topic that has filled and will continue to fill volumes of business books. Arrogantly, US companies have often underestimated the importance of developing a detailed knowledge of the attributes of local culture, and in many cases have been taken by surprise when local people did not embrace American methods of business. Cultural misunderstanding is sometimes reflected simply by a lower rate of productivity in the foreign business entity. A reduced level of production or higher costs are not due to any lack of capability or deficit in the ability of individuals; it can often be attributed to a lack of commitment and investment by the US-based management to educate employees in western business techniques or US methods that may not be intuitive to other cultures.

To implement a global capability using a creating customer value model – which is a prerequisite for developing a mass customization competency – corporations must cultivate or acquire a more comprehensive perspective on the aspects of global cultures. Customizing a product to meet the expectations of multiple demographic market segments within one country is difficult, as any multinational corporation that has tried it during the past 50 years knows. As pointed out elsewhere, Coca-Cola's introduction into the highly fragmented market of India was a famous blunder. Established in India in the early 1990s, Coca-Cola has not been a success in beverage sales, discovering its product at forty-first on the list of customer-preferred drinks despite Coca-Cola's massive initial investment.[13] Coke's miscalculation of the Indian market stems from a less than rigorous evaluation of the actual potential market for the beverage (the bulk of the Indian population is what can be described as 'rural poor'), dietary issues (never to be underestimated) and income. These facts – compounded by consumption preference issues, such as taste and sweetness – further diminished the success of the introduction. From the standpoint of a synergistic economy, the existence of many fragmented micro-market segments made it difficult to identify the actual existence of something that can be called 'an Indian market'.[14]

Attempting mass customization on a global scale is similar to applying a single product across the marketplace of India; it requires a framework which reflects multicultural preferences and the inclusion of demographic data. The ability to apply products to targeted micro-market segments avoids unnecessarily high start-up costs. The overall cost of introducing products into a variety of global markets can be reduced through carefully controlled experimentation even if an in-depth knowledge is not easily acquired from employees or external sources. Figure 1.3 illustrates the contextual relevance of social preferences.

Developing a corporate competency for sensing multicultural social preferences is critical for companies operating in a synconomy. Given that each business entity acts like a node on a network, one must be aware of the idiosyncrasies of adjacent nodes in order to establish a two-way dialogue for commerce. Therefore, regardless of whether a firm is engaged in a product-selling model or is in transition to a creating customer value model, the need to connect with partners, access global customers and interact with geographically dispersed suppliers requires a much broader knowledge of regional, cultural, religious and local issues.

Figure 1.4 illustrates the idea that corporations operating in a synconomy must strike a balance between product standardization and customization. However, few companies have the ability to do so. Additionally, a similar balance must be maintained between the needs of macro-level global customers and those of a more localized group of idiosyncratic tastes, also depicted in Figure 1.3. In both the product-selling and creating customer value business models, the main goal is consistently to provide good value for money regardless of the customer's individual preferences. Handy identified providing good value as one of the prime objectives for organizations operating in a changing business environment:

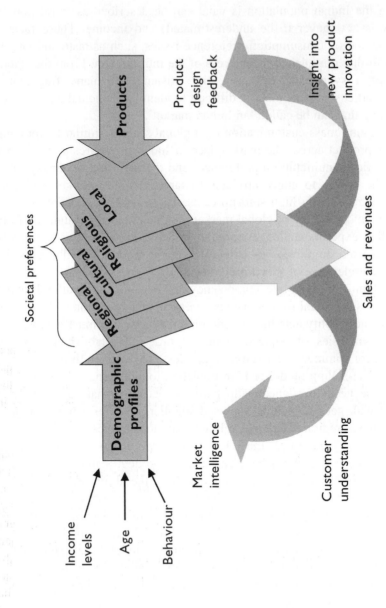

Figure 1.3 Societal preferences

Income levels

Age

Behaviour

Demographic profiles

Regional

Cultural

Religious

Local

Societal preferences

Products

Product design feedback

Insight into new product innovation

Sales and revenues

Customer understanding

Market intelligence

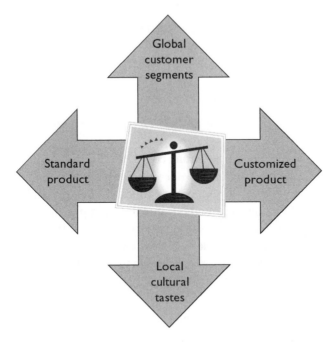

Figure 1.4 Market segmentation and product customization

Business, any business, has multiple objectives which include providing good value for its customers, offering a worthwhile job and opportunities for personal growth for its workers, investing in its future stream of products, respecting the needs of the local communities in which it operates and the environment in general, and, of course, making sure of a proper return for its financiers.[15]

Many organizations believe that in today's modern society a global corporate value proposition can be fashioned by creating a generic product that has a basic appeal to everyone in all cultures. The business press is filled with examples of western corporations, armed with technology, aspiring to sell mostly US-conceived products to seemingly hungry foreign markets. However, these same corporations are surprised when products fail to achieve sales rates and growth figures that often are established by sales and marketing personnel who typically are based in locations far removed from the target markets. In the closing decades of the twentieth century, many multinational firms learned that sagging product sales could be attributed to five elements:

1. lack of local acceptance of the product

2. economic conditions changing, making the product more costly in the local currency

3. sociopolitical unrest

4. changes in trade regulations

5. the introduction of a similar product by a local competitor.

One could argue that corporations could develop a generic global value proposition based on a set of societal values which transcend cultures and geopolitical boundaries. These cross-cultural values are indeed rare but can be explored by considering the following example: the basic composition of a product's value proposition may be equated with the values at the heart of the cultural roots in a historical context. In Keynes' viewpoint, individuals are motivated to save and spend by subjective social incentives. Motivations for saving include:

■ precaution (against contingencies)

■ foresight (to provide future relations with income)

■ calculation (saving now for spending later)

■ improvement (to increase expenditure gradually)

■ independence

■ enterprise

■ pride and avarice.

Impetuses for spending comprise:

■ enjoyment

■ short-sightedness

■ generosity

■ miscalculation

■ ostentation

■ extravagance.[16]

Although today's business leaders have been claiming the rise of a new economy, the Keynesian recognition of consumers' motivations continues to be true. Even when these motivations are projected against a backdrop of a changing family structure (from a nuclear family to a fragmented network of relationships), the basic needs, wants, desires and motivations identified by Keynes have not changed.

If one takes the seven deadly sins as yet another example of primary motivations associated with the basic fundamentals of human needs, weaknesses and fragilities, one can find that a product's primary value proposition must be formed in association with these sins. That is not to say that this model of value is all-inclusive. It is simply a mechanism for exploring the relevance of value. An understanding of these basic motivations is thus essential for developing cross-cultural value propositions. Additionally, an understanding of what appeals to basic needs, wants and desires can be fundamental to interpreting human responses to how products are sold and distributed. A human–technological interface with products is the focus of research at the Integrated Media Systems Centre at the University of Southern California, which is designing technologies that measure the interactions of people with technologies, such as combining facial recognition systems with automated teller machines (ATMs) to verify identity. Using genetic algorithms, consumer buying behaviour can be monitored and measured to determine the overall desirability of a global product along sociodemographic lines.[17] However, the argument here is that corporations should no longer think solely along the lines of demographics, product features and other characteristics traditionally used to sell products to customers. Organizations must build mechanisms to sense customer preferences on three levels:

1. a generic application across cultures and market segments that appeals to the most primary human desires and needs

2. a societal preference level that caters to the trends and preferences within a society

3. a focused individual need or highly refined micro-market segmentation.

On the primary level, the seven deadly sins provide a convenient framework in which to segment product and service attributes. This can also be viewed through a cultural lens, and later compared to ascertain similarities and differences. Table 1.1 looks at the seven deadly sins from two perspectives: customer behaviour; and corporate behaviour.

Table 1.1 The seven deadly sins		
Attributes	**Applied to customers**	**Applied to business**
Envy	Peer pressure	Follow the leader
Gluttony	Overconsumption and a debt-based culture	Product dumping, hedging inventories
Greed	Shifting from long-term investors to impatient speculators	Excessive compensation deals
Lust	Desire and the complex decision process between need and want	Growth agenda fixated only on mergers and acquisitions
Pride	Retail therapy	'Not invented here' syndrome and corporate egos
Sloth	Slow adoption and adaptation of products to lifestyles	Unwillingness to change core business processes
Wrath	Distrust of product or service falling short of expectations	Price cutting, cartels

Envy

For example, take Handy's insight into the excesses of capitalist behaviour in his observations of Asian economic activity:

> Capitalism falters if demand diminishes, when we move beyond our needs and can't be persuaded to want more than we have. A faltering consumer demand was Japan's problem in the Nineties, when the government even considered giving people vouchers to tempt them into the shops. New products and product upgrades titillate our appetites and keep demand alive. So does the desire to have what we see others having, or to have what they don't have. Fashion, boosted by advertising, is an important stimulus to demand, as is envy.[18]

On an individual customer level, envy naturally brings to mind fashion, fads, peer pressure and a host of characteristics of needs based on luxury or semi-luxurious products. If social envy is examined at a granular level, for example, it leads us to questions such as: does any eight-year-old child really need an £80 pair of trainers? Need versus want notwithstanding, it appears that peer pressure is a prime motivator in the purchase of consumer goods, in many cases transcending cultures or ideologies. Although it is not a good example of how a culture or people within a nation state would like to be perceived, envy does have an important part in product appeal.

Envy is not restricted to consumers; it also permeates the corporate environment in organizations which fall into the same trap of keeping up with their competitors, even when they know they should simply rethink their strategy in order to continue to achieve competitive parity. Evidence of envious corporate behaviour was manifest during the late 1990s, when companies without any comprehensive financial measure of benefits raced to develop websites. When asked why, the reply was either 'so as not to be left out of the new economy', or 'my competitor has a better site'.

Sloth

Consumer sloth can be identified in the way in which consumers are slow to adopt new products and technologies and, in many cases, even slower to adapt new technological capabilities into their everyday lives. This cond-ition is not true for every type of consumer. In fact, consumers can be segmented by behaviour into five distinct categories in graduated order of slothfulness: innovators, early adopters, the early majority, the late majority and laggards. In each market segment, a consumer's ability or inability to adapt to new products is similar and follows a predictable pattern influenced by the same buying stimuli.

Although typically the smallest group, *innovators* (being the least slothful) are the first ones to welcome improvements and are willing to try new product offerings. Exhibiting a behaviour which often transcends global cultures, they indicate that they are eager to experiment with new ideas, are often well informed and can afford the financial risks associated with adopting the new product or service.

Customers classified as *early adopters*, only slightly more slothful, repre-sent a larger group of the population and are, in many cases, more socially active in their local communities or belong to organizations that have shared interests. The behaviour of early adopters varies slightly across global cultures but demonstrates common attributes; a higher level of education, in a more influential social class, with a greater diversity of interests.

Members of the *early majority* subsegment begin to demonstrate true slothful behaviour. Typically the second largest group, they adopt a new product innovation only after the early adopters have begun to broadcast its tangible benefits. Customers in this subsegment are more cautious, although not 'slow' in the proper sense, as they take longer to decide on the value of a new product because they ponder its benefits to their lifestyle. Culture, religion and social factors play a greater role in motivating this group and, consequently, it has the greatest variability in product preferences.

The largest subsegment is the *late majority*, who classically delay the adoption of a new product chiefly due to scepticism related to its perceived value. Their reluctance to adopt a new product or technology is often surmounted by a feeling of strong societal pressure, a sense of being left behind. This group has a similar sociodemographic profile as the early majority, but their product preference variability is less because they simply adopt the products of the early majority and so are less of an influence on new product designs.

In the last category, which, as a percentage of the population, varies dramatically from culture to culture, are the market *laggards*, whose slothful approach to technology is governed by their conservative nature, one which can be found across cultures, age groups and demographics in many countries. These consumers are likely to adopt a new product at the end of its value to all other market sectors. Globally, laggards are remarkably dissimilar in their reasons for not adopting a new product and surprisingly similar in their mistrustful attitude towards new products and their perceived benefits.

When organizations and sometimes industries become complacent, one could say that they also suffer from the sin of sloth. At the birth of a company, a group of founders establish a process and create a set of behaviours that in turn produce a product or service. During the life of the company, as the product volumes go up and customer requests become more complex, additional staff are required to perform the work. As the organization grows, informal actions become institutionalized into business processes and ultimately into some form of business procedures or a complete description of how the product is created. This process is documented to reduce the training given to new personnel and to establish mechanisms to monitor and control the process. As the organization matures, these formalized rules become the chief architect of corporate sloth; the operating procedures often hinder the organization's ability to rethink its processes or invent new products. Over time, people become used to the process and are threatened when change is introduced, not because the new process is harder to perform than the old set of organized tasks, but simply because it is unfamiliar.

The net result of organizational sloth leads firms which are continually slow to market with new products to miss repeated opportunities to reduce operating costs because they become more concerned with following the process than with the output of the process. In a synergistic relationship between two firms, each organization must endeavour to balance the adherence to the process with the ability to update the process and the product it creates. The traditional assembly-line approach to thinking about process is founded on building a statistically standard product, changing the least number of parts for the maximum throughput of profits. In a synconomy, the nature of product demand from a global marketplace is no longer static; it is a dynamic process of continual invention and reinvention. Products must evolve and thus be tailored to specific sociocultural preferences. The underlying business processes must be restructured seamlessly and rapidly.

Gluttony

From a consumer point of view, in a capitalistic society you can never have too much of a good thing. Overconsumption of the world's natural resources by western nations is brilliantly discussed in Packard's *The Waste Makers*:

> estimates have suggested that the average American requires, for his style of life, ten times as much raw materials – not counting food – as the average citizen of the rest of the free world.[19]

Forty years have passed since Packard's book, and the rate of consumption has steadily increased, exacerbated by the wealth created by the baby-boom generation. Once again, Packard reminds us of a seemingly American phenomenon that has spread to some degree to other global cultures: 'Most Americans above the really poor like to splurge and can splurge most easily if they can assure themselves that somehow they are getting a bargain.'[20] The act of gluttony is not confined to western cultures, although it is most visible there due to the numerous avenues of media. In many other countries, the sin of gluttony is present to some extent but less noticeable as private, older money speaks softly, with less desire for attention. Nevertheless, the primary need to want more is not restricted to any one social class in the global society.

Gluttony is not always intentional, as one can see in a company's supply chain. In a classical company, the sales and marketing department makes a forecast of goods to be sold during the next period. The sales forecast is interpreted by various people in the production and operations departments, each with a different level of trust towards sales and marketing's ability to forecast accurately. Different departments develop a method of hedging inventory levels in turn. In many cases, managers fearing a stock-out situation of parts needed for the production line will add a few extra quantities in order to take a cautious position in their inventory stocking levels. This methodology continues throughout the organization, often resulting in an increasing quantity of excess inventory and, more damaging, excess cost. Other forms of corporate gluttony are product dumping, executive pay packages and merger or acquisition activity.

Wrath

Consumer wrath is uncompromising. Once a customer's trust in a company is broken, the cost of replacement is almost unreachable. Volumes could be written about consumer behaviour towards firms which have violated a sense of trust or undermined a customer's confidence in a product. In a synconomy, customer wrath is magnified because of the pervasiveness of the ever-present global media, which can quickly tarnish a corporate brand image or perceived public trust.

Competitive pressures often bring out corporate wrath when organizations engage in strategies centring on price cutting or when they form cartels. Businesses subscribe to the concept of developing a competitive strategy that pits them against their corporate competitive enemy and will go to great lengths to steal away customers under a guise of developing product or brand loyalty. What companies sometimes forget is that the definition of strategy is 'planning and directing an operation in a war or campaign'.[21] Noticeably absent from the broad definition of strategy is profitability, customers, collaboration and corporate morality, which are often overlooked in the heat of battle with a competitor. In a global economy, firms that at first glance appear to be competitors can be transformed into new channels to market and willing collaborators if their value proposition is compelling.

Pride

From a consumer perspective, pride goes hand in hand with envy. Customers will purchase goods not only because others have goods which they do not have, but also because consuming, in today's society, is linked to the idea that a person himself or herself is perceived as more valuable due to the material goods he or she owns. The idea of 'retail therapy' is rooted in that of shopping to satisfy a need to become happier about oneself.

In what concerns corporate pride, the 'not invented here syndrome' is typically accompanied by a hierarchy of corporate egos, and creates a condition of higher long-term cost because it forces organizations to learn internally through continuous trial and error. Firms operating in a collaborative synconomy learn that the transfer of knowledge is a two-step process in which an organization establishes a dialogue to acquire knowledge, insight or a specific understanding, usually technical in nature. Firms then realize that they must develop a method of applying the knowledge to the business agenda at hand. Stewart rightly observes that:

> If there is one management lesson that the last dozen years taught above all others, it is the importance of uncovering, managing and improving business processes, those sequences of handoffs and events that snake through organizations and connect the work of one function to another.[22]

The application process is, in many cases, a product of the combined knowledge of the individuals in a firm or it could be called the output of the human capital employed. The continual insertion of knowledge, ideas and insight from external sources is paramount for companies to innovate generations of products, reduce long-term operating cost and evolve as business conditions change. Organizations often hedge the process of applied knowledge by hiring consultants who may bring either broader industry knowledge of an application or a specific technical/scientific skill that is not resident in the firm.

Lust

Unless you have been living on another planet orbiting the sun for the last century of more, you know that sex sells products. In countless societies, the lure created by lust is often incorporated into products to attract a consumer's attention. Sex is often used as a mechanism for lust in two key ways: as a cloak to disguise a poorly crafted value proposition, or in products in which the cost of educating the customer to the applied benefits is higher than simply appealing to a primary stimulator. Although using lust as a mechanism to sell has been a traditional mechanism in western capitalistic societies for decades, it is not widely accepted in cultures that have a more religious or fundamentalist orientation.

Corporate lust or desire can take many forms. However, the most prevalent in recent times is the voracious appetite for corporate mergers and acquisitions, predicated on the popular belief that they create value in achieving some level of operational synergy. However, in many instances, mergers and acquisitions fail to deliver significant shareholder value because of their inability to reach a synergy in which the newly formed organization's combined output is more than either company could produce separately. Sceptically, one could argue that the merger and acquisition activity during the past two decades of the twentieth century was more about testosterone than shareholder value.

Greed

Greed may be the most prevalent force in today's capitalist society, and its presence can be seen each day in almost every major newspaper. Individual greed, as Moschandreas observed, is a component of consumer behaviour that centres on choice during times of certainty or economic stability: 'The axiom of greed: This states that a consumer's wellbeing improves as the quantity of goods acquired increases.'[23] Individual greed is most visible in the rise in corporate executive compensation. A famous example is Webvan's agreement with its CEO George Shaheen, who appeared to receive lavish benefits while investor losses mounted.[24] It could be argued that greed is, to some extent, the underlying motivation behind shareholders moving from long-term investors to short-term speculators. A speculator focuses on predicting the movements in price relative to the market for the security, independent of a firm's ability.[25] Without rummaging through tomes of discourse on corporate greed exhibited by firms such as Enron, it can be said that, at times, greed (sometimes disguised as stockholder pressure for higher earnings) bypasses an executive team's ability to assess right from wrong. However, not all companies that exhibit greed can be said to be fraudulent.

As CEO of Giordano International Ltd, Peter Lau applies a variation on the seven deadly sins to service management. In his observations, organizations commonly commit seven fundamental behavioural flaws during the execution of their business models as a product of their combined corporate individual behaviours. To operate in a synconomy, a firm must strive to overcome these organizational shortfalls by proactively avoiding the development of these less than desirable traits. Lau identifies seven key behaviours:[26]

1. Short-sightedness, described as having an approach that focuses on nickels and dimes over a short planning horizon, often inhibits an organization's ability to meet long-term profit and service objectives;

2. Unhappy front-line service personnel ultimately lead to unhappy customers. Personnel must be managed as an asset, with motivations, compensations and benefits which demonstrate their importance to the organization;

3. Bloated management egos often alienate front-line workers from managers who need continuous customer service feedback to make key decisions;

4. Lack of customer-friendly policies, such as exchange and refund policies which empower employees to resolve customer problems without the need to refer a complaint higher up the chain of command;

5. Disregard for career-building skills development often places organizations at risk of experiencing high turnover in personnel which erodes productivity and increases overall cost. Training and skill acquisition must occur at regular intervals with a eye towards management development and succession planning;

6. Management that does lead by example and fails to communicate on a daily basis creates a condition in which self-imposed barriers are erected between customers, front-line employees and the management team;

7. Organizations that are complacent or satisfied with the status quo face a slow competitive death, not realizing that their market differentiation is gradually eroding to a point of reduced or non-profitability.

Regardless of their results, corporations all start with the same fundamental motivations, goals and objectives. Businesses and the individuals employed by companies do not intentionally adopt the characteristics of the deadly sins as their modus operandi. They merely fall victim to the attributes of behaviour when business conditions meet a variety of problems. Businesses themselves are driven by behavioural motivations, as Keynes pointed out:

   ■ The motive behind enterprise – to secure resources to carry out further capital investment without incurring debt or raising further capital on the market;
   ■ The motive of liquidity – to secure liquid resources to meet emergencies, difficulties and depressions;

- ■ The motive of improvement – to secure a gradually increasing income, which, incidentally, will protect the management from criticism, since increasing income due to accumulation is seldom distinguished from increasing income due to efficiency;
- ■ The motive for financial prudence and the anxiety to be 'on the right side' by making financial provisions in excess of user and supplementary cost, so as to discharge debt and write off the cost of assets ahead of, rather than behind, the actual rate of wastage and obsolescence. The strength of this motive mainly depending on the quantity and character of the capital equipment and the rate of technical change.[27]

In summary, businesses operating in a synconomy must consider all these factors in the context of today's capital market activities and consumer behaviours. Products aspiring to achieve a global appeal must strive to satisfy a desire, want or need that is applicable to all cultures. This does not necessarily imply that products will seek to create cultural homogeneity. Corporations developing products for global cultural markets or taking existing products to world markets should incorporate the fundamental elements of basic human needs, wants and desires into their products and add extra properties to achieve local cultural appeal. This method of defining a value proposition based on primary needs is not a simple guess at what people might like; it requires a detailed sociodemographic awareness and the ability to configure product options quickly and cheaply. A highly customized, culturally aware product can become too costly if not managed effectively. In a synconomy, businesses have the opportunity to provide global customers with products which fall into two distinct categories: culturally neutral products appealing to primary needs, wants and desires; or customized products focused on fulfilling localized individual needs. The true test for businesses and technology will be to create products that fulfil basic needs while celebrating cultural diversity. In some cases, corporations using global partners can do both, and as they develop a network of value-added partners, the structure of the internal organization changes to accommodate the new process, as we shall see in the next section.

The New Structure of Business Capabilities

There is no doubt that today's business world is undergoing a fundamental change. Where business is conducted is a matter of technology, how business is performed is a function of collaborative skills, and what business produces is dictated by changing global consumer demands. These factors, coupled with the new global reach of business, raise the question: if every-thing is changing, should the structure of an organization remain the same? Changing market forces are (and always have been) altering the structure of the organization, if not by design, then by a firm's need to tackle the growing competitive pressures. Traditionally, the operating model used by a firm is contrasted with its organizing structure as a framework for under-standing how value is generated by the activities of the company. Although this method provides a perspective on the characteristics of value generation, in a synconomy, a corporation's view of itself must be taken in the context of a single global market. Therefore, a firm's oper-ating model and structure must be viewed through a lens of a global operating form which reflects its relationship with international factors and cultural environments. To explore this line of thinking, the subject is examined in three stages: an inward look at corporate operating models and organizational structures; an external examination of various aspects of global functional forms; and a view which incorporates elements of organizational structures, business models and their influence on global functional forms, coupled with the external corporate forces that are facili-tating a change in form, structure and model.

Organizational Structures and Business Models

Stabell and Fjeldstad observe that there is a direct relationship between the way in which an organization is structured and its ability to change from one corporate objective to another.[28] The type of business process used by an organization (described as its 'business procedures') requires that indi-viduals should possess a number of skills in order to execute the tasks asso-ciated with adding value to the product or service. One could argue that the structure of the firm may at times be in conflict with its ability to harness its resources on a given set of tasks and objectives. As Stabell and Fjeld-stad point out, organizations fall into three broad categories of structure:

1. a value chain (in which the focus of the organization is the production or fulfilment of a product)

2. a value shop (whose focus is to bring together resources to complete a specified task or event)

3. a value network (in which the capabilities of the organization are a node connecting a series of processes or acting as a nexus in which to aggre-gate processes).

Value chain organizations typically have a time-honoured, hierarchical organizational structure fixed on producing single or multiple product lines. The underlying business processes are, in many cases, the physical embodiment of the value proposition adding incremental value during each step of the process. Porter described a value chain as comprising five fundamental functions: inbound logistics; operations; outbound logistics; marketing and sales; and service, coupled with a set of secondary activities – such as procurement, human resource management, technological development and infrastructure – to provide support to the primary process.[29] An oversimplification of Porter's value chain can be to see all business processes in a company following a familiar pattern: purchase raw materials; perform a set of tasks that add value; and distribute or sell the product, which is the case example of manufacturing companies.

Alternatively, a *value shop* is a matrix structure in which the line organization and cells of specialization provide combined resources to fulfil a specified task or event.[30] Value shop organizations typically focus on single, often temporary opportunities which culminate in a specific, desired end state. This type of organization is represented by a motion picture company which brings together a wide range of varying talents to create a feature film. Consulting companies are typically organized as a value shop in a matrix structure, and can rapidly mobilize resources in response to a client's requests.

A *value network*, as seen by Nalebuff and Brandenburger, is a structure strikingly similar to that of a medieval guild, where individuals are organized in cells of competencies throughout the firm.[31] Each cell acts as a node of capability, providing services to specific business process components or acting as a mechanism connecting individual components as a process, as depicted in Figure 1.5. Cells of competency also act to aggregate other cells and/or bring together or bundle disassociated process components into new processes. A value network achieves its value proposition when it effectively organizes and harnesses resources to execute a business process or exploit an opportunity. Value networks typically focus on fulfilling specific customer needs.

To achieve efficiencies, corporations organized in a network structure using cells of competencies must use collaborative technologies to link with suppliers, customers and other skill groups. If a firm elects to remain in the traditional hierarchical structure and perform like a networked organization, its profitability and capacity to compete will depend on its ability not to simply use, but also to leverage technology to facilitate interactions with other cells of competencies. In the latter case, technology's value proposition must be greater or equal to the efficiencies gained by

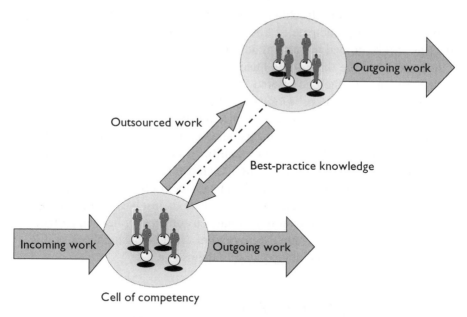

Figure 1.5 Cells of competency

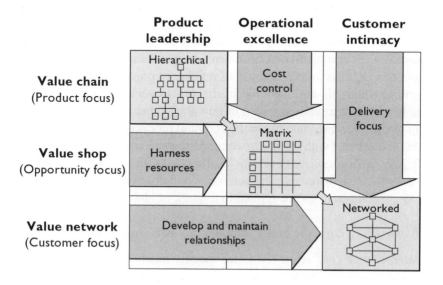

Figure 1.6 Operating models and organizational structures

Source: Adapted from Stabell and Fjeldstad (1998)

moving to a networked structure. If the efficiencies are not present, a hierarchical firm can participate in a network of value but, over time, profit margins will be eroded because of additional costs.

In Figure 1.6, the three value business models are contrasted against a framework such as the one offered in Treacy and Wiersema's *The Discipline of Market Leaders*.[32] Observing the matrix, one can surmise that although organizations excel in a specific discipline such as product leadership, operational excellence or customer intimacy, the structure of the organization may hinder the firm's ability to do so efficiently or for a sustained length of time. Firms trying to achieve customer intimacy using a traditional hierarchical structure handicap themselves from achieving process efficiencies. Corporations that organize themselves into a network of competencies can more rapidly facilitate customer, supplier and partnership relationships and measure the product of the relationship because it is similar to the way in which they measure themselves.

Aspects of Global Functional Forms

In *e-Leadership*, Mills defines global corporate forms as complying with one of five basic functional structures: exporter, international company, multinational, transnational, or world enterprise.[33] Corporations operating in the global environment rarely assess their own functional structures relative to the changing business conditions in a proactive manner. Adjustments to their basic operations at this level often occur as a reaction to a catastrophic change in their competitive environment, reorganization due to a merger or acquisition or, more rarely, because of regulatory pressure by a host nation. Executive teams (if not everyone in the firm) operating in a syncomony need to have a clear understanding of how their functional structures allows them to compete, facilitate transactions, brand products, engage local workforces and interact with diverse government perspectives on commerce.

Briefly, Mills describes each global functional form depicted in Figure 1.7 as possessing distinctive characteristics and different approaches to how corporate competencies are applied to the task of global competition:[34]

1. *Exporter* – a domestic outlet shipping products from a home country;

2. *International company* – replicates specific functions found in the home country to a foreign location, usually sales, sometimes production; few links to sister companies; seldom cross-fertilizes management approaches and is generally managed centrally from the home country;

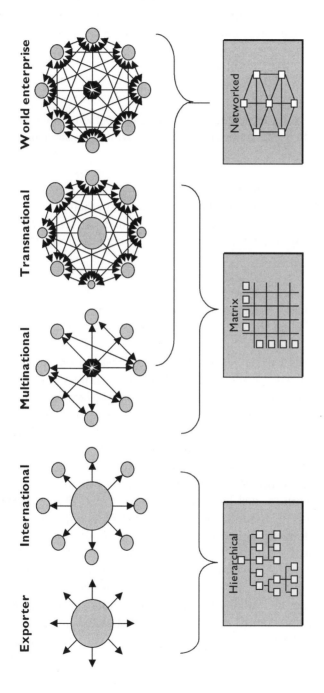

Figure 1.7 Five general forms of a global organization

Source: Adapted from Mills (2001)

3. *Multinational* – clones operations to many countries, links national subsidiaries although there is often little communication between them. A
   host country manager often interfaces with the home country;

4. *Transnational* – distributes specific competencies to many country locations creating subsidiaries and manages them centrally from a home
   country;

5. *World enterprise* – decentralized competencies dispersed to many countries, creates a free market within the firm, whilst considering itself
   non-national.

Mills argues quite convincingly that only two forms (exporter and world
enterprise) will ultimately survive the test of long-term viability under the
new conditions of global commerce, because of their inherent ability to
reduce the complexity of interactions using a lean organizational structure
and lower overhead costs.[35]

Value Streams

A different view on the structure to support transnational process, which
Hines et al. called 'value stream', is described as:

> those sets of tasks and activities required to design and make a family of products
> or services that are undertaken with a group of linked functions or companies
> from the point of customer specification right back to the raw material source.[36]

A value stream establishes a network of suppliers that share some level of
resources, being driven by the 'pull' of demand from the customer origination point. This structure reduces operating costs because as customer
demand occurs, the information on customer orders flows downstream to
each supplier, triggering a 'just-in-time' distribution event. The key benefit
of the value stream is the minimization of inventory in the pipeline leading
to final customer delivery. However, this approach does require an accurate and time-critical exchange of customer orders, product design and
other key elements of information. Manufacturing companies have practised this approach with varying degrees of success in the past, and have
been limited by either their ability to integrate computer software systems
or the software manufacturers' reluctance to collaborate with competing
vendors. However, the value stream and its related approach to management does provide a map to how most organizations operating in a
synconomy must approach the generation of value to customers. Starting
with the identification of customer demand, rapidly assembling a network

of partners and establishing measurements to control the final process, the activities are basically the same.

Global Approach to Structure

When organizations adopt any of the aforementioned global structures (an exporter being a possible exception), cultural values, corporate morality and individual ethics play integral roles in the success of an organization's engagement in the competitive challenges of a single global market. That said, even the exporter must be aware of cultural values when establishing the trust needed for international exchange. As organizations outsource more core and non-core functions, they must develop a clear definition of how the firm will be structured, processes that will be dynamic enough to be rapidly altered to react to changes in business conditions and, more importantly, people who can interpret strategic intent to take the appropriate tactical actions needed to execute these processes daily. The new organizational structure, with its propensity to extend beyond the traditional corporate boundaries, calls into question what must be measured both inside the firm and in the external relationships with partner organizations.

The generation of value in today's business environment is rarely accomplished without some form of business collaboration. How a partner adds value is, in many cases, equal to the value generated by the primary company. This is especially true when the completion of the overall value of the product is solely dependent on the relationship. However, Champy observes that there is an associated risk in partnerships when change in the outsourced business process triggers a re-engineering of the partner's business processes.[37] Establishing measurements within the growing labyrinth of business partnerships is further complicated when organizations collaborate or co-design products and their contributions result in a new product. In many cases, the partnership may include shared amounts of equity in the final product. Regardless of the complexity of the business process relationship, the activities of each organization must be measured, both individually and as a total producing entity. Organizations often tend to simply establish measurements which record transactions between organizations (and within an organization), forgetting that the goal of companies operating in a synconomy is to produce an output greater than the sum of their two or more parts. Without a comprehensive set of measurements which reflects the activities of the partnership in total, disagreements eventually occur when unpredicted peaks or troughs in demand suddenly disorientate the partners. The cost of production is typically a continuing source of concern within a network of partners. To reduce the cost of transnational collaboration, organizations will need to invest in predictable, robust technological infrastructures which enable the organization to co-design, co-engineer and engage in partnered manufacturing and other activities found in their network of value.

One key mistake that organizations are making as they endeavour with partners in a network of value to achieve higher levels of customization with global consumers is, as Pine and Gilmore point out, that customizing a product inevitably turns it into a service.[38] Few companies realize that once they begin to tailor products for global marketplaces, they must invest in a process, system or partnership that can provide service levels comparable with the additional costs associated with the added contact required by customers during and after the customization. One issue rarely considered is the supplementary customer service cost relative to the direction of the customized product. For example, if the product is meeting fierce competition and is on its way to becoming a commoditized product with higher volume and low margins, does the additional cost of service erode the margins faster because of the weight of the initial investment cost? In a global synconomy, this can be exacerbated as multi-language, additional hours of operations and other incremental costs erode margins slowly over time. It is clear that as business continues to evolve, new structures will emerge to facilitate the new transnational nature of commerce made possible by technology. The next section takes the discussion of global business structures and considers the question: does everyone want to collaborate, and are some cultures naturally more collaborative than others?

The Collaborative Nation State

If the key to long-term business viability in a connected world is that each firm is a part of one or more networks of value, then collaboration is a cornerstone to adding value as a network member. If one considers that as corporations evolve their behaviour becomes similar to the maturity cycle experienced by nation states, one must ask whether factors such as culture, economic wealth, environment or levels of education can either accelerate or hinder an organization's progress during the maturity cycle.

Usually, it is understood that people and corporations collaborate because they are motivated by profit. However, one could argue that, in some cases, the extent to which a firm collaborates spontaneously may be a product of its culture and less a mechanism of simple monetary reward.

This raises the question: do some cultures collaborate more naturally than others? It could of course be argued that the success of collaboration or the act of collaborating is directly proportional to the motivation and gains anticipated by the participants. Additionally, one can visualize collaboration between groups of workers, small and medium-sized enterprises, multinational corporations and nation states, given the right motivational conditions and joint goals or aspirations. Reich points out that the motivations of collaboration indeed transcend the visible boundaries of nationhood and corporate structure by either the conscious design of corporate entities and governments or the unconscious force of an individual's desire to be in an environment that promotes success:

> power and wealth flow to groups that have accumulated the most valuable skills in problem-solving, problem-identifying, and strategic brokering. Increasingly, such groups are to be found in many places around the globe other than the United States. As the world shrinks through the efficiencies of telecommunications and transportation, such groups in one nation are able to combine their skills with those of people located in other nations in order to provide the greatest value to customers located almost anywhere.[39]

Reich brings up a good point which many people have not yet realized: during the twenty-first century, individuals may well be able to select which nation state provides an environment, culture and values which best suites his/her personal lifestyle choices. As will be discussed in Chapter 4, the role of the nation state and one's national identity are changing, and the ability to collaborate, adopt and adapt are becoming increasingly important. Today it is said that people are a company's most valuable asset. However, in reality, companies are not investing as much as they claim in their employees' training and skill development. In a synconomy, highly skilled professionals will indeed be a highly valued asset to a corporation, regardless of from whence they come.

A nation state traditionally represents a group of people who share, to varying degrees, aspects of culture, language, costumes and a common past. Although human migration has turned the nation state into a symbolic collection of individuals rather than a realistic group of people sharing common values, there are still some predominant cultural characteristics which make a nation state a clearly identifiable collection of individuals. This brings forth the question: why are some nation states more inclined to collaborate than others? Is collaboration a product of western or eastern philosophies? Hampden-Turner and Trompenaars brilliantly jettison any preconceived prejudice by establishing a cultural topology, according to which cultural characteristics are either universalistic (rules, codes, laws and generalizations) or particularistic (exceptions, circumstances and relations).[40] This categorization is particularly helpful because it assumes that no single culture is dominant and that all nation states have a varying degree of attributes in each cultural perspective. The cultural topology is extremely useful to companies which are becoming transnational, because it allows them to map cultural and social values as characteristics to target markets in which they are collaborating with network partners. Additionally, cultural and social observations should be factored into the strategic thinking of globally focused firms because they identify traits which influence customer and organizational behaviour, as Hampden-Turner and Trompenaars note:

> Competition is easy for American companies but cooperating is harder, whereas for Southeast Asian countries like Singapore, Malaysia, and China cooperation is easy but competing with other teams is harder and must be learned.[41]

Just as some cultures may have a natural social tendency to collaborate, some corporations may be better at collaborating than others, having developed the ability to capitalize on highly agile teams. Teams collaborating within a corporation are a micro-example of the behaviours needed for international, multi-organizational collaborations. However, there may not be sufficient models for cross-cultural collaboration. Businesses have discovered over the last half-century that empowered teams are essential in the global coordination of resources to fulfil business objectives, as Lipnack and Stamps observed:

> For goal-oriented, task-based business organizations, teams are the 'cells'. At work, we interact with others for largely task-orientated purposes. We cannot avoid teaming. We can only team well or badly, consciously or unconsciously.[42]

The key to collaboration is the bi-directional communication of ideas, logistics, information and know-how. Technology makes communications across geographies easy and cost-effective. Although technology provides a means to collaborate, it also creates an obstacle by distancing people from a basic face-to-face interchange of ideas. Is the expression of an idea limited by using technology, or is one's ability to use technology to express ideas the limiting factor?

Organizations can employ technology to build intellectual equity by using it as a means to propagate ideas, discussion and dialogue in addition to simply building a repository of information. The value of collaborative technology is to build and continually refresh intellectual equity in areas such as product design knowledge, branding strategies, customer behaviour identification and marketing intelligence. Collaboration can occur within a firm in activities such as mentoring, using technology as a communications vehicle and intra-organizational product development. External collaboration – in which intellectual capital is exchanged – is seemingly harder because, in most cases, a clear understanding of how the knowledge will be used in the future must exist between the parties. Once goals are clarified, collaboration occurs in two ways: passively (when organizations share infrastructure); and actively (in activities such as multi-company product design, profitability collaboration, collaborative product commerce and direct joint actions with customers and suppliers). Outsourcing, on the other hand, enables a firm to collaborate in two very different ways: simple collaboration (in which the outsourcing provider supplies services which maintain and enhance a specified business process or processes); or complex collaboration, which includes a bi-directional exchange of knowledge between personnel in both parties, such as skills development or a joint effort to redesign the original business process or processes.

Corporations operating synergistically with partners who transcend geopolitical boundaries must achieve new levels of collaboration in order to compete in the world market. An organization such as the Massachusetts Institute of Technology Media Lab's ThinkCycle provides an example of a group that is engaged in supporting distributed collaboration and design challenges, utilizing global resources to solve problems in communities in need.[43] Unlike ThinkCycle's global interests, governments have a national interest in accomplishing domestic goals when they collaborate with business, which is achieved by adapting economic policies which encourage collaboration between transnational businesses. The real opportunity for national, regional and local governments is to foster an environment in which collaboration is an essential element in economic growth, by encouraging joint ventures, among other practices.

Economic growth at a macro-level is a goal rarely understood by shareholders demanding a better return on investment during the next quarter year. Companies must achieve collaboration between individuals, processes and other organizations by using technology to leverage their combined experiences into a knowledge base of intellectual assets that can be exploited into profitable activities. Organizations leverage their intellectual assets when they establish a culture whose philosophy and motivations act as a catalyst in the exchange of knowledge. However, in order to share knowledge and collaborate on an inter-company or intra-company basis, knowledge needs to be defined, prioritized and valued. Davenport provides a good definition of knowledge which a company can use to assess value:

Knowledge is a fluid mix of framed experience, values, contextual information, and expert insight that provides a framework for evaluating and incorporating new experiences and information. It originates and is applied in the minds of knowers. In organizations, it often becomes embedded not only in documents or repositories but also in organizational routines, processes, practices, and norms.[44]

One key advantage of an organization that holds collaboration as its cornerstone may be the fact that information and knowledge are shared formally and, more importantly, informally. Within the corporate structure, a formal exchange of knowledge takes the form of mentoring and the development of communities of practice. In a community of practice, individuals who work in similar disciplines are brought together in a frequent dialogue to exchange ideas and learn new techniques, as discussed elsewhere.[45] To achieve this operational state of intra-learning, deliberate commitments from management must reinforce the value of knowledge to the organization's performance. Additionally, organizations can achieve noticeable increases in individual competency when they provide an environment and/or the means to facilitate an informal network of sharing, which, in many cases, is simply providing technology such as intranet newsgroups, discussion areas, a practitioners' electronic library or Internet-like chat rooms. That said, in all cases, the key to establishing a leveraged, knowledge-sharing organization is to create a sense of trust and institute a compensation system or other motivation to shift the organization's behaviour. Employees must be encouraged to share knowledge and not feel threatened when they share what they know.

This all leads to collaborative commerce, which has little to do with technology. Yet, it employs technology to facilitate electronic transactions, information and data and therefore establishes an irrevocable dependence on technology. One could argue that collaborative commerce has been achieved to some degree by cartels, monopolistic firms and companies that cooperate in establishing pricing schemas which ultimately are interpreted as unfair trading practices. However, not all intra-market activities need to be viewed sceptically to interpret corporate behaviour as malevolent. Typically, cooperative organizations seek out partners for three distinct reasons:

1. to reduce costs by utilizing the combined resources of each firm to fulfil a customer demand as a mechanism to level product demands

2. to reach new markets, thereby distributing their products over a greater population

3. to leverage a relationship that provides access to resources which cannot be obtained independently by either firm.

Collaborative commerce requires that each firm should develop a set of principles in which the goal of the collaborative effort executes the expressed goals of each firm while satisfying the implicit objective of fulfilling customer demand. Collaboration at this level requires a tight integration of business processes, the dynamic exchange of data and the global coordination of people. The nature of today's business activities and increasingly co-mingled processes demand effective collaboration across organizational and geographical boundaries, as Naisbitt points out:

> Cooperation is taking the form of a vast array of economic strategic alliances. Products can be produced anywhere, using resources from anywhere, by a company located anywhere, to a quality found anywhere, to be sold anywhere. This is being done through webs of strategic alliances. One of the reasons for the growth of strategic alliances is companies avoiding getting bigger.[46]

Although collaboration between transnational organizations in a network of value is at times difficult to establish and must be governed by multilateral agreements, in turn it gives firms enormous flexibility in altering their products and services. This is because the initial partnering typically focuses on one specific activity and can be easily modified to engage the larger capabilities of the partnering organizations. Bruce and Ireland noted that collaboration leads to an increase in corporate agility, which is yet another advantage of collaboration.[47]

The collaborative business model is important to companies because it represents the future state of how companies will operate in a synconomy. Today, organizations are already poised to rethink the way in which they collaborate internally as they realize that a firm, in reality, has three distinct functions:

1. to innovate products

2. to maintain a relationship with customers

3. to provide an infrastructure in which the business activity can occur.[48]

Organizations must establish formal and informal mechanisms of collaboration to meet customer demands. Therefore, the single most important competency a firm must develop to participate in a synconomy is the ability to collaborate both internally and with external entities. The important thing to remember is that the key to collaboration is fourfold:

1. an appreciation of cultural values

2. regular communications throughout the organization

3. a robust technological infrastructure

4. a clear definition of the intended goals of the relationship.

Companies must thus codify the factors of culture, communications and infrastructure into a process which can be used to assess the level of collaboration required to engage external partners. Simply, the characteristics of the internal organization can be used as a template for external relationships which can be modified to reflect variations in cultural values and the purpose of the external relationship. Moreover, the criterion for transnational collaboration in a synconomy is to perfect internal collaboration first, and then move on to external collaboration.

The new era of business is undoubtedly one of increased collaboration and transnational business activities. However, collaboration is simply the means by which to accomplish value-adding activities. Collaboration does not generate value by itself; it merely enables an organization to produce beyond the traditional confines of the organizational structure. In short, a company's value proposition starts with the perception of the value of the firm's output by the customer and, in most cases, the perceived value is relative to cultural, socioeconomic and even political factors, as we will see in the following chapter.

Notes

1 See J. DiVanna, *Thinking Beyond Technology: Creating New Value in Business*, Basingstoke: Palgrave Macmillan, 2002.

2 M. Hammer and J. Champy, *Reengineering the Corporation: A Manifesto for Business Revolution*, London: Nicholas Brealey, 2001, p. 67.

3 P. Evans and T. Wurster, 'Strategy and the new economics of information', in D. Tapscott (ed.), *Creating Value in the Network Economy*, Boston: Harvard Business School Press, 1999, p. 15.

4 Moschandreas, *Business Economics*, London: Routledge, 1994, p. 63.

5 Moschandreas, *Business Economics*, p. 67.

6 J. Champy, *X-Engineering the Corporation: Reinvent your Business in the Digital Age*, London: Hodder & Stoughton, 2002, p. 2.

7 The effect of the Internet in its broadest definition has been prophesised as a process merging global societies into one homogeneous culture. Contrary to this popular belief, this book defends the viewpoint that the Internet provides an opportunity to bring the diversity of cultures to individuals, making them more culturally aware and engaging society in an exchange of beliefs and values.

8 J. Pine and J. Gilmore, *The Experience Economy: Work is Theatre and Every Business a Stage*, Boston: Harvard Business School Press, 1999, p. 72.

9 M. Roche, *Rethinking Citizenship: Welfare, Ideology and Change in Modern Society*, Cambridge: Polity Press, 1992, p. 165.

10 Moschandreas, *Business Economics*, p.16.

11 The Conference Board, *The CEO Challenge: Top Marketplace and Management Issues 2001*, New York: the Conference Board, 2001, p. 18.

12 B. Benoit, 'Wal-Mart finds German failures hard to swallow', *Financial Times*, 12 October 2000, p. 25.

13 D. Gardner, 'Slim pickings for the global brand in India', *Financial Times*, 11 October 2000. See also DiVanna, *Thinking Beyond Technology*, pp. 171–2.

14 E. Luce, 'Hard sell to a billion consumers', *Financial Times*, 25 April 2002, p. 14.

15 C. Handy, *The Elephant and the Flea: Looking Backwards to the Future*, London: Hutchinson, 2001, p. 128.

16 J. M. Keynes, *The General Theory of Employment, Interest and Money*, London: Macmillan – now Palgrave Macmillan, 1946, pp. 107–9.

17 Y. Chen and C. Shahabi, 'Improving user profiles for e-commerce by genetic algorithms', Los Angeles: Integrated Media Systems Centre and Computer Sciences Department, University of Southern California, available at http://imsc.usc.edu/research/, November 2002.

18 Handy, *The Elephant and the Flea*, p. 122.

19 V. Packard, *The Waste Makers*, London: Longmans, Green, 1960, p. 195.

20 Packard, *The Waste Makers*, p. 135.

21 A. S. Hornsby, *Oxford Advanced Learner's Dictionary of Current English*, Oxford: Oxford University Press, 1991, p. 1270.

22 T. Stewart, *The Wealth of Knowledge: Intellectual Capital and the Twenty-First Century Organization*, London: Nicholas Brealey, 2001, p. 181.

23 Moschandreas, *Business Economics*, p. 166.

24 The *eCommerce Times* reported on Webvan's compensation to former CEO George T. Shaheen of US$375,000 per year for the rest of his life, as part of a supplemental retirement package that was negotiated before Shaheen began his employment with the company. See *eCommerce Times*, Sherman Oaks: Triad Commerce Group, 17 May 2001, available at www.ecommercetimes.com/perl/story/9804.html.

25 R. Hagstrom, *The Warren Buffet Portfolio: Mastering the Power of the Focus Investment Strategy*, New York: John Wiley, 1999, p. 202.

26 P. Lau, 'The seven deadly sins of service management', in D. Dayao (ed.), *Asian Business Wisdom: Lessons from the Region's Best and Brightest Business Leaders*, Singapore: John Wiley, 2000, pp. 193–7.

27 Keynes, *The General Theory of Employment, Interest and Money*, pp. 108–9.

28 C. Stabell and Ø. Fjeldstad, 'Configuring value for competitive advantage: On chains, shops and networks', *Strategic Management Journal*, **19**(5) 1998, p. 413.

29 M. Porter, *Competitive Advantage*, New York: Free Press, 1985, pp. 11–15.

30 Stabell and Fjeldstad, 'Configuring value for competitive advantage', pp. 413–35.

31 B. Nalebuff and A. Brandenburger, *Co-opetition*, New York: Doubleday, 1996, pp. 16–19.

32 See M. Treacy and F. Wiersema, *The Discipline of Market Leaders*, Reading, MA: Perseus Books, 1997.

33 D. Mills, *e-Leadership: Guiding Your Business to Success in the New Economy*, Paramas: Prentice Hall, 2001, pp. 124–36.

34 Mills, *e-Leadership*, pp. 126–31.

35 Mills, *e-Leadership*, p. 134.

36 P. Hines, R. Lamming, D. Jones, P. Cousins and N. Rich, *Value Stream Management: Strategy and Excellence in the Supply Chain*, Harlow: Pearson Education, 2000, p. 5.

37 Champy, *X-Engineering the Corporation*, p. 133.

38 Pine and Gilmore, *The Experience Economy*, p. 70.

39 R. Reich, *The Work of Nations: Preparing Ourselves for 21st-Century Capitalism*, New York: Alfred A. Knopf, 1991, p. 111.

40 C. Hampden-Turner and F. Trompenaars, *Building Cross-Cultural Competence: How to Create Wealth from Conflicting Values*, Chichester: John Wiley, 2000, p. 13.

41 Hampden-Turner and Trompenaars, *Building Cross-Cultural Competence*, p. 112.

42 J. Lipnack and J. Stamps, *Virtual Teams*, New York: John Wiley & Sons, 1997, p. 234.

43 ThinkCycle, *Open Collaborative Design*, available at www.thinkcycle.org/.

44 T. Davenport and L. Prusak, *Working Knowledge: How Organizations Manage What They Know*, Harvard Business School Press, 1998, p. 5.

45 DiVanna, *Thinking Beyond Technology*, pp. 81–95.

46 J. Naisbitt, *Global Paradox*, London: Nicholas Brealey, 1994, p. 50.

47 R. Bruce and R. Ireland, *Migration to Value Chain. Collaboration through CPFR*, VCC Associates, available at www.vccassociates.com, p. 2.

48 J. Hagel III and M. Singer, 'Unbundling the corporation', *Harvard Business Review*, March–April 1999, Reprint 99205, p. 2.

CHAPTER 2

The Relativity of Value

In this chapter, the discussion centres on how customers perceive value and how organizations develop value propositions which are increasingly shaped by cultural preferences and other social factors. Why one product is perceived to be more valuable than another has perplexed marketing professionals for decades. How can a product which was revered as extremely valuable lose its value over time, only to have its value reinstated at a later time? This can be observed in the fashion industry, where clothes go in and out of style in successive generations or from country to country. The question of what makes products valuable and how customers perceive value has challenged even the most determined marketing executives, frustrated senior executive teams and provided vast opportunities for academics to analyse the behaviours, attitudes and decision-making processes of large varieties of people.

It can be said that organizations harness and combine resources to generate value by adding a component, brokering a relationship and/or performing a service which adds a distinct incremental value to a core product or service. Therefore, in the most abstract view, organizations add value, whereas products simply are valuable. The difficulty lies here: investigating a plethora of business books, it is difficult to find agreement on the definition of value. Yet, there are several definitions which companies must consider when defining strategies in a synergistic economy. The definition which best captures the fundamental element of value comes from Buckminster Fuller:

> If you are in a shipwreck and all the boats have gone, a piano top buoyant enough to keep you afloat that comes along makes a fortuitous life preserver. But this is not to say that the best way to design a life preserver is in the form of a piano top.[1]

The concept exemplified by Buckminster Fuller's life-preserving piano top is that value is relative. Not only is the value of the piano top relative – it makes a good life preserver – but also the individual who takes advantage of it – others might have drowned, not realizing that the piano top can be used as a floating surface. One can infer that a product's value is that of perceived worth, being the root of demand, and in many cases not stable and decidedly temporary. Sombart brilliantly puts the issue of the relativity of value into the context of necessity and luxury:

> Luxury is an expenditure in excess of the necessary. Obviously, this is a relative definition which becomes intelligible only when we know what constitutes 'the necessary'. This again may be determined in either of two ways. We may view 'the necessary' subjectively, with reference to some judgement of value (for example ethical or aesthetic), or we may attempt to establish an objective standard to serve as the measure of 'the necessary'. Such a yard stick is found either in man's physiological needs or in what may be called his cultural wants. The former vary according to climate; the latter, according to the historical period. As regards cultural wants, or cultural needs, the line may be drawn at will; however, this arbitrary act should not be confused with the above-mentioned subjective evaluation of 'the necessary'. In this case, luxury has two aspects: qualitative and quantitative.[2]

Sombart's discussion on the importance of culture in the context of purchasing is extremely relevant to all firms engaging in global commerce and synergistic relationships with geographically distant partners. One lesson learned from the dot-com experience is that in a global environment not all US business models and products meet the expectations of customers in diverse geographies. Different types of product, such as commodities or primary goods, are influenced to greater or lesser degrees by cultural idiosyncrasies. Luxury goods tend to move towards a more standard global appeal because they are equated with power and affluence, making them an easy measurement of personal wealth across national identities.

The Equation of Value

In terms of value and how to generate it, Treacy and Wiersema put forward the viewpoint that in order to create value effectively and efficiently, a firm must concentrate on one of three value disciplines:

1. product leadership (meaning the best product available in its class);

2. customer intimacy (signifying fine-tuning products and services to the needs of customers);

3. operational excellence, which means providing the lowest overall cost.[3]

Most corporations try desperately to achieve a high level of proficiency in each of the three disciplines. Unfortunately, as Treacy and Wiersema point out, firms typically waver between these operating states as changes in consumer behaviour force them to spread valuable resources in all directions. The same symptomatic problem is experienced by companies trying to serve multiple countries in a synconomy, each requiring varying levels of discipline. Companies considered best in class often excel in one discipline while maintaining an operational parity with competitors in the other two. It is in the pursuit of a single-minded focus in one of the three value disciplines that distinctive value is produced. However, even the achievement of a single value proposition can be eroded over time as customer demand changes, as Franczak pointed out:

> While organizations can focus on and maintain their value discipline, consumers have an entirely different perspective – their tastes, desires, and needs vary widely. Consumers can appear schizophrenic – they purchase high-quality clothing, low-cost food, high-service banking, and so on. In addition, consumers are continually changing their mind, making impulse decisions and influenced by a wide range of factors – salespeople, advertising, product image, and other individuals (friends, associates, family).[4]

Companies operating synergistically in a network of value-added partners can reduce the cyclical nature of product demand and dearth by developing intelligent distribution systems that level product stocks, recruiting them to global customers.

The value of a product or service and its resulting value proposition is an asset which must be created, monitored, maintained and, most importantly, managed. Wiersema places corporate value generation into a linear chronological perspective comprising three stages. In stage one, the 1970s and 80s, customers perceived value in higher quality products, demanding better goods for their money. In stage two, the 1990s, customers increased their appetite for better, cheaper, more consistent products, thus leading corporations to focus on optimizing core business processes and new product development. Firms embraced the need to incorporate customers' new demands by focusing on one of the value disciplines which, coupled with re-engineering, inspired many organizations to concentrate their efforts on delivering either the best product, the best total cost or the best total solution.[5] For many companies, re-engineering became the focus of senior management's attention during this time.

Wiersema's third stage comprises our present-day pursuit for a value shift towards developing an in-depth knowledge of customer needs. Often described as mass customization, the drive to excel at meeting customers' growing demand for individual specificity on product options presents new challenges in the way products are ultimately valued. Conversely, a case could be made that the greater the level of product individuality, the lower its intrinsic value as a product for the entire customer base. That is, if a product is highly customized, the perceived value to the individual customer is high, but the potential value to other customers is low unless they share some similar buying characteristics. This dichotomy compels organizations to endeavour continually to strike a balance between standardization and customization. This can be expressed in an adaptation of the basic value proposition formula, as shown in Figure 2.1. Since a value proposition is relative to a target customer, the perceived value can only be delineated by customer segments.

The notion of value or the relativity of a product's intrinsic value proposition is a result of customers' subjective and often illusive perception of its value. In a synconomy, technologies such as the Internet can be used to reduce the unpredictability of demand by allowing customers to order and customize products in advance. The question remains: are customers willing to trade convenience for price? For example, would a customer order a product unavailable for two or three months only to save a percentage of the price? The ratio of time to price is determined by a firm's production cost/schedule. In this sense, on the consumer's side, the value of a product is based mostly on personal preference and rarely on specific economic benefits. A product's value proposition could be summarized as consisting of a varying degree of appeal in one or more of three key factors: convenience; product lifespan benefits; and service efficiency. In the case of industrial purchases, a manufacturing specification or other type of value

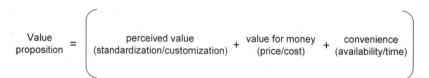

Figure 2.1 The value proposition equation

measurement chiefly dictates that the value proposition should meet similar criteria (on-time delivery, direct application during engineering changes in the product and the ability to reduce post-sales service calls).

Tangible and Intangible Value

Unfortunately, when corporations construct their formula for value, they often fail to consider their relationships with customers, suppliers, employees and partners – essential components in a synconomy. Traditionally, relationships have been categorized as intangible assets because, in many cases, they lack qualitative and quantitative measurements. Organizations create such measurements when they enter relationships such as partnerships, but they fail to reassess the effectiveness of the measurements and create new ones to reflect changes in the business environment which has influenced the activities of the relationship. Kaplan and Norton identify that the creation of value stems from two sources; intangible assets (such as the combined knowledge of the people a firm employs, the technologies applied to the production of a product or the technological infrastructures used to support the process of business); and the tangible

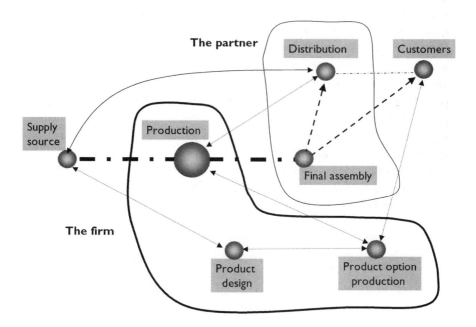

Figure 2.2 The characteristics of a relationship

assets of the firm (such as raw materials, land, equipment and items that have an intrinsic value or cost).[6] Their research indicates that intangible assets enhance a company's value proposition when they are applied to the underlying process of business. An asset's specific value is difficult to assess separately. Furthermore, Kaplan and Norton surmise that the overall value of tangible assets is more easily understood because their contribution to profitability can be measured by direct costing.[7] The key observation they make is that value is created when tangible and intangible assets are combined, producing a product which is greater that the individual stand-alone value of the sum of the component parts.

Consulting the overabundance of publications on value propositions found in most bookshops, one can see that there is no consensus on a formula that represents the basic value proposition of a firm. This is simply because the creation of value is relative to a combination of customer demand, organizational competency, product design, marketing, and the ability of a firm to distribute the product at a cost attractive to customers. However, one issue on which sources agree is that value starts and ends with the customer and the customer's perception of the product's value. Value is perceived in two ways: either a product has similar characteristics to another product, or the attributes of the product are unique. Product similarity provides value by enabling the customer to compare and select, based on the external characteristics of a product such as price, quality, delivery and service, because all other attributes are the same, thereby nullifying the competition's differentiation. When a product is uniquely different, the attributes which make it dissimilar must be compelling enough to justify any additional cost. Factors such as brand identity play a critical role in shaping customer perception, in some cases masking product shortcomings or, in the case of bad publicity, punishing product demand, as Moschandreas pointed out:

> Product differentiation refers to the extent to which products are perceived by buyers to be different. Whether they are different or not, in reality is immaterial. What is sufficient is that buyers believe them to be different. Furthermore, the more differentiated products are believed to be the more likely it is that consumer attachment to a particular product (brand loyalty) may exist, which has important implications for market behaviour and competition.[8]

However, in a synconomy, a network of value built on partnerships offers corporations new ways of leveraging the value equation by assigning value to business relationships – with customers, partners and even shareholders. Camrass and Farncombe argue that trust is the key differentiator, which firms must achieve to compete in a global market, as indicated in their formula for shareholder value which states that:

> shareholder value is equal to customer intimacy combined with the value of networking multiplied by the organization's capacity to innovate, the sum of which is raised to the power of the customer's perception of trust. Simply, shareholder value is generated by focusing on what a customer considers valuable such as the product, service or a combination of both, coupled with a network in which to complete a dialog with a customer. In each case, the value is magnified by the organization's ability to continually innovate by adding incremental value and as a product of these endeavours consistently raise the level of trust between corporation and the customer.[9]

In this model, trust represents three possible variants: a customer's confidence in the brand, the trust between partners in a network of value, or the inter-company trust to mobilize resources effectively to innovate products needed by the increased trust in the relationship with a customer. For companies operating in a synconomy, although it may be difficult to measure it qualitatively and quantitatively, trust *must* be managed as an asset. Therefore establishing an implicit and explicit level of trust must not be left to chance; it ought to be planned, executed, monitored and managed.

The Topography of Value

Another approach to the value equation is offered by Shillito and Marle, who break down value by assigning a relative value to each component of a product, ranking the contribution of each to the entire product value index while linking each specific element of desire to the customer perspective.[10] Shillito and Marle's value index is important for companies operating in a synconomy because it provides a convenient framework which can be used to establish a product topography, identifying which product characteristics are valued in each market, customer segment, geography and culture, triggered by factors such as customer behaviour, local taste, price sensitivity and competitive characteristics. If the value index is applied to transnational product strategies, a corporation can use this data to drive marketing campaigns, adjust the product based on local or cultural product feedback, factor cost considerations within each market and a host of analytical assessments, as summarized in Figure 2.3.

A firm's value proposition to customers must reach beyond the physical product and its life cycle to include the intangible aspects of a firm such as service, customer perception and partnerships. During the product's life

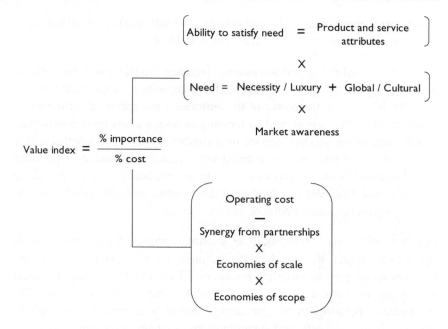

Figure 2.3 The value formula

Source: Adapted from Shillito and Marle (1992)

cycle, the value equation must be revisited periodically to ensure that it is still generating not only value to customers but also to shareholders. A product's value proposition erodes from unforeseen changes in business activity, a competitor's similar products, product unsuitability or its association to some previously unanticipated association with a hazardous by-product, resulting in alienation of the customer base. For these reasons, products and their customer value propositions must be established in the context of a complete suite of offerings by a firm to assess their relative value.

The Value Equation

It is vital for any company operating in a synconomy to define its value proposition as a two-sided equation of value, consisting of a differentiated customer value and an incremental shareholder value. Customers are seeking the highest value for their money while shareholders demand that a firm maximizes their return on investment, as illustrated in Figure 2.4.

Corporations under continual competitive pressure must balance these two seemingly opposing forces by increasing their performance at every

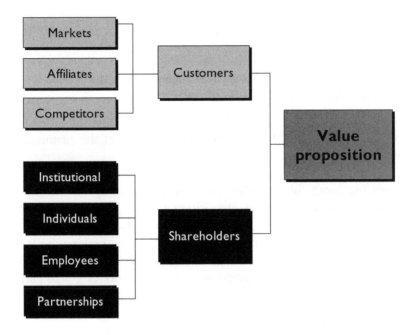

Figure 2.4 The value equation

opportunity. Half the value equation consists of efficiencies in production that are reflected in the price of the product and other attributes of value to the customer and its associated profit margin is in return redirected to shareholders. This market-driven value philosophy is not based on cost-plus accounting, but on balancing production costs against global market forces. The second component of the equation centres on shareholder value, described as the delta between the value of a firm's output realized in total revenues subtracted from the cost of the raw materials and the components or services which the firm adds to the bought-in material to produce the output. In other words, the efforts of the organization must result in supplying products that the market needs at a cost that delivers a reasonable return to those who invested in the organization. This is by no means a new concept; it is the fundamental aspect of basic capitalism and has not changed, regardless of the new capabilities which technology has introduced. What is different in a synconomy is the way in which business must deliver value, the mechanisms it uses to achieve the productivity required to be competitive and the structure which firms adopt to achieve their goals.

In what concerns value and the 'new economy', the boom–bust dot-com cycle provided several interesting new lessons:

1. the fundamentals of aspects of business have not changed even if the economy is given a new label (that is, corporations must return reasonable profits);

2. value propositions must be based on achieving long-term market viability, not simply acquiring short-term market share;

3. competing in a global marketplace requires a market differentiation that is clear and discernable throughout the diversity of the customer base and shareholders.

To meet the competitive challenges of the new century, businesses must continually assess their value proposition to both customers and shareholders. The measurement must establish the relative value of external factors to a firm's value proposition by weighing and ranking the factor's influence on the customer's perception of value, profitability and a firm's ability to deliver, using its competencies or its network of global partners. To interpret accurately customer behaviour, social, political, technological and cultural trends, firms must proceed to the direct observation of customer actions and a comprehensive analysis of the relativity of their wants, needs and desires, as seen in Chapter 1. Individuals need to develop process knowledge and consider this array of factors in order to develop strategic initiatives to determine a company's value proposition. In a synconomy, the sources of value emanate from a global marketplace requiring firms to increase the level of transnational partnerships to form networks of value. The dynamic nature of business in a global synergistic network is altering the structure of a firm, the way it organizes its activities to produce value and how it employs technology to achieve its value proposition, as shown throughout this chapter.

Sources of Value and the New Structure

Without delving into a detailed debate between economic structuralism and behaviourism, the interdependencies of a synconomy bring forth a question of how to achieve equilibrium between corporate commercial activities across geographical boundaries. Simply, as consumer demand rises and falls, organizations linked together synergistically strive to balance their throughput by increasing and decreasing their industrial capacity to other connected partners in a technology-enabled network of value. Moschandreas noted that a transnational partnering phenomenon is not a product of technology, it is a corporate behaviour resulting from the need to strive continually to reduce operating cost, made ever-more possible by the frequent advances in technology:

> Limitations in human rationality, for example, coupled with complexity and uncertainty, create transaction costs which may lead firms to expand by internalizing transactions, thus affecting the number and size distribution of firms in the market. Thus, behaviour affects structure. But at the same time a more concentrated structure implies the existence of small numbers of traders which coupled with information asymmetries can induce opportunistic behaviour and prostrated bargaining situations which create substantial transaction costs. To avoid or reduce these costs firms may decide to supersede the market by producing their own requirements rather than buying them from third parties. In other words, structural features affect the size of transaction costs which in turn affects business behaviour and market structure.[11]

One could argue that the present need to reduce operating cost, rather than technology, actually promotes business and consumer behaviour towards globalization. Technology only provides the means to realize the goal and increase an organization's ability to cope with the greater complexities generated as a by-product of this behaviour. As stated earlier, Porter offers two views that must be placed at the forefront of corporate competitive thinking; there is no 'new' economy, just the old economy with advanced technological capabilities; and adopting a business model approach is not a strategy, just as generating revenue is not the same as creating economic value.[12] These distinctions are vital for businesses operating in a synconomy, needing to be fully understood and integrated into strategic thinking. What Porter and others reveal is that the Internet is a technology which fundamentally changes how business activities will function in a transnational environment; however, the *nature* of business (which is to optimize costs, deliver value and generate a return on investment) has not changed.

In a synconomy, organizations must readdress their value chain and business model to incorporate advances in technology as a means to implement strategic initiatives. The failings of many dot-com companies and traditional firms that followed the technology mantra of the Internet were because of technological myopia, in which companies viewed the Internet as a mechanism to replace all other means of facilitating business activities. Just as television did not eliminate the radio, newspapers and other news media, the lesson is that the Internet must be used in conjunction with all other mechanisms to access markets, serve customers, market products, ship products and facilitate a bi-directional dialogue between customers, suppliers and partners. Therefore, corporations must period-ically deconstruct their value chain and rebuild it from the perspective of the customer, and not grow complacent about their value proposition, by re-evaluating the value to customers to ensure alignment with changing market conditions, as Evans and Wurster noted:

> The changing economics of information threaten to undermine established value chains in many sectors of the economy, requiring virtually every company to rethink its strategy – not incrementally but fundamentally.[13]

Within the value chain, information plays three fundamental roles that are valued by the organization: data within a transaction has value such as order quantity or invoice amount; information about the transaction has value such as items shipped or total cost; and information about the infor-mation has value such as an aggregation of bank accounts to determine a consolidated cash flow. Information is the linchpin, providing an inherent value *within*, to and about transactions. Each information type has a value relative to its application to the business process, the partner that facili-tates the transactions and the entity that is the recipient of the inform-ation. Corporations operating in a synconomy must develop a competency to sense the market, react to changing customer behaviour, adapt to cultural preferences, accommodate evolving regulations and be responsive to the needs of partners in a network of value, as Rayport and Sviokla observed:

> Creating value in any stage of a virtual value chain involves a sequence of five activities: gathering, organizing, selecting, synthesizing, and distributing information.[14]

To achieve business process synergy, it is necessary to categorize process activities into three forms:

■ Processes which are self-contained and can be executed within the firm or outsourced in their entirety;

■ Processes with core subprocesses which depend on external partner-ships and can only be executed by a synergistic relationship with resources outside the firm;

■ Processes with non-core subprocesses which can be externalized on demand.

Corporations externalize business processes not because it is the latest business trend, but because of two key incentives: cost efficiencies (economies of scale); and a broader market reach (economies of scope), each resulting in a bottom-line benefit to shareholders and customers. To achieve lower operating cost, corporations externalize self-contained processes. This is not a trivial undertaking, as it requires individuals within the firm to adopt a process perspective and an in-depth understanding of the measures, controls and ways in which to adjust the process when unanticipated external factors facilitate the need to change the basic process. Even more difficult is the externalization of core processes, because now the firm must develop a cultural/behavioural adoption of a process focus and typically unlearn the compartmentalized specialization of post-industrial age thinking and disassemble their traditional structural hierarchies to a leaner networked approach of linked competencies, as observed by Naisbitt:

> Downsizing, reengineering, creating networking organizations, or the latest, the virtual corporation, whatever it is called, it comes down to the same thing. Companies have to dismantle bureaucracies to survive. Economies of scale are giving way to economies of scope, finding the right size for synergy, market flexibility, and above all, speed.[15]

Fortunately, outsourced non-core processes appear to be the easiest of the three tasks, although also demanding that the non-core process should have a comprehensive set of measures which are clearly understood by both organizations. Outsourcing customers have learned that they achieve a higher efficiency and have a long-lasting relationship with providers when they outsource processes, capabilities or functions in which they already excel, and which they can easily measure and understand. When firms outsource processes that have traditionally been a problem area, outsourcing them often leads to failure because expectations are never met, no matter what the vendor does to accommodate the requirements. All external relationships carry an element of risk as core and non-core processes suddenly rely on partners to perform the associated business activities. Corporations operating in a synconomy must develop a method for assessing those risks quantifiably on a relative scale in order to prioritize alternative providers and formulate a partner-hedging strategy, as conceptually illustrated in Figure 2.5.

In order to achieve a broader market reach, corporations develop partnership agreements which can be described as hybrids because they often encapsulate the typical elements of a joint venture with that of an outsourcing contract. An 'economy of scope' is a new phenomenon

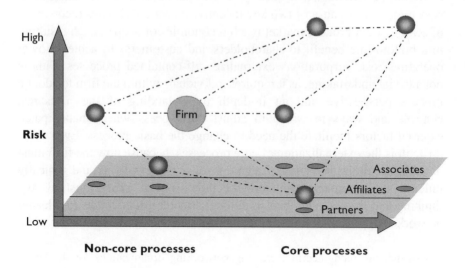

Figure 2.5 The value of relationships

describing firms that have multi-product offerings which span markets, geographies and sometimes industries, which can be achieved in a network of value, using partnerships, affiliations and associations. Jarillo defines a strategic network as:

> an arrangement by which companies set up a web of close relationships that form a veritable *system* geared to providing product of services in a coordinated way. These networks are becoming dominant in more and more industries, and the reason is that these can meet the current competitive requirements better than old ways of organizing economic activity.[16]

Regardless of the underlying structure of the organization, value can be created and costs reduced when subprocesses or entire processes are executed by external resources in business relationships such as partnerships, affiliations or associations. As stated above, Rayport and Sviokla identified five essential value-adding processes (gathering, organizing, selecting, synthesizing and distributing) which transform information into a matrix of applied value.[17] Extending this line of thinking to the maturity cycle of relationships within a network of value, it can be argued that each activity must be exercised in a different manner as the nature of the relationship changes and matures, which is the subject of the following section.

Value-added Relationships: Partners, Affiliates and Associates

Above it was shown how individuals within a company or nation state tend to collaborate at different levels in different organizations/countries. Here, how companies partner, affiliate and associate to add value to customers is discussed. Just before the dot-com boom, Reich made an observation on the changing nature of corporations that is not only true today, but also should be foremost in the minds of executives operating in the newly forming global synconomy:

> The high-value enterprise has no need to control vast resources, discipline armies of production workers, or impose predictable routines. Thus it need not be organized like the old pyramids that characterized standardized production, with strong chief executives presiding over ever-widening layers of managers, atop an even larger group of hourly workers, all following standard operating procedures.[18]

Companies in the twenty-first century are rapidly realizing that a substantial part of their value proposition depends on their ability to forge relationships with other firms in order to add value to their customers. In a global synconomy, these relationships between companies take the form of partnerships, associations, affiliations and joint ventures, migrating from transnational links with suppliers to cooperative ventures with would-be competitors. This phenomenon, which Nalebuff and Brandenburger labelled 'co-opetition', is a direct result of technology reaching a state in which it is now cost-effective to construct these relationships in a network of value.[19] However, as corporations develop a new, higher level of extra-company transnational relationships, they are quickly realizing that these relationships become increasingly complex over time, as the nature of competition continues to change and the inter-company relationship matures. Each type of relationship is typically governed by a legal contract which defines the limits of the relationship. The key idea to remember is that all relationships thrive on an increasing level of collaboration and bi-directional communications. Additionally, all relationships must be forged on a common set of clearly stated goals and objectives, which stipulate to both parties the value of the combined efforts. Within each type of relationship there is also a varying degree of mutual trust, which is often tested by the willingness or unwillingness to share data, information and knowledge. This new level of business co-dependence reduces the total number of activities to be performed within the firm and, as an expressed goal, lowers the total operating cost. Many companies consider the exis-

tence of these integrated value-added activities as an asset, either because
it allows them to focus on areas in which they are most likely to be better
skilled, or because it increases their ability to concentrate on their
customers. Like any asset, relationships must be actively managed to
maximize the investment made at their inception and development and to
measure effectively the value added to the product or service.

In order to formulate strategic relationships, organizations must first
educate the executives in each party on the extent of the arrangement,
define a set of clearly understandable objectives and secure executive
sponsorship or ownership of the relationship. Next, each organization must
master the art of communication. The essential ingredient to maximizing
the value in these newly emerging relationships is to view the individuals
involved from both parties as a joint team whose loyalty is pledged to the
customer, with a set of core objectives that are mutually beneficial to each
organization but are a by-product of fulfilling a customer's needs. Therefore, the activities of the joint team members must be governed by an
objective set of performance metrics which incorporates not only the
primary qualitative objective of serving the customer, but also quantitative
measurements establishing levels of profitability, rewards and other cooperating values.

Davidow and Malone emphasize an important point that companies
often overlook when assessing their strategic relationship, that of the
duality of risk in the relationship with suppliers and business partners:

> In the business model of the future, customers will have far fewer suppliers.
> The just-in-case supply philosophy will be increasingly obsolete. A supplier's
> failure to adequately support a customer will be a serious problem. On the
> other hand, suppliers will be dependent on fewer customers. A customer's
> failure will be extremely damaging to the supplier's business.[20]

Companies engaged in a network of value must thus assess the benefit
in the relationship with suppliers and value-added partners as well as the
inherent risk of the external entity's inability to deliver. For example, if a
firm enters into an outsourcing relationship for technology services and its
outsourcing partner has in turn outsourced a number of the key business
processes and the end outsourcing company fails to deliver, what is the
inherited impact to its operation? More importantly, do the contracts
contain sufficient clauses to guarantee business continuity?

Corporations in a synconomy are learning that partners within the
network of value must have a good understanding of their products and
services. Partners are not order-taking suppliers; they must have compre-

hensive knowledge of the product in order to act in true partnership. Firms now realize that, in order to reap the efficiencies of scale and scope, they must educate, to some degree, their suppliers and distributors. This in turn creates an opportunity for many firms to set up quasi-consulting groups which not only educate network partners, but also can act as authoritative sources of information on the application of products for customers. Organizations migrating towards solution selling now understand that they must provide three distinct value-added components: the product itself; the knowledge of the product's application to business; and a higher level of customer service. Recognizing that a firm can extend its resources dangerously thin, organizations have been able to leverage their internal intellectual property by investing in technologies which educate their partners, effectively expanding their product knowledge reach and providing alternative sources of information for customers. In many cases, this propagation of product knowledge often occurs at points closest to large customers or in geographies with a high density of customers.

The Functions of a Value-based Partnership

Porter's description of a value chain breaks down a firm into the primary activities of inbound logistics, operations, outbound logistics, marketing and sales, and service, requiring a firm to take a process view of its enterprise.[21] According to Porter, a number of secondary activities – such as procurement, human resource management, technological development, and infrastructure – must also be performed to sustain the value chain and provide support service to the primary processes. In the past, corporations used to outsource many of the secondary process activities such as technology, human resources and other traditional administrative functions to firms which provided a similar service to other companies. In the post-dotcom business climate, a small number of firms externalize primary business processes with partnerships, affiliations and associations. Their relationships are distinctly different from outsourcing because they are founded on mutual cooperative goals and financial objectives that cannot be attained without either of the partners. An outsourcing relationship often decays over time into an adversarial tenor in which the outsourcing provider is viewed as merely a supplier of services. Synergistic business process behaviour is successful when both parties conclude that to achieve a specific goal, such as introducing a product to a regional marketplace, both firms need to be operating in an integrated fashion.

In their observations of the Italian textile industry in the Prato region between 1970 and 2000, Malone and Laubacher explore the characteristics of a network of value. The textile production in this region has evolved into a network of 15,000 very small, employee-owned firms which have been operating using a variety of cooperative ventures. The firms exist in co-opetition with each other, thus leveraging the strength of the group whilst maintaining differentiation through product design. Their cooperative association centralizes non-core processes such as the acquisition of raw materials and customer order taking to reduce operating cost, making the region competitive in a global marketplace.[22] This cooperative series of relationships is more than an association but less than a formalized corporate entity. It does illustrate, however, the fundamental need that firms now have to collaborate in order to maintain a competitive edge. The Prato network also uses brokers (called *impannatori*) to facilitate the numerous transactions between manufacturers (firms) and buyers (customers). The brokers, as identified by Malone and Laubacher, are fundamental for the Prato network, as they help to coordinate the design and manufacturing processes, ensuring customer satisfaction with the final product. They have also created an electronic market which acts as a clearing house for information about the process and products, allowing the textile production capacity to be approached as a commodity.[23]

Partnerships, associations and affiliations do not necessarily imply that over time collaboration and cooperation will lead toward cartels, price fixing and monopolistic behaviour. Within a collaborative partnership, each member is keenly aware of their role in the creation of the end product and the contribution to the bottom line of their organization. More importantly, members should also know how their contribution influences the profitability of each member in the network of value. That is, in a process-oriented relationship, each node on the network that provides a value-added service must have a comprehensive understanding of the total process. Business process knowledge is paramount to delivering the applied value of an individual firm at every step in the process. Members of the assembled network must act in harmony when addressing issues of changes in the price of the finished product, not to set market pricing like a cartel, but to react in unison to upward and downward pricing pressures exhorted by the marketplace. In addition, they must keep in mind the changing prices within a firm as well as the added operating expense, because the labour associated with instituting the change is compounded across the value partners, adding incremental cost to each member in the value network. Therefore, actions such as price changing, cost cutting, setting new production targets, demand volumes and other factors that influence the rate of the process require a higher degree of coordination between each value partner. The goal is to achieve a dynamic process that rebalances the price/cost ratio at each step in the value-adding process during times of price instability and market uncertainty. Organizations operating synergistically, and collaborating to such a degree that the free exchange of information between the members allows them to maximize their profit margins and leverage interchangeably economies of scale and scope, must avoid looking like a cartel. Establishing proactive mechanisms which clearly state the limits and boundaries of agreements and that the data associated with each relationship is held in the strictest of confidence, each member of the network is important in the provision of services not only to the members of a single group of network partners, but to many members of many networks. One could argue that to avoid cartel-like behaviour (or the perception of a cartel), an organization needs to be engaged in many value-added networks, with a distinct stated policy on the firm's behaviour to all members of all networks.

It has been said that England, for example, is a nation of shopkeepers, with a vibrant market of small and medium-sized enterprises (SMEs), which are considered the backdrop of the British economy. If one considers each SME as a stand-alone entity, establishing a network of value in the UK can be accomplished, firstly, by creating a robust and predictable technological structure. The second step is developing a mechanism that encourages the adoption of a standard mechanism for exchanging relevant information. The third step would be to provide a means for commerce to engage in the intra-country exchange of goods and services, finally expanding this network of value beyond the confines of the country.

China, on the other hand, is a nation of traders. For centuries, Asian companies have capitalized on Asian values, which Li described as a remarkable work ethic, a disciplined commitment to saving and education and strong support for governments.[24] Li also points out that the traditional Chinese enterprise – be it large or small – is, for the most part, a member of an informal or formal network of relationships, often stemming from a family enterprise. Asian business is based on combining strong cultural values and a networked structure, which does have its shortcomings but often surprises western businesses by its ability to rebound and adapt. Chinese businesses display characteristics which at first glance appear to be a composite of many, often-admired 'western' traits in business excellence, such as agility, competence and the capacity to deliver.

Corporations today are less encumbered in their business by the gradual removal of tariffs and quotas under agreements such as the General Agreement on Tariffs and Trade (GATT) and the creation of free-trade blocs such as the European Community. The media hype of the Internet's ability to enable trade has waned, but the true value proposition of the Internet has only just begun to be harvested. One could argue that the greater journey towards a highly leveraged, synchronized, interactive business cycle is yet to begin. The rapid rise and fall of the dot-com companies is a mixed blessing. On the one hand, it did raise awareness of the potential that technology has to streamline business. On the other hand, it demonstrated that a great deal of money can still be wasted if companies do not acquire and/or develop clear directions and strategic intent aimed at solving a specific business need and global customer demands.

Value Network Characteristics

Becoming a member or node in a network of value can give firms distinct advantages over purely domestic enterprises with a local market, because of companies' ability to exploit regional-specific opportunities. In an environment of closely linked business partnerships, the coordination of activities such as marketing can be orchestrated with partners in a selected region so that local consumers see the product everywhere.

As a node in a network of value, a firm's ability to leverage relationships is directly proportional to three factors: technology; collaboration; and the quality of information that a firm exchanges with other members of the network. Information once again plays a key role because it is valued by others and provides the necessary components for process synchronization between companies (Figure 2.6). Process synchronization in a network of value is essential for two key reasons:

1. to increase the capability to service a customer segment, market niche or special product requirements which have become clear on the Internet through the emergence of virtual communities;

2. to achieve a level of business continuity that creates a technological hedge against catastrophic failure by interoperating core processes to the extent that a technology outage can be redirected to another node to complete the process activity.

This decentralization of business process activities, coupled with the higher utilization of external resources to perform the tasks within the processes, requires that organizations should address the fundamentals of business

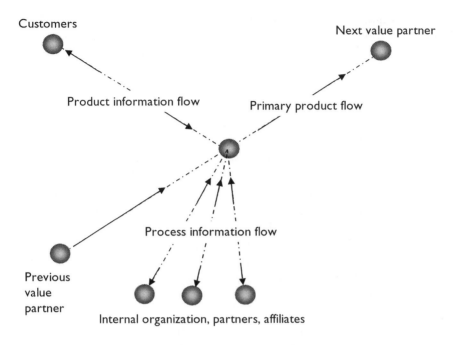

Customers

Next value partner

Product information flow   Primary product flow

Process information flow

Previous value partner

Internal organization, partners, affiliates

Figure 2.6 Information relativity

leadership to control geographically dispersed activities and re-engineer their organizational structures, which is now discussed.

Distance Leadership and Evolving Organizational Structures

As the structure of business changes and traditional hierarchical organizations give way to a network of coordinated cells of competencies, leaders must find new ways of guiding the organization towards its goals and objectives. Complicating the leadership challenge is the fact that organizations now span more geographies, cultures, regulatory authorities and corporate entities as workforces become intermixed resources which are no longer owned by the corporation. Business leaders in the new transnational environment must be able to orchestrate globally dispersed activities into a cohesive process which results in the desired output of the organization. This is not simply a matter of project management; leaders must adopt a fundamentally new method of leadership style, focusing on leveraging the abilities of knowledge workers to achieve operational synergy within the firm and with external entities such as partners, suppliers and customers. Leaders are realizing that as activities and functions that were traditionally part of the internal workings of a firm are now being performed externally, the command and control structure of a hierarchical organization no longer applies.

A globally dispersed business process, regardless of whether each value-added process step is performed by an internal or external organization, requires not only the coordination of activities, but also a strategic leadership that transcends the entire process. The lack of distance leadership is often the result of either a poor understanding of the process in its entirety or the mismanagement of the many relationships between each value-added provider. Parikh argues that in order to manage effectively a set of complex relationships, one must achieve a 'detached involvement' in the activities on which the relationship is based. Parikh claims that the ability to effect change and make process decisions is directly influenced by our learned beliefs, which in turn often cloud objectivity because of factors such as ego and other hidden, self-centred motivations:

> We generally tend to prove ourselves right rather than improve ourselves and, therefore, we need to detach and liberate ourselves from our belief system. This freedom will in turn enhance the proactive courage we need to keep our minds open to a different level of thinking, feeling and doing – making our relationships more meaningful and effective.[25]

Parikh's observations are essential for senior managers managing the global coordination of decentralized and increasingly complex business activities that comprise newly forming synergistic business processes, because managers cannot easily observe the process in its entirety from within the process itself. Senior management in an organization engaged in a synergistic relationship with other value providers must exhibit process mastery, which can only come from balancing resources and relationships with external and internal market forces. Again, Parikh puts the attainment of a detached-involved relationship into perspective:

> Now, consider the way you hold the steering wheel of a car while driving. When you were still learning how to drive the car, you must have held the wheel tightly. There were so many variables to cope with while driving that, as a learner, you must have held on to the wheel tightly – an illusion of control! But once you had been driving for some time, how would you hold the wheel? Much more lightly, with mastery – a balanced 'detached-involved' relationship with the wheel.[26]

One could then argue that the true role for senior managers is to become process leaders who are detached from the actual day-to-day process operations. Detachment gives them the ability to view the process holistically, impartially and objectively. Information regarding the process performance and process exception handling can be combined with the experiential knowledge of the senior management team, yielding market wisdom. This strategic perspective is broadcast back to the members in the organization in the form of advice indicating the basis of observations, not as edicts to diminish the decision-making at the process level.

Distance and Trust

In a synconomy, where colleagues and collaborators are often separated by distance, a new approach to leadership must be employed, based on a trust. Once senior managers establish the necessary environment and set up associated business processes, they must trust individuals within the firm and the external partners to perform activities under the prescribed guidelines. Furthermore, senior managers must trust employees to interpret the guidelines to do what is best for the company when business conditions initiate events or actions that go beyond the guidelines. On the other hand, individuals or the firm must master trust management to steer the operations of the firm towards viable, long-term profitability. Trust is paramount in forging relationships within the firm and with external entities. Acting as a bonding agent, trust is based on knowledge, as Handy describes, requiring limits in the form of boundaries, the need to have mechanisms for adaptation, and should be considered an impersonal commodity.[27] Handy identifies one of the new challenges that technology brings to managing and directing people, that of distance leadership:

> We will also have to get accustomed to working with and managing those whom we do not see except on rare and prearranged occasions.[28]

Trust is the cornerstone of collaboration, which cannot be used as a substitute for trust, only as a mechanism to enhance trust in a relationship. Handy reminds us:

> That attitude becomes a self-fulfilling prophecy. 'If they don't trust me,' employees say to themselves, 'why should I bother to put their needs before mine?'[29]

As organizations realize that their participation in a synconomy is predicated on establishing and nurturing a set of relationships, which are built on layers of trust over time, they also become more aware that trust in itself is changing shape in the emerging global economy. Trust is a product of growing confidence in each partner's ability to perform within the boundaries of expectations. Therefore, expectations are fulfilled and managed when the rules which govern trust are known and understood by each partner in the relationship. Firstly, trust is not blind, it is actually based on knowledge and linked to an individual's ability to perform and react to change in a predictable manner. This, in turn, stimulates confidence in the partner because under a given set of conditions, the partner is capable and willing to do the right thing. The boundaries of trust establish the extent of the relationship and must be extended or decreased as the relationship matures. As time passes and the level of trust increases, organizations operating in a connected network of value-based relationships must have the ability to change or adapt, based on trust. This reflects the need for trust to be based on a continual process of learning, in which each party becomes more comfortable with the other's ability to interpret factors that influence the relationship, such as changes to the business model or a sudden shift in customer demand.

However, trust – or, more specifically, the act of trusting – is a complex system because trust is built on the delivery of expectations as business conditions change, and expectations often remain fixed. To prevent the undermining of trust in a relationship, companies must communicate changes and reset expectations in order to allow trust to grow and organizations to become more confident in their ability to interoperate. Here again, Handy makes an important identification regarding trust: it needs to be the bond between organizations and communication must be the metaphorical glue, which binds organizations together in a continuous dialogue. In many cases, the elements of trust are realized in the physical manifestations of mission statements, goals and other documentary forms, which act as markers or reminders of the limits/extent of trust. Therefore, trust needs to be based on a continual measurement of performance against objectives viewed relative to the boundaries in which each party operates. The confidence in each partner to do the right thing at the right time becomes almost second nature, and it is at this time that boundaries become less important.

Distance and Communications

Organizations traditionally forget these fundamental building blocks of a relationship. Communication between parties requires different media or technologies to facilitate the various types of interaction in a maturing relationship. Although they are considered the bane of modern corporations, periodical face-to-face meetings are vital when organizations are engaged in international commercial activities, because they are tactile experiences in which both parties can participate, as Handy notes: 'Paradoxically, the more virtual an organization becomes, the more its people need to meet in person.'[30] Teleconferencing, eMail and other technologies play an important part in facilitating transactions but, in many cases, the personal interactions of a meeting are needed to refresh the relationship of trust and leadership.

The new approach to leadership is actually not new, it simply requires more effort on the part of management teams to lead by direct example. Bruce and Ireland of VCC Associates identify five essential attributes that senior managers should consider in practising new leadership:

> The senior management leadership must champion a collaborative culture by demonstrating their commitment to the Internet initiatives, encouraging internal and external collaboration, openness in trading partner relationships, risk taking with Internet related projects, and fostering the development of stronger bonds between the IS [information systems].[31]

These attributes are not unlike traditional actions that management teams have had to perform. They are, however, more transparent because technology now makes these actions more accessible to employees. The message is simple; if a management team determines that collaboration is a key component of the value proposition of a firm, the best way for them to demonstrate its value to all persons within a firm is by using the technique itself. Leveraging technology to support leadership, communications and geographic compression is best introduced by senior managers setting the example.

In order for corporations to disseminate decision-making to the lowest level of the organization responsible for specific process execution, individuals possessing the kinds of skill that can interpret formulated strategies and facilitate strategic execution must accomplish the combination of empowerment and collaboration. Kaplan and Norton have observed that the key to operationalizing strategy is to make it understood by the entire organization:

> In this era of knowledge workers, strategy must be executed at all levels of the organization. People must change their behaviors and adopt new values. The key to this transformation is putting strategy at the centre of the management

process. Strategy cannot be executed if it cannot be understood, however, and it cannot be understood if it cannot be described. If we are going to create a management process to implement strategy, we must first construct a reliable and consistent framework for describing strategy. No generally accepted framework existed, however, for describing information age strategies.[32]

Strategic thinking in prior generations of business was an activity reserved for either top management or a select group of strategists, often set apart from the mainstream activities of the corporation. In a corporation engaged in a global syneconomy, strategic thinking skills must be present at all levels of the organization. This is not to say that everyone will be engaged in the development of corporate strategies, such as product development, brand identities, merger activities or others in the formulation of strategic initiatives. However, individuals will be responsible for the implementation of strategic actions and thus must have a clear understanding of the fundamentals of strategic thinking. People at all levels must have the basic skill of assessing the actions and risks associated with a strategic manoeuvre in order to capitalize on the benefits. This does not imply that everyone in a firm must run off to business school and get an MBA in order to work on everyday business activities. Rather it

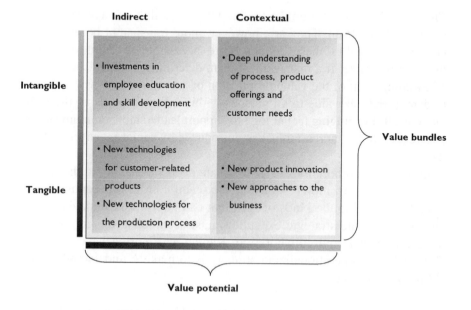

Figure 2.7 The relativity of value

Source: Adapted from Kaplan and Norton (2001)

does indicate that one of the essential roles of management is reading strategic thinking to the organization by articulating in plain language the intent of a strategic manoeuvre. Simply, management must place the strategic action into a context that is understandable by every group within the firm and, more importantly, act as an educational resource to enhance strategic thinking skills throughout the firm. Management teams should view each strategic initiative as another chance to upgrade the entire organization incrementally to be more cognizant of how each organizational, product or competitive change brings the firm closer to its intended goals. A company's ability to operationalize strategic thinking is a critical element in establishing its receptivity to distance leadership.

As firms become more like an association of geographically dispersed cells of competencies, the role of management becomes less associated with bundling intangible and tangible assets into bundles of value, instead assuming the role of an agent for matching assets. Here, senior management behaves like a corporate clearing house for asset matching, identifying assets that are indirect or contextual, and assessing their degree of tangibility to the business process, as illustrated in Figure 2.7. The source of the assets in each category can come from the internal organization or from external sources. As matchmaker managers assist the line of business units, middle-level managers explore the possibilities of asset combinations and provide corporate guidance on the feasibility of the asset combination's value potential. The key is that in order to avoid growing into a bottleneck in which operating units vie for permission to fund and confirmations on how to proceed, management must become a strategic information resource to be used by business units which are executing predesigned strategic initiatives. These strategic initiatives in most cases depend on leveraging technology to produce the desired outcomes. This use of technology becomes the critical factor in the realization of the value equation as the distance between the cells of competency increases, which is the subject of the next section.

The Convergence of Technology and Geography

Synergistic relationships are exemplified by traditional US banking institutions which, as part of their value proposition, provide third party or co-branded insurance products to customers. Banks have realized that they can make higher margins by acting as selling agents for existing insurance companies than if they were to do the insurance underwriting themselves. The banking industry is ideal for the development of leveraged synergies such as found in the aggregation of financial services, which are vital in a synconomy. Simultaneously, this same corporate behaviour can also lead insurance companies to sell or provide reciprocal financial products under the same basic agreement structures. In the US, the 1999 Financial Services Modernization Act provides the stimuli needed for this type of synergistic behaviour, raising the question of whether financial services firms operating across international political boundaries will eventually need similar, internationally agreed regulations in order to operate in an optimized competitive environment. However, such ground-breaking international cooperation is not on the horizon and, in a lot of cases, existing regulations in many countries stand in direct contradiction to the Financial Services Modernization Act. Early opportunities for synergistic behaviour may be seen in financial services, but are also emerging in a variety of other industries.

One could say that the internationalization of business on the Internet has only just begun. Businesses which have adopted a less aggressive competitive stance due to the dot-com failure may be prematurely making themselves less competitive. In the post-dot-com era, technology bridges geographic distances slowly and in more subtle ways by creating connections that have yet to be fully understood by most consumers. For example, if you want to send a dozen roses from New York to Rio de Janeiro, you can go to the Internet and do it electronically. America On Line (AOL) offers a link to a vendor called FTD. On the site www.ftd.com, one can select international deliveries and find one dozen roses (available only in a simple glass vase) that can be delivered in Brazil for US$99.00 with a $9.99 service charge and a $12.00 international fee, totalling US$120.99. However, also using AOL, one could go to AOL Brazil and visit the site www.uniflores.com and order the same dozen roses (without a glass vase) for R41.00 (today the equivalent to US$11.17) with free delivery, saving US$109.82. Even with no knowledge of the Portuguese language, one can perform the transaction with ease by recognizing international icons such as the checkout basket, credit card and so on. As more companies begin to make their websites multilingual, even shopping at a foreign company's website will become less of an inconvenience. The Internet is continually exposing consumers to value propositions which were built on previous generations of technology and outdated business practices, such as international flower buying. However, once this gap in value is identified, it presents an opportunity for businesses to fill the gap with a redefinition of the service, based on the new technological advances. For example, it would be easy for FTD or a competitor to forge affiliations with florists around the world (which they already have), similar to www.Amazon.com, without any large capital investment, linked by reciprocal relationship agreements, providing a worldwide one-stop shop for flowers. This requires shifting a firm's focus from a multinational view of business to a transnational perspective, which is discussed in Chapters 4 and 6.

The transnational view of a firm requires, in many cases, a rethinking of how individual technologies are applied to business processes. Companies must also consider that multiple technological capabilities are converging to create new capabilities or new business opportunities which they must exploit synergistically with global partners. More importantly, how the reapplication of technology fits into the context of the firm's future business state must be driven not by streamlining existing business practices, but by consciously designing business with a single world marketplace perspective. Technology vendors are realizing that the role of technology is no longer simply to automate an existing business process, but to either act as a bridge between corporate capabilities or provide new capabilities which must be integrated and ultimately nurtured into new corporate, connective, business process competency. Leveraging technologies – especially infrastructure technologies – into the competencies required to participate in a network of partnering organizations demands that technology should permit firms to develop not only collaborative skills, but products which are agile enough to meet changing customer needs. Product agility becomes critical when products span geographies, cultures and lifestyles.

For example, corporations, such as IBM, have now introduced hybrid products, which do not simply offer a technical solution but come complete with an end user, business product strategy. IBM's application of product hybridization in financial services provides an insight into how technology must not simply enhance existing business processes, but also assist firms in embracing new processes and in some cases new business models:

> In order to protect and expand domestic and international markets, the banks are having to create and sell a range of products in both traditional and new areas. The idea of bundling financial services is not new, but the idea of offering products which cross financial boundaries, known as hybrid products, is in its infancy.[33]

IBM's approach indicates that hybrid products are indeed unlike commodity products; they have become invisible to the banking customer, now merely facilitating a continuous relationship between customer and financial institution, built on trust, security and mutual confidence.[34] At first, hybrid products within the financial services industry assisted customers in facilitating a specific lifestyle such as young middle-income couples' total financial needs managed under a single-relationship account. The application of hybrid products is not limited to larger organizations such as big banks. The same basic need exists in SMEs that have fewer funds to invest in technology and face the same degree of competitive pressure. Technology is not only altering how SMEs engage in global commerce; it also influencing how firms operate within their local economic marketplace. One could argue that the leaders of smaller countries could capitalize on the same opportunities presented to these companies. Walsh describes the economic and business challenges of small country markets as:

> Small countries have less influence over international market structures than large ones, and tend to have relatively fewer firms with the economic and commercial capacity to be successful in international markets.[35]

These challenges are very similar to those of small firms operating in large country economies, and present the same opportunities to leverage a shared technoeconomic market infrastructure. Firms operating in smaller countries – and indeed the countries themselves – must collaborate on an unprecedented scale to secure a prosperous economic future. The same risks, benefits and opportunities that technology has presented to business must also be taken into account by governments. This requires that the leadership of smaller countries and lower volume capital markets should work together to develop synergistic operating relationships, which in turn act as gateways for the corporation operating within their borders to have access to global customers, investors, labour pools and resources. Walsh argues that one area that may be a good candidate for intra-country collaboration is innovation and research.[36] Usually an area reserved for corporations with large budgets, the cost of technological innovation could often be spread across many firms working collaboratively in a multi-country infrastructure, enabling co-opetition between participating firms. Participating nations would agree on proportionate investments and costing mechanisms for firms using the infrastructure. In this scenario, collaborating government agencies in effect act as venture capitalists, regulating infrastructure investment and working with businesses to create an economic entity that can compete as an equal player in the global marketplace.

As venture capitalists, small countries participating in a synergistic economy will need to establish an infrastructure baseline as a foundation or core set of services such as specialized labour pools, natural resources and other items that differentiate businesses and people in the labour market in which more local special interests can be leveraged. This of course requires that participating countries should agree on a basic level of infrastructure, complete with technology, legislation, tax incentives and other economic stimuli, coupled with the ability of each country to prioritize the additional investments needed to accentuate the specialties of the companies operating within their borders. For example, a country with a highly educated labour pool specializing in computer software support services will require a robust communications/Internet infrastructure in order to provide services to global customers. Conversely, in-country corporations providing access for multinational firms to acquire goods in local markets will require a less-sophisticated technological infrastructure but more robust logistics capabilities such as airports, highways, rail systems and intercity freight handling.

Regardless of the current, inherent complexities of achieving multi-country agreement as to what requires a comprehensive economic vision and concurrence on the foundation of services, mounting evidence indicates that, at some point in the near future, small countries will need to address this issue or face a growing number of local companies which will be economically challenged in the global marketplace. The raison d'être for this cooperative technoeconomic infrastructure is twofold: to provide a gateway of access to local goods and services; and offer an easy, convenient mechanism for local firms to find sources of external investment capital.

If individual corporations make up the wheels of commerce, then capital investments must be the lubricant which keeps the wheels turning. All businesses, regardless of geography, need investment capital to grow, expand and take advantage of ongoing opportunities. Regardless of size, corporations operating in a synconomy must be able to acquire capital from a diverse group of investors, which traditionally have been limited to a single operating environment. Large financial services companies have enjoyed a near monopoly in gaining access to foreign investment markets, because they can readily offset the additional fees associated with international share trading and absorb fluctuations between currencies. However, with the steady and relentless advance of technologies designed to facilitate international electronic commerce and the interconnection of stock exchanges and other investment vehicles, the average investor will eventually be able to participate in geographically distant investments, which is discussed in Chapter 3.

Notes

1 R. Buckminster Fuller, *Operating Manual for Spaceship Earth*, New York: Arkana-Penguin Group, 1991, p. 9.

2 W. Sombart, *Luxury and Capitalism*, Ann Arbor: University of Michigan Press, 1967, p. 59.

3 See M. Treacy and F. Wiersema, *The Discipline of Market Leaders*, Reading, MA: Perseus Books, 1997.

4 P. Franczak, 'Value is in the eye of the beholder', *Consumer Markets*, KPMG LLP, August 1999, available online at www.usserve.us.kpmg.com/cm/article-archives/actual-articles/value.html, November 2002.

5 F. Wiersema, *Customer Intimacy*, London: HarperCollins, 1998, pp. 13–14.

6 R. Kaplan and D. Norton, *The Strategy Focused Organization*, Boston: Harvard Business School Press, 2001, p. 66.

7 Kaplan and Norton, *The Strategy Focused Organization*, p. 68.

8 M. Moschandreas, *Business Economics*, London: Routledge, 1994, p. 16.

9 R. Camrass and M. Farncombe, *The Atomic Corporation: A Rational Proposal for Uncertain Times*, Oxford: Capstone, 2001, p. 91.

10 M. Shillito and D. Marle, *Value: Its Measurement, Design, and Management*, Chichester: John Wiley, 1992, pp. 50–9.

11 Moschandreas, *Business Economics*, pp. 48–9.

12 M. Porter, 'Strategy and the Internet', *Harvard Business Review*, March 2001, p. 73.

13 P. Evans and T. Wurster, 'Strategy and the new economics of information', in D. Tapscott (ed.) *Creating Value in the Network Economy*, Boston: Harvard Business School Press, 1999, p. 19.

14 J. Rayport and J. Sviokla, 'Exploiting the virtual value chain', in D. Tapscott (ed.), *Creating Value in the Network Economy*, Boston: Harvard Business School Press, 1999, p. 36.

15 J. Naisbitt, *Global Paradox*, London: Nicholas Brealey, 1994, p. 14.

16 J. C. Jarillo, *Strategic Networks: Creating the Borderless Organization*, Oxford: Butterworth-Heinemann, 1993, p. 7.

17 Rayport and Sviokla, 'Exploiting the virtual value chain', p. 46.

18 R. Reich, *The Work of Nations: Preparing Ourselves for 21st-century Capitalism*, New York: Alfred A. Knopf, 1991, p. 87.

19 See B. Nalebuff and A. Brandenburger, *Co-opetition*, New York: Doubleday, 1996.

20 W. H. Davidow and M. S. Malone, *The Virtual Corporation. Structuring and Revitalizing the Corporation for the 21st Century*, London: Harper Business, 1993, p. 153.

21 M. Porter, *Competitive Advantage*, New York: Free Press, 1985, pp. 11–15.

22 T. Malone and R. Laubacher, 'The dawn of the e-Lance economy', in D. Tapscott (ed.), *Creating Value in the Network Economy*, Boston: Harvard Business School Press, 1999, pp. 60–1.

23 Malone and Laubacher, 'The dawn of the e-Lance economy', p. 61.

24 D. Li, 'Chinese family values in transition', in D. Dayao (ed.), *Asian Business Wisdom: Lessons from the Region's Best and Brightest Business Leaders*, Singapore: John Wiley, 2000, p. 160.

25 J. Parikh, 'Managing by detached involvement', in D. Dayao (ed.) *Asian Business Wisdom: Lessons from the Region's Best and Brightest Business Leaders*, Singapore: John Wiley, 2000, pp. 21–5.

26 Parikh, 'Managing by detached involvement', p. 24.

27 C. Handy, 'Trust and the virtual organization', in D. Tapscott (ed.) *Creating Value in the Network Economy*, Boston: Harvard Business School Press, 1999, pp. 112–14.

28 Handy, 'Trust and the virtual organization', pp. 110–11.

29 Handy, 'Trust and the virtual organization', p. 111.

30 Handy, 'Trust and the virtual organization', pp. 114–15.

31 R. Bruce and R. Ireland, *Migration to Value Chain: Collaboration through CPFR*, VCC Associates, available at www.vccassociates.com, p. 2.

32 Kaplan and Norton, *The Strategy Focused Organization*, pp. 65–6.

33 *Financial Services Hybrid Products: Marketing the Second Wave*, London: IBM Corporation White Paper, 2001, p. 2, available at www.ibm.com/industries/financialservices/, September 2002.

34 *Financial Services Hybrid Products*, p. 14.

35 V. Walsh, 'Technology and competitiveness of small countries: review', in C. Freeman and B.-A. Lundval (eds), *Small Countries Facing the Technological Revolution*, London: Pinter Publishers, 1988, p. 40.

36 Walsh, 'Technology and competitiveness of small countries', p. 44.

CHAPTER 3

The Global Flow of Capital

Global businesses competing in a synconomy now realize that the flow of capital will follow talent, innovation and resources to any part of the world. Capital is a requirement of business for growth and development; it can come from many sources, for reasons known only to the investor, with a variety of commitments in time. In this chapter, the discussion centres on the influence of micro-level corporate value propositions to spawn new business activities, with yet to be seen implications for macro-level, socioeconomic relationships between companies and nation states.

If one looks into a socioeconomic and technological crystal ball and imagines the future of capital markets after, say, 20, 30, or 40 years of technological integration, it is not hard to picture a single global capital market trading 24 hours a day, every day of the year, supplying much needed funds to companies in all parts of the world. Although this picture is easy to envisage, its implications are far more difficult to predict. Today, investment capital flows to companies in all parts of the world through a somewhat antiquated network of financial services products, relationships and channels. In the future, the flow of capital will have a direct bearing on a firm's ability to attract capital and the quality of life enjoyed by the people working for a company. Therefore, one could argue that a fundamental shift is occurring from the quantity of capital available within a nation state to the quality of the people's ability to produce. The global syncolomy is about adding value and achieving more as collaborating groups than could be accomplished by independent business entities. The higher degree of collaboration is predicated on having a robust technological infrastructure and highly skilled people. Nations must either create environments which attract skilled people, or invest in upgrading the skills of indigenous people. Like nations, corporations must also attract skilled personnel or periodically upgrade their employees in order to remain competitive. Therefore, just as businesses must invest in educating employees to meet changing competitive conditions, nations must endeavour to produce higher skilled workers, as Reich observed:

> national savings increasingly flow to whomever can do things best, or cheapest, wherever located around the world. 'National competitiveness' is thus less dependent on the quantity of money that a nations' citizens save and invest than it is on the skills and insights they potentially contribute to the world economy.[1]

Concerning businesses, the point to consider is the change from a company's ability to gain access to investment capital, which has been monopolized largely by western companies and investors, to its potential to be a contributing member in a world economy. For example, a small start-up company located outside Pittsburgh, Pennsylvania can draft a business plan and within a short period of time acquire venture capital to bring a new product to market. The venture capital firm provides a channel for investors to apply their money to good ideas that have undergone a degree of due diligence to establish the potential profitability; the exchange of funds is relatively straightforward. Alternatively, an established firm can simply issue additional shares and find a ready market for investment capital without much effort. Other, larger firms can issue new shares and use investment capital channels such as the NASDAQ to attract investment from individuals living in many parts of the world. However, the same is not true for similar firms with similar ideas and inventions operating just outside Prague, Jakarta or Rio de Janeiro. Geographically distant firms have a more difficult time attracting capital and almost no access to investors in, say, the US. Yes, larger firms can be traded using American depository receipts (ADRs) or larger investment firms, but they do not have the same free-flow access to investors that US companies enjoy today. In the future state of a connected world capital market, companies operating in a synconomy must rethink their capital acquisition strategies and contemplate who is the best type of investor for their company, and how to attract investors and manage their expectations. This interlinked global flow of capital may make acquiring capital a more competitive task between global firms, but it may also give firms the ability to assess the type of investor that best meets their needs.

Capital is a fundamental requirement for all corporations, regardless of where they operate. Firms actively seek out investors by private and public mechanisms to fund activities that enable them to grow and prosper. This

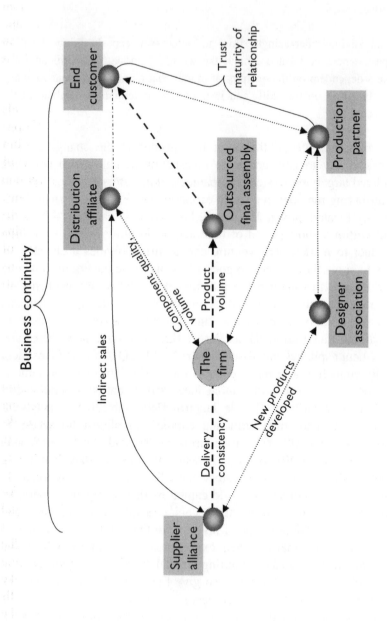

Figure 3.1 Capital flows mirror information exchanges

process is not a product of modernity, but one that transcends business models, cultures and time itself, as observed by Bernstein:

> Apparently, most features of market behaviour today are little different from market behaviour in the seventeenth century. Speculators still speculate, while the risk-averse still hedge. But, it is not just the conduct of investors that is so strikingly similar to what we see today. Even the instruments traded and the mechanics of settlement have barely changed with the passage of time.[2]

In a synconomy, a firm's use of capital centres on facilitating various levels of business continuity in which the firm may have to augment its relationship with suppliers and distributors by establishing equity positions within the partnering company, as illustrated in Figure 3.1. Access and use of global capital such as information now spans geography and corporate entities and is rapidly becoming a means to enhance external relationships. Although the flow of global capital is becoming less encumbered by technology, legislation and regulation, it can also make dissolving partnerships more complex. One of the many roles that governments play is that of facilitating environments that provide the greatest number of mechanisms and sources to capital. The role of governments and the effects of globalization on capital sources are now discussed.

Globalization and the Quest for Capital

For centuries, governments have been concerned with the regionalization of capital, particularly as this is an important ingredient in creating economic growth. Access to capital combined with highly educated workforces is a breeding ground for entrepreneurism and the birth of new companies. An organization such as the Local Futures Group is developing an in-depth understanding of the drivers that enable the knowledge economy and, more importantly, placing these factors into a local socio-economic context.[3] An understanding of this type of research is essential for organizations developing comprehensive human capital plans because it enables corporations to pinpoint the most likely sources of new talent. The important point for our discussion is that talent attracts capital, and capital attracts talent. Pike reports that 'The ability of different regions to take advantage of the new economy varies dramatically, with substantial skills gaps in many areas',[4] indicating that old population centres are still the dominate sources for an educated workforce and are best equipped to compete in a knowledge-based economy. The Local Futures Group subscribes to the view that the knowledge economy delivers global competitiveness and local social cohesion. The growing body of business experience and academic research indicating that – at least within the UK – many areas are ill prepared to compete on a global basis supports this view. If the same research methodology was applied to business, entities large and small would assess their readiness for global competition, could be ranked, and deficits in capabilities identified. The ongoing indications of the Local Futures Group's research highlight the following issues:

- the essential ingredients for the knowledge economy are located in large cities and this attracts talent away from rural and suburban areas;

- the number of jobs created by the knowledge economy is not keeping pace with the annual rate of university graduates entering the job market;

- the changing needs of urban and rural communities must be addressed by changing the focus of the government's modernization of public services.[5]

Stock markets, favourable tax laws, a ready educated workforce and a regulatory authority that fosters trust are the foundation for an environment that stimulates a competitive playing field. The global reach of capitalism is, here again, relative to how a corporation wishes to engage it in commercial endeavours. Do all firms need global sources of capital? Do all investors need international investment opportunities? A family-owned retail store in a small country hears about globalization from a variety of media sources and will do little about it until the bulldozers appear and start constructing a Wal-Mart down the street. Globalization is a relative phenomenon. To a similar sized firm in the same country, globalization provides an opportunity to export goods and services to new markets, using multinational distribution channels that would normally be too costly if tried individually. To this company, globalization brings additional jobs, higher volumes and new management challenges.

For the most part, the general discourse on globalization comes from three sources:

1. Various factions in western business, such as management gurus, technology industry advocates, journalists and academic sources describing the benefits of cross-border commerce.

2. Western academics, journalists and government policy makers primarily located in the US and Europe reporting on the detrimental effects of globalization on economically emerging nations.

3. Social dissident groups identifying globalization as similar to western economic imperialism, primarily as a means to promote their locally driven self-interest.

Regardless of the motivation, dissatisfaction, benefits, problems and hidden agendas surrounding globalization, businesses still need convenient sources of capital investment in order to grow. Consequently, the need for global capital is also relative. For example, a small business research firm in Portugal expanding to address the needs of a client in Spain may require significantly less investment that a biotech research firm in Silicon Valley expanding to fund one project. The needs of the firm in Portugal are the same as those of the firm in California, and although the investment amounts may differ, the access to global investors should be the same. Even though the Portuguese company may have been in business for 60 years and the Californian firm for six months, chances are that under the current system, investors who are looking for diversity in their portfolios will never hear of the Portuguese company's need for investment. Therefore, access to capital is indeed relative to two factors: investor awareness; and access within the locally focused investment marketplace. Handy identifies that value and economic need are relative to the economies in which one operates and lives:

> Global capitalism also makes a few of us happier. Ironically, it is the poor rather than the rich who say that wealth brings happiness. In a series of surveys around the world, there is some evidence that a per capita income of $10,000 a year is the point of diminishing returns. Below that level, roughly where Greece and Portugal are today, more money buys more of the basic comforts of life and increases one's satisfaction. Above that level any additional dollars don't appear to make us more cheerful, probably because we are now into rat-race territory, comparing ourselves with our neighbours, or with what we could be, rather than where we come from.[6]

One could argue that it is not the erosion of social ideals that is at the heart of the dissatisfaction surrounding globalization, but rather the rapid spread of business activities and the plethora of new desires that it generates in local people, creating the desire to reach economic or material goods parity with their social counterparts in another culture. An oversimplification of this complex subject is as follows: capital stimulates business by providing the necessary funds to expand. A portion of this growth may be attributed to customer growth which is external to the operating geography of the firm. Select segments of customers in one country want to replicate all or part of a lifestyle from another country or region representing a social desire for a lifestyle. The aspiration to copy selected attributes of cross-cultural lifestyles ultimately results in an economic change of cultural values and an overall increase in the pace at which society seems to be moving, relative to traditional social values. This hybridization of cultural values adds an additional level of complexity to the pre-existing family and social hierarchies, being interpreted as a negative influence on the population's ability to enjoy life. Therefore, one could say that the dissatisfaction with globalization expressed by special interest groups is not the increase in the gap between the haves and the have-nots, but the sudden rise in cross-cultural awareness and the drive to achieve economic parity between citizens in diverse nation states.

One of the many reasons why there is a rising tension surrounding globalization is the existence of local self-interest groups who use globalization as a mechanism to preserve the status quo, cloaked in the guise of protecting a traditional lifestyle. World leaders acknowledge the need for economic cooperation, and yet individual countries often act with their own self-interest in mind. For corporations operating in a global business environment, tensions represented by special interest groups pose a potential threat to long-term economic viability and, possibly, physical disruption in the production of goods and services. Corporations need to factor local dissatisfaction into strategic plans in order to reduce the risk of social disapproval while operating in a specific geographic region. This can be accomplished by actively communicating a firm's community value proposition in more than simple monetary terms. Localizing brand image and corporate identity will accentuate links with the community and show compliance to local cultural values.

The Value of Culture

Local cultural values also reshape the role of government, transforming it from a mere provider of social services to a more accountable public entity which also facilitates international commerce while empowering citizens. Exemplifying this rise in electronic-based social services is Malta's eGovernment initiative. In October 2000, the government of Malta published a White Paper describing a vision and strategy for the attainment of electronic government, relating its short and long-term goals not as a simple provider of services, but as a catalyst for a socioeconomic rethinking of the government's relationship with society:

The Government, however, has a responsibility that goes beyond the provision of its own services. This responsibility embraces a wider national picture and entails the creation of an information society via initiatives that will ensure universal digital literacy and the widespread adoption of e-commerce in the private sector, within a legal framework, as the means for social and economic development in Malta.[7]

The Maltese approach engages government in public–private partnerships by addressing the requirements of a synconomy under three distinct initiatives:

1. establishing an infrastructure to facilitate global commerce (which will be discussed in greater detail later in this chapter)

2. increasing technological literacy in order to participate in the knowledge economy (to be explored in Chapter 5)

3. providing the legal/regulatory framework to reduce barriers to trade.

Yet another example of growing synergistic behaviour is the regulatory agenda of capital markets, specifically the stock market, which provides companies with access to much-needed capital. The market also provides access to investors who are continually seeking opportunities to invest their capital in ventures and entities which show a good chance of achieving a better return on investment than can be found from other sources. One could argue that in the future, investors will find technology which will facilitate the establishment of a virtual, global or intra-linked regional capital market that enables short-term speculations to literally follow the sun while long-term investments will find promising companies in all parts of the world. If one considers Keynes' observations on market behaviour, the extension or interconnection of capital markets could act as a balancing mechanism to level the results of local economic crises:

> Let us recur to what happens in a crisis. So long as the boom was continuing, much of the new investment showed a not unsatisfactory current yield. The disillusion comes because doubts suddenly arise concerning the reliability of the prospective yield, perhaps because the current yield shows signs of falling off, as the stock of newly produced durable goods steadily increases. If current costs of production are thought to be higher than they will be later on, that will be a further reason for a fall in the marginal efficiency of capital. Once doubt begins it spreads rapidly.[8]

A good example of governments working in unison to establish and facilitate commerce is the Eastern Caribbean Security Exchange (ECSE). Established in 2001, the eight member states – Anguilla, Antigua and Barbuda, Dominica, Grenada, Montserrat, St Kitts and Nevis, St Lucia, and St Vincent and the Grenadines – developed and passed the Securities Act 2000, which provides uniform legislation and a supporting legal and regulatory framework to govern the operations of the ECSE. The exchange receives its oversight from the Eastern Caribbean Securities Regulatory Commission, the Eastern Caribbean Central Securities Depository, and the Eastern Caribbean Central Securities Registry. This multinational legislation also governs all securities business by intermediaries, issuers and investors in the eight member territories of the Eastern Caribbean Central Bank currency area. The ECSE provides a trading platform for the buying and selling of stocks, bonds and government-backed securities. The formation and primary mission of the ECSE is similar to that of other regional approaches:

- Promote economic development in the region;
- Promote the private sector led development of the economies of the member countries of the ECCB, through the development and expansion of a market-based economic system;
- Promote broader domestic ownership in the region's economy;
- Mobilise regional capital resources for regional enterprise development;
- Create a vehicle to accelerate privatisation in the region; and
- Promote increased foreign investment in the region's economy.[9]

The ECSE is an early illustration of synergistic behaviour within a region because the investment in infrastructure and the associated risks are shared across national entities bonded by common goals and objectives. This market will function best when all parties reach operational parity. Simply, it will be valueless to offer listed shares of a firm in one country if the order cannot be filled on or between the exchanges. Therefore, the success of the group depends on each member working together to ensure that the infrastructure brings continuity to the markets, while striving to achieve their individual corporate goals. Regardless of the means of transporting capital from investors to corporations, investing is a common need shared by all firms operating in a capitalist environment. As discussed in the next section, while technology brings an eventual state of continuous access to capital markets, it also initiates new requirements to measure business activity in order for investors to achieve an understanding of a firm's potential to generate returns and leverage its assets.

The New Levers of Finance and Business Measurement

Corporations face a new global reality which demands that companies should compete in a global marketplace, continue to meet higher levels of customer-centric customization, while keeping ever-vigilant as to the cost of production, reinvestment in the business and delivery of benefits to stockholders. The nature of business is becoming increasingly complex, with the introduction of co-opetition, collaborative commerce and other new dimensions of co-mingled business interplay. Senior management teams have been turning to even more complex computer models to assist in the decision-making process. However, one could argue that although computer models offer analytical syntheses of data and information, management teams need simplistic mechanisms in order to place this new level of information into a context that can be easily understood by everyone in the organization. As corporations restructure themselves into networks of value, they no longer have the luxury of placing the levers of control solely in the upper levels of management. Senior management teams must strive for mechanisms that can be implemented so that decisions can be pushed downwards to the lowest level within the organization which can effectively handle the problem. It should be the expressed goal of the management team to define, create and disseminate the mechanisms of control, and not to be the point at which all controls converge in order to facilitate decision-making. Measurement in its simplest form is illustrated in Figure 3.2.

Although Figure 3.2 is a necessary oversimplification, many companies are surprised by the results of the simple exercise of analysing the graphic when this is conducted with individuals at various levels within the organization. What the model does achieve is a means by which senior managers can engage the organization in a dialogue free from hidden agendas. If you only have three strategic moves on each side of the line for the survival of the firm, actions that improve the entire organization become more important than gains within an individual group. This exercise is often conducted with many groups in the firm and then synthesized by senior management into common or similar actions that can be put into operation quickly.

Measurement is a key aspect for firms operating in a synconomy, because to assess the output of strategic partnerships accurately, one must be able to measure the production of both the firm and the partner individually and in total. If business process synergy is to be achieved, the combined output of both must be greater that the sum of both parties' individual production. Measurement (both qualitative and quantitative) is

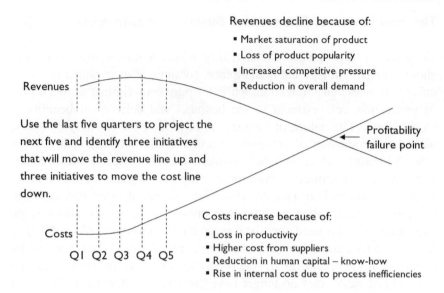

Revenues decline because of:
- Market saturation of product
- Loss of product popularity
- Increased competitive pressure
- Reduction in overall demand

Revenues

Use the last five quarters to project the
next five and identify three initiatives
that will move the revenue line up and
three initiatives to move the cost line
down.

Profitability
failure point

Costs increase because of:
- Loss in productivity
- Higher cost from suppliers
- Reduction in human capital – know-how
- Rise in internal cost due to process inefficiencies

Costs

Q1 Q2 Q3 Q4 Q5

Figure 3.2 The simplistic measurement: profitability

essential because it establishes a mechanism for understanding the behaviour of process components. This is uniquely true for organizations trying to achieve synergy in a network of value because the examination of the combined competencies, coupled with the measurement of the process components, makes possible the discovery of new ways to achieve fundamental business activities, reflecting Buckminster Fuller's observations on synergy:

> There is an important corollary of synergy which postulates that the known behavior of the whole system and the known behavior of at least three of the parts of the system makes possible the discovery of the other parts of the system and their respective behavior.[10]

Buckminster Fuller's principle postulates discovering unknown components based on the behaviour of known components, leading us to identify key skills which organizations must develop into corporate competencies: the ability to detect factors which can be rapidly understood and turned into corporate intelligence. For example, by observing the behaviours of individual market subsegments and correlating them to previously purchased product options, one can project product volumes dynamically. The dynamic nature of free-market capitalism across transnational boundaries has previously only been part of the strategies of large multinational corporations. However, now that all firms will achieve some degree of global reach, these factors must become part of their planning activities, especially organizations engaged in a network of value. The behaviour of corporations at a macro-level is similar to that of national economic ideologies which have demonstrated the repercussions of misunderstanding the dynamic nature of the world's socioeconomic systems, as Mead points out:

> Capitalism is the world's most powerful form of social organization because it is the most revolutionary. Capitalism did not defeat communism because capitalism is more stable; rather, the frozen stability of planned communist society was unable to match the social and economic dynamism of capitalistic activity.[11]

In a synconomy, corporations must emerge from the surprisingly similar corporate centralized planning activities and decentralize strategic thinking to line organizations that can leverage the dynamic nature of transnational commerce. Simply, firms must transition strategy from a centralized corporate function to a fundamental skill that managers at all levels must possess to leverage their combined knowledge. Unfortunately, the tools that corporations are using to embrace the dynamic nature of today's commerce, such as balance sheets and income statements, are backward-looking. These instruments measure the past. It is like driving a car forward while looking in the rear-view mirror. A fighter pilot in a high-speed jet flying at low altitude would rarely consult his or her rear-focused radar to detect a rapidly approaching mountain range. Likewise, corporations operating the new global environment must adopt and adapt new measures and mechanisms to sense what is ahead and use what is known about the organization's past performance to steer the course into future opportunities or sidestep potential problems.

Business Intelligence

Although the technology industry has recently adopted the term 'business intelligence' as the next manifestation of mechanized decision support tools, corporations in a synconomy must develop the process of business intelligence as a core competency. Management teams have to work to assist other functional groups within the firm and, in some cases, external partners to create an environment that senses and interprets external factors and enables the organization to adjust dynamically to the new competitive state. Business intelligence must be achieved along four distinct disciplines:

1. Sales organizations must be customer focused (market sensing).

2. Products demand continual observation of operating conditions and customer behaviour that influences design, production and sales
   (cost/value, behaviour sensing).

3. Attention to quality (adherence) is crucial to maintain product and brand
   images especially when core processes are externalized.

4. Production methods and costs must be frequently revisited to address
   improvements (process optimization).

Technology obviously plays a pivotal role in accumulating, synthesizing, aggregating and consolidating information to support the business
intelligence competency, requiring organizations to make significant
investments in infrastructure and specialized software applications to
develop the required data and skills. Business units that are becoming
culturally aware transnational entities must now weight an increasing
number of factors, interpret their influence on the firm's business model
and then seek advice from senior managers, looking for strategic actions to
maintain profitability, as Moschandreas observes:

> While economies of scale and scope may co-exist it is important to distinguish
> cost changes associated with the output mix from cost changes associated with
> the size of the firm. It would be of some significance, for example, for manage-
> ment to know that total cost may be reduced by altering the output mix
> (economies of scope) rather than by expanding all production lines proportion-
> ately (economies of scale).[12]

Tateisi identified several key issues that organizations must address to
circumvent the abundance of what he calls 'big business syndrome', a
condition in which organizations find themselves displaying the following
symptoms:

- a highly centralized bureaucracy;

- proliferation of special forms to conduct routine decisions;

- rising numbers of meetings to reach decisions;

- transference of matters between departments.[13]

To address the big business syndrome, Tateisi suggests an approach that is
strikingly similar to a solution which should be at the core of operating

behaviour for firms engaged in synergistic business practices. Firstly, firms must decentralize decision-making by reforming the company into smaller autonomous units that act as individual businesses and making top management a regularly accessible resource. Secondly, business units become, in effect, a consultative resource for senior managers when a line manager deems that a decision extends beyond the scope of the single entity. This ends up giving the top management team the ability to react quickly while making informed consolidated decisions because now it is removed from the traditional, routine, decision-making process and can act as a strategic resource aggregating the needs of all business units.[14]

Old and New Business Measurements

Business processes and transnational relationships both demand new comprehensive, dynamic measurements to meet changes in the competitive environment. The effectiveness of the measurement is relative to the organization's ability to synthesize the depth of the information into the context of the firm's business model and operating strategies. Traditional measurements, such as earnings per share, earnings before interest and taxes, return on equity, return on capital employed, return on process, return on investment and economic value added, all have their specific relevance and companies should use them within their appropriate context to validate decisions and act as a bridging mechanism back to shareholders and industry analysts. However, these traditional measurements must now be used in concert with other mechanisms, such as Kaplan and Norton's 'balanced scorecard', to give senior management teams a holistic representation of all the factors that influence strategic decisions, as Chattell points out:

> Balanced scorecards can enable companies to understand what's driving their performance. In addition to financial performance, they can keep track of softer factors such as customer satisfaction, the time it takes to get products to market, and employee satisfaction.[15]

The effectiveness of a corporation's strategy and the contribution to the bottom line is the intention of financial measurement, linking the financial objectives of individual business unit strategies to specific measurements which can vary during the different stages of the business life cycle (grow, sustain and harvest). As business units pass through each stage in the cycle, different measurements are required, principally to tell the story of the unit's strategy, objectives and actions to deliver the desired long-term financial performance. A customer's perspective requires both qualitative and quantitative measures such as customer satisfaction, retention, acquisition, profitability and market share to reflect the performance of the organization to key objectives. An internal business process perspective divides the critical processes of the firm into two distinct areas of focus: processes of innovation (such as product design and development); and processes of operations, such as marketing, manufacturing, quality and service. In order to take a 'learning and growth' perspective, an organization must examine the firm's infrastructure – people, systems and organizational procedures – to determine any existing shortfalls in capability and develop measures to reduce any deficiencies.

Probst et al. make a key observation for companies operating in the new synconomy:

> The concept of the balanced scorecard does not include a method of operationalizing the knowledge dimension, nor does it offer indicators of knowledge. Each organization must work out its own set of indicators, designed to suit its own circumstances, to record and control the variables that are important to it.[16]

Therefore, the metric needed to reflect the value of human capital or, more precisely, the combined potential of intellectual capital that can be applied to the corporate value proposition, must consist of indicators that are relevant to the organization's need for process competency.

The New Parameters

Achieving business process operational synergy in a network of value-added partners could be rephrased as mutual help or co-dependent assistance between normally disassociated corporate competencies. It is irrelevant that the competencies should be internal or external to the firm. In all cases, they must be linked into a value chain to deliver any value. Therefore, in the context of strategic thinking, the ownership is not important. The key to operational synergy with partners is the adaptive control in which the measurements of the processes and the external business environmental factors are brought together using preconceived rules online to estimate and adjust the control parameters of the co-dependent processes. This level of control can only be achieved by a sophisticated, robust technological infrastructure. To achieve synergy is, in essence, to attain local process stability of the adaptive process controllers or control mechanisms. Simply, the mechanism that senses changes in the business environment must alter the process conditions quickly to bring the process back towards its optimal design parameters. Therefore, synergy is achieved when the process treats external anomalies as merely new inputs to the operation, and not as exceptions that require additional intervention.

Businesses fail to achieve operating synergy between network partners not because changes in the external business environment go beyond the limits of their business processes, but because of ill-conceived relationships between the firms and/or a misunderstanding of how the parameters of each organization's business processes will react to the dynamics of the external factors. The business environment of today carries a high degree of competitive instability due to a plethora of social, political, economic and technological factors. Waiting for external forces to generate instability within the business process and then reacting to it by hastily making tactical corrections is not acceptable behaviour in a global synconomy. This is because this line of thinking is corporation-centric, reflecting a time when all the associated assets of the process were contained within the confines of the firm. Business process synergy occurs when the measurements can identify and classify external factors into a schema of preconceived scenarios which enables the business processes to reconfigure the underlying business model and/or process to adapt to the new business conditions.

When corporations operating in a network of value achieve this level of business process synchronization, considerable benefits can be realized in business agility and cost efficiencies. Operational excellence in a synconomy is not simply measuring the output of organizations operating in a network of value, it is measuring these organizations' performance to adapt and produce economies greater that the sum of their parts. When organizations reach this level of business conductivity, they will reduce the uncertainty of the business caused by external factors. However, to reach this goal, management teams from each organization must work together to develop a comprehensive set of business scenarios which can be used by the business units as mechanisms to derive tactical manoeuvres. When corporations apply this level of business process control, it gives them the ability to construct subprocesses of value that can be applied to niche market segments and other opportunities with smaller investments of capital and resources, which is the subject of the next section.

Micro-financing and Macro-brands

An area of economic activity which has been largely ignored by global financial institutions is that of financing and commerce by small and medium-sized enterprises (SMEs). The Internet, with its ability to facilitate eCommerce transactions, provides SMEs with a wide variety of growth opportunities in which they can meet new competitive challenges. Competition in the SME market comes from three sources:

1. other SMEs (normally in the same geography although in progressively distant locations)

2. big businesses looking to expand by either capturing additional market share or acting as a consolidator with a fragmented marketplace, frequently using mergers and acquisitions as a vehicle for growth

3. foreign sources (which are typically similar organizations providing products and services constructed around a similar value proposition).

In all cases and regardless of source, today's SMEs face greater competitive pressure than their multinational counterparts. Due to their size, the SMEs sometimes have difficulty in accessing capital. This is because either most SMEs cannot meet the financial requirements established by local and distant stock exchanges, or when they do meet the requirements, they are unable to market economically to potential global investors other than big institutions. However, what financial institutions must realize is that the SMEs' compact size does make them far more agile than larger corporations, giving them the ability to change direction and objectives rapidly. Much has been written on this topic, using examples of western economies and US businesses, which is why this global problem is illustrated here with an example of Islamic and other economic systems.

The synergies found in financial systems – comprising governing regulations, banks, lenders, tax authorities and other institutions involved with the regular, predictable and timely transfer of monies – serve the community in which they operate by providing a socioeconomic conduit which enables businesses to transact, consumers to buy, the government to collect taxes and individuals to save. Mills and Presley have noted that the objectives of western and Islamic societies are, in the main, the same: the achievement of an adequate level of social and economic justice.[17] It is in this sense of social and economic justice that Warde sees little difference between the classical Keynesian approach to market capitalism and Islamic economic objectives, with the exception of *falah*, translated as well-being, in which the socioeconomic systems strive for an equitable, purposed redistribution of wealth.[18] The key differences between western and Islamic economic systems is that the morality of the participants within the system rests on a social obligation to create meaningful employment, not to make every individual a consumer, as in western societies, but because full employment impacts individuals' dignity within society.[19] If this basic differentiation between free-market ideologies is taken within the context of micro-financing, one can see that there are indeed a number of striking similarities between western capital lenders and SME investors, and the *mudaraba* (which commend a partnership or financial trade) and the *musharaka* (longer term, equity-line arrangements).

To avoid an in-depth dissertation on the idiosyncrasies of Islamic finance, these variables will be oversimplified to focus on the central point. Micro-lending in any economy is vital to achieve the overall implied goals of socioeconomic activity to better conditions for businesses and citizens participating in economic exchange. The western ideals of financing SMEs are defined within the boundaries of simple and small capital loans and/or access to small venture capital providers. If a small business needs additional capital to achieve its goals, it can take out a loan, issue public or private shares or seek out venture financing. The transactions are complete when the capital is repaid with the pre-agreed rate of interest. In contrast, within the Islamic system, businesses must weigh the objectives of the firm while considering the needs of the community, being able to take advantage of more fluid mechanisms of financing which resemble their western counterparts but are fundamentally different, as they act as proactive mechanisms to self-redistribute wealth. When *fahal* is combined with two other key ideological differences, that of *riba* (the taking of interest) and *gharar* (the prohibition of certain counter-cultural values on exchanges and/or gambles), they illustrate a set of principles which global businesses should bear in mind, not simply within the boundaries of Islamic economies. The point to consider is that a firm must not simply adapt its business processes to embrace an Islamic customer; corporations must develop connective mechanisms that enable them to adopt, to some degree, the different requirements of all external cultural idiosyncrasies. The issues found in local cultural commerce must be taken into consideration for the broader implications of a rising sense of corporate moral and social responsibilities.

Local commercial activities often comprise highly fragmented marketplaces, which is ideal for studying synergistic business behaviour. A good example is the micro-credit programme for small, often family-run businesses in Bangladesh, which have the same fundamental problems as western SMEs. In the Bangladeshi market, micro-lending is used as a mechanism to reduce poverty by supplying capital to stimulate economic growth and increase local incomes. Traditional banks and other institutional lending sources typically ignore the needs of small businesses and individuals desiring self-employment because of the lack of perceived collateral – physical or other – to secure a loan. The goal of micro-credits and other cooperative programmes is to assist self-employed people or people desiring self-employment who are typically not serviced by traditional financial institutions. In many ways, the problem of self-employed credit in Bangladesh is similar to the financial challenges faced by western SMEs, small start-up companies and individuals identified as self-employed, sometimes called 'free agents'. However, in Bangladesh, as Khandker observes, the Grameen Bank has developed a micro-credit programme which has unique value propositions:

> The bank's group-based lending scheme has two important features that attract the poor: borrowers are allowed to deal with a financial institution through a group and members self-select their own group.[20]

In Khandker's opinion, the group's default rate is lower because members experience peer pressure to maintain their standing in the group. The value proposition to the Grameen Bank is a reduction of risk because it can pool resources and spread its risk across community groups. Another key observation is that home-based workers, which in most cases are women in Bangladesh, are the best candidates for micro-credit but are often not able to participate because of one of three factors: lack of training in entrepreneurism; low literacy rate; or social restrictions.[21] The lesson here for corporations operating in a synconomy is that the traditional view of the small loan market in Bangladesh ignores a large customer segment; the cultural value of pride within the community, which is a qualitative factor, substitutes for the traditional western quantitative requirement of collateral. Therefore, in terms of a synconomy, one must realize that it is a rare occurrence when corporate behaviour or market value propositions are truly unique. We can see that although the mechanisms for micro-lending are, on the surface, fundamentally different in each case, they share the same basic premise: to provide the western SME with a conduit to capital, the Bangladeshi with a means to group lending, and the Islamic SME with a *wadi* (stream) of financing.

Micro-credit is just one example of how corporations must learn to adopt and adapt their transnational business processes to engage diverse cultures and not bypass them because the value proposition is not readily noticeable. Global businesses and the rising cross-border business process activities create another condition that must be placed in the context of affecting local and cultural values – that of branding.

Macro-branding, Micro-brands and Culture

In the evolving synconomy, the challenges of culture and branding must be considered in the broader context of cross-corporate integration and differentiated product identity. To achieve a clear market differentiation, firms operating in a synconomy must balance the synergistic relationship between information and other tangible and intangible assets which are shared or integrated between partners and those aspects of a product or service which are unique to a firm in an open global marketplace. Collaboration between cooperating firms must be based on an understanding of when, how and what to exchange between partners. This is especially true with product or corporate branding. One can argue that global connecting technology increases the local consumer's awareness of local brands more cost effectively than that of their globally branded multinational counterparts. Since the overall effectiveness of the Internet to attract and retain customers is still relatively unknown, in that few internal, customer-specific studies have been conducted to draw any quantitative or qualitative conclusions by industry, the Internet levels the competitive playing field between large and small brand identities. The uncertainty of the Internet's total effectiveness is evident by the deep reduction in advertising spending in the post-dot-com business climate. Underhill observes that not just technology is challenging a firm's ability to leverage a brand image; consumers' attitudes towards brands are also changing:

> Simultaneously, we are witnessing the erosion of the influence of brand names. Not that brands don't have value, but that value is not the blind force it used to be. A generation or two ago, you chose your brands early in life and stuck by them loyally until your last shopping trip.[22]

In a globally connected business environment, corporations must develop a brand image that communicates value using three primary channels:

1. the physical world or the traditional mechanisms to demographic markets

2. the Internet or virtual world, which can be used as an alternative means for attracting customers and increasing levels of services

3. the newly emerging interconnected network of value partners, providing and receiving value from brokered relationships between partners, affiliates and associated organizations.

Each distinct channel must allow the firm to develop either a corporate brand, product brand or value-based brand. In all cases, a brand image must carry a clear value proposition to customers, that is, a differentiation that is recognized by indigenous people in a specific geography. The brand identity must be formulated to combine the overall objectives of the corporate brand strategy and local or cultural attributes.

In a synconomy, brands represent not simply the image of a firm or product; they are a corporation's identity to regional markets and local consumers. As corporations become partners in a network of value, they must make branding decisions, such as co-branding, special market branding, niche branding, cultural branding, religious branding and other non-traditional brand forms, to either cater to global cultures and market subsegment tastes or develop a strong central or corporate brand image. Brands are an essential mechanism that will engage customers, introduce products to markets and communicate a corporate trust. As a firm enters into partnership relationships, it must remember that the partner and its actions will often alter its brand image and may communicate unintended messages to customers. How the brand identity is used between partners must be clear to all parties to avoid future misunderstandings when devising marketing campaigns and other joint activities. Co-branding with newly formed public–private partnerships with government agencies also raises a number of questions about how products and services are brought to the market. Corporations must think of the strategic implications to brand and corporate images in the context of how it will be interpreted by the global consumer, especially as governments move to a more intimate role in facilitating transnational and regional commerce. It is to this topic that we now turn.

Facilitating Commerce and the New Role of Government

Globalization, technology, and changes in social attitudes worldwide present governments with a new set of challenges which require rethinking not only the role of government, the services it provides, and the nature of taxation, but also the effectiveness of elected leadership to achieve the goals of society. As international boundaries become less physical in definition and more cultural and economic in form, governments, like their business counterparts, are becoming transparent, in the sense that their actions and use of public funds are under increased scrutiny by the press and their citizens. World and local leaders must now consider the role of government in a global marketplace, being no longer simply an organization that supports only local agendas.

In this sense, one measure of government's effectiveness will be the economic competitiveness of those governed. Compounding the government's role in the twenty-first century economy is the erosion in the overall perceived power of the nation state to act as an effective control mechanism in a free-market economy, as we will explore in Chapter 4. Today's global economic climate is increasingly growing in complexity and uncertainty, as the more integrated financial markets become, the greater the degree of volatility between them. Seemingly, this ripple effect is due in part to the ability of technology to facilitate information at ever-increasing rates. However, one could also argue that the ripple effect is due to the interconnected volatilities between markets which have always existed, now being magnified by technology. One thing has become clear in a synconomy: in the new interconnected global economy, more cooperation and collaboration between nations is needed in order for the world as a whole to progress towards economic prosperity and cultural parity.

Governments should act proactively to facilitate commerce and stimulate economic growth by working in partnership with businesses to develop the infrastructures needed to give all companies within a region access to the global marketplace. German Chancellor Gerhard Schröder professes that the new economic policy needs to be forward-looking, creating an environment for competition and jettisoning its historical use as a mechanism to promote individual products.[23] A key benchmark that citizens should use to measure the effectiveness of government is not the imposition of single-market regulations or tariffs, but the government's ability to facilitate corporate growth by reducing barriers to markets and enacting policies which serve as an agenda for economic growth. Growth in a synconomy depends on an increased level of collaboration between governments and industries within an economic region and in conjunction with all regions of the world. One role of government will be to identify, broker or manage public and private sector partnerships not only in their home country, but also in what concerns external counterpart organizations. Government agencies must act as a broker of trade – not a regulator – offering advisory services which enable corporations to examine the partnership in the context of their individual interest and as part of a cohesive national economic agenda. This brokering relationship must extend beyond the traditional geographic borders to facilitate transnational behaviour.

In the UK, this new view of government has been embraced by the Department of Trade and Industry's White Paper on enterprise, skills and innovation entitled *Opportunities for all in a World of Change*, which prioritizes the transition to a knowledge economy, innovation and the establishment of business clusters as a first step towards an integrated world economy.[24] Businesses operating in a synconomy must view government agendas as a framework in which to synchronize their activities, to some degree, with these initiatives. For example, a UK business that has identified a demand for its products in a foreign marketplace can reduce the total investment needed to establish its external business presence by using the opportunity to broker a partnership with its counterparts in the target region, thus leveraging the government's objective of participating in a global economy.

As governments act to facilitate commerce in a synconomy, the traditional relationships between corporations, customers, financial institutions, investors, commercial activity, taxation and regulation get nearer to being on a collision course with the forces of globalization and disintermediation. Business activity at each step in the value chain needs to have a clear value-added proposition so that consumers and businesses can determine the overall applicability of an underlying product or service. Recent corporate scandals, declining market activity and other global factors present an opportune time to rethink how companies are measured for performance and regulated to quantify their integrity. More importantly, as citizens and businesses become more global, they will continue to challenge our traditional mechanisms for measuring risk and performance. The impending opportunity for world governments is to develop a standard set of measurement criteria and monitoring mechanisms which can be applied not only as a method of regulation, but as a conduit for international interchange. If one considers that a small but growing company in a developing nation is not unlike a small start-up Internet company or subsidiary of an existing organization, a set of benchmarks could be developed to assess the risks across the entire economic sector, with ranges or 'tolerances' applying to specific areas of market activity. To carry this line of thinking further, we could develop an assessment matrix that would determine not only the risks for a firm, but also a 'relative' risk for the global sector. This is similar to how stocks are assessed with multiple indicators (for example a price earnings ratio, yield and share price). Regulatory agencies and other connected organizations could easily establish a global consortium and set the boundaries of measurement and the mechanisms for rating corporate behaviour within the guidelines, effectively providing a global risk benchmark that operates independently of geopolitical regulations.

In a capitalist society, the government's ability to facilitate commerce is directly proportional to its trust in the activities of business and, more

importantly, in the fidelity of the information used to report those activities. If we look again at the objectives of Malta's eGovernment, it is clear
that two of Malta's goals are to provide a legal framework in which businesses can operate and a technological infrastructure initiative to move the
country quickly into the information age. More significantly, the eGovernment has made a concerted effort to engage citizens. The Maltese plan for
an information society and information economy establishes two distinct
objectives: the creation of a national environment providing the necessary
legal, educational, technological and new organizational structures, and a
set of eGovernment initiatives detailing specific steps which will be taken
to achieve their goals:

> The government is committed to raising the quality of life of the Maltese to the
> highest attainable levels. In striving for this goal it will actively promote and
> utilize Information and Communications Technology to the widest possible
> extent, as the means to strengthening the economy, creating jobs, ensuring
> social equity and enhancing education and culture. The Government will
> ensure that all citizens participate in the creation of, and benefit from, the addi-
> tional social, cultural and economic wealth that will be created.[25]

Malta's objectives go beyond simply building websites for government
agencies; they demonstrate the beginning of a complete rethinking of the
role of government from a passive provider of social services to an active
participant in reshaping the sociotechnological business environment. For
businesses operating in a synconomy, Malta's eGovernment initiatives
provide insights into a technological infrastructure framework which
describes how the public and private sector can work synergistically while
optimizing the cost of the infrastructure.[26]

   Although it is difficult to pinpoint any one direct factor to be identified
as the root cause in changes occurring in the relationship between business,
society and government, demands for government to take a more comprehensive but less intrusive role in business are nevertheless happening
sporadically around the world. Initiatives such as the 'eEurope 2003' docu-
ment, in which European governments acknowledge the rising change in
the attitudes of their citizens and recognize that a key role of government is
to ensure long-term economic stability for the European Union (EU) and
any candidate countries, are very rare indeed.[27]

   The European Commission (EC) has identified that the solution to delivering a substantial change in the functions of government is in the creation
of an information society based on establishing a robust technical infrastructure, a highly skilled workforce and incentives to foster an increased

level of international collaboration. At the vanguard of this approach is the identification of three essential components – technology, skills and motivations – which will create the conditions for growth within the information society. These issues are the same for businesses operating in a synconomy and must be incorporated into strategic initiatives as part of a holistic approach to competing in a quasi-collaborative marketplace. The EC rightly identified three critical components for the information society to flourish:

1. A relatively secure, high-speed technology infrastructure linking people, centres of learning, businesses, government agencies and other non-EU countries, provided by either public or private sources or both.

2. A comprehensive and proactive approach to educating young people in obtaining the skills needed for the next generation of business, coupled with a continual education process for individuals to develop the skills required for participation in a knowledge-based economy.

3. A directed effort at using the Internet for eCommerce, electronic access to public services or eGovernment, the facilitation of health care online, the development of European digital content for distribution inside the EU with the intention of exporting a large percentage of information to world peoples, and the creation of an intelligent transport system.

On the other hand, Darrell West of Brown University points out that in the US – a nation state which has been viewed as the leader in eGovernment and eEducation – a survey of 1,813 US-based, eGovernment websites shows that the vast majority of these sites fall short of providing a comprehensive suite of government services:

> In general, we find that the e-government revolution has fallen short of its potential. Government websites are not making full use of available technology, and there are problems in terms of access and democratic outreach. E-government officials need to work to improve citizen access to online information and services.[28]

The conclusions drawn by West identify a central problem which also exists within businesses conducting trans-border eCommerce: the lack of a standard place to find common information. In the case of the eGovernment survey, finding basic information such as human services across all 50 states was almost as taxing as going to their physical bureaucracies. This is not to say that all states must agree on a technology standard in order to provide services to citizens; it merely reflects that like their European government counterparts, the focus has been on access, not effective use. One could argue that the next wave of eGovernment initiatives will focus on information navigation, inter/intra/extra-agency integration and the aggregation of self-service citizen information. Government initiatives worldwide will need to address two universal components to eGovernment solutions: privacy and security. All government agencies, large and small, international and domestic, must develop a level of security and privacy that offers citizens a level of confidence that their information will not be unduly disclosed or misused. Darrell West notes that a recent project at Brown University revealed that an overwhelming majority of US state and federal websites lacked effective security and privacy policy statements, with 15 states having no security policy statement and 10 states having no privacy policy statement.[29] Sadly, although all governments share this technological challenge, few are working towards developing a standard mechanism or means to safeguard this information collaboratively. Government services could save millions of dollars by establishing a global standard for security and privacy that would not only reduce costs because of economies of scale, but also reduce long-term integration and interchange costs. That said, in the UK, the Office of the eEnvoy was established to actively address the development of standards and other means of facilitating commerce in the emerging economy:

> We are working towards enabling the right market framework for e-commerce. Legislating only where necessary, and looking at industry-led self- and co-regulation where possible. We are also working closely with partners in Europe to develop the international e-commerce market framework.[30]

The UK's eCommerce initiative, coupled with innovations such as its Government Gateway,[31] which allows users of government services to register using a central identification and send secure authenticated transactions to any government agency, is a forerunner of the type of taxpayer-centric services that will be developed globally. Corporations should review this model of information-based portals to services because it provides an insight into how centralized, user-focused design enables the direct reduction in operating costs because of its ability to allow a user to traverse the myriad government services using one identity.

It often seems that simple technological solutions evade the strategies of governments and businesses alike when contemplating how to improve the communication and interactions between government and citizen or company and customer. A review of government and corporate websites reveals that many do not actively contain effective mechanisms for eMail contact, mailing address information and inwardly directed search engines. It goes without saying that even fewer US government websites offer multilingual services. These technologies are not difficult, exotic or expensive, but they do require a robust infrastructure to support rises in volumes and an organizational discipline to ensure that the use is not interpreted as additional work to the organization but as *the* work of the organization.

Fortunately, the EC again has identified key weaknesses in eGovernment implementations, thus challenging members and potential members of the EU to embrace a comprehensive set of guidelines for cross-cultural implementation of a pan-European technical infrastructure. The EC is linking aspects of social inclusion for new EU members, prioritizing digital inclusion as a mechanism for participation in a competitive, knowledge-based economy:

> In emphasising digital inclusion, the European Commission aims to distinguish the European approach to the information society from other regions of the world. It is no secret that the United States for example outperformed Europe in the initial speed with which industry and citizens took up the Internet. eEurope is now, however, helping Europe catch up, channelling efforts at regional, national and European levels to ensure that the digital economy brings benefits to all European citizens and to put a European stamp on the Internet.[32]

For businesses operating in a synconomy, these new government initiatives translate into higher levels of information exchange between private and public sectors, ultimately increasing the level of data security required to protect sensitive customer and citizen data. The EC identified 20 services targeted at both citizens and business which will influence not only business activities throughout Europe, but will also determine the future of non-European firms' ability to interface with European partners. The public citizen services include: income taxes, social security contributions, personal documents, car registration, building permission, declarations to the police, public libraries, birth, marriage and death certificates, change of address and health-related services. As for businesses, the services include among others: social contribution for employees, corporation tax, VAT, company registration and customs declarations.[33] Each country in turn must internalize how the knowledge economy will be achieved. In Scotland, for example, a three-pronged strategy is envisioned, bringing together academic research and corporate enterprises to form Scottish enterprise clusters.[34] This strategy centres on commercializing research by reducing the barriers between academic institutions, government and private industry, by developing a technological infrastructure comprising collaborative clusters, as stated by the Scottish Office:

> Progress towards a more competitive position must be made on technology innovation and productivity improvements. The Government's policy emphasis is therefore on knowledge, skills, creativity and the pressing need to transfer knowledge from the scientific and engineering base into the market place.[35]

The establishment of infrastructure-sharing business clusters is a vital first step in building the economic, social, legal and technological mechanisms required by large and small businesses within a nation to engage in global business, as demonstrated by the commerce initiatives of His Highness Sheikh Mohammed Bin Rashid Al Maktoum, crown prince of Dubai in the United Arab Emirates.[36] The comprehensive Dubai strategy is threefold (interacting with the government, education, and infrastructure), spanning myriad government functions, all aimed at fulfilling clear value propositions:

> Ease the lives of people and businesses interacting with the Government and contribute in establishing Dubai as a leading economic hub.[37]

The three components of the eGovernment strategy are as follows:

1. To reduce the difficulties sometimes encountered by local business and external corporate entities in interacting with government agencies. The initial eGovernment initiative provides direct links with the Chamber of Commerce, Department of Civil Defence, Economic Development, Department of Electricity and Water, Al-Awqaf Department, Tourism and Commerce, Dubai Municipality, Naturalization and Residency, Civil Aviation, Land Department, Jebel Ali Free Zone, Dubai Ship Docking Yard, Development Board, Dubai Port Authority, Dubai Police, Dubai Airport Free Zone Authority, Dubai Courts, Public Prosecution Dubai, Health and Medical Service, Department of Information, Dubai Ports and Customs, in an effort to streamline activities such as starting a business, finding a house, paying bills and fines, and new arrival services.[38]

2. The IT Education Project, built in conjunction with the Ministry of Education. This project addresses the need to develop a higher education programme tailored to focus on the new skills required in a technology-networked world of commerce by converting the standard educational system into an eLearning system.[39] The project establishes partnerships

with leading international technology companies to provide high-quality technology-based learning.

3. To develop public–private infrastructures to assist new commercial activities such as the establishment of the Dubai Internet City[40] complex (a free-trade zone for technology companies and eBusiness a few kilometres outside Dubai) and the Dubai Media City[41] (the first city devoted to creativity and the media industry).

Sheikh Mohammed's vision does not stop with merely providing a vibrant government structure that is continually changing to meet the emerging needs of global businesses; his strategy also includes seeking out the best ideas to integrate the local vision into the greater global context, with events such as the Dubai Strategy Forum.[42] The Dubai vision demonstrates the new role of government in a synconomy; its strategic initiatives are centred on economic development which brokers relationships, establishes public–private partnerships and provides mechanisms to integrate local business activities directly into a transnational commerce infrastructure.

Governments in all parts of the world are now rapidly experimenting and forging new relationships to reinvent themselves and provide services tailored to acclimatizing domestic business to the competitive levels needed to participate in a network of value-added partners. Some approaches are more proactive than others, and require greater or lesser amounts of investment capital. However, they all share a common idea: that commerce and trade is the key to economic growth and an increase in the standard of living for a nation's citizens. As governments reassess their capabilities, realigning their services to better support the needs of citizens and business, corporations are rethinking the mechanisms for reporting performance in the emerging business environment, as we shall see in the next section.

Corporate Performance Reporting and Organizational Morality

> Capitalism is the astounding belief that the most wickedest of men will do the most wickedest of things for the greatest good of everyone.
>
> *John Maynard Keynes*

In the wake of the dot-com meltdown and the spectacular implosion of corporations such as Enron and WorldCom, investors, regulators and the press rekindled their love affair with corporate morality. During the 1990s, the ethics of senior management teams, the morality of firms and the social responsibilities of multinational enterprises simply took a break, as the quest for rising market capitalizations became the single measure for investors. The behaviours of corporations resulted in two distinct reactions by investors: the industry and government agencies established the need to restore confidence in the quality of information within the financial markets; and the development of a heightened awareness towards corporate social, moral and community obligations by various segments of investors. This is not to imply that all firms lost a sense of obligation to the communities they serve, it simply reflects that companies responded to the priorities of private and institutional shareholders. Here again, we find that this type of market behaviour is not a product of modernity, technology or the dot-com phenomena, but a natural part of the cyclical nature of business, as observed by Kevin Phillips:

> Near the peak of the great booms, old economic cautions are dismissed, financial and managerial operators sidestep increasingly inadequate regulation and ethics surrender to greed. Then, after the collapse, the dirty linen falls out of the closet. Public muttering usually swells into a powerful chorus of reform – deep, systemic changes designed to catch up with a whole new range and capacity for frauds and finagles and bring them under regulatory control.[43]

A predictable reaction during times of economic downturn is to bring firms under closer scrutiny. Companies are made accountable not only for their financial performances, but also for their contribution to society in important social issues, such as environmental policy, human rights, regional economic impact, activities with business partners and corruption. The bursting of the 1990s stock market bubble made clear that the generation of shareholder value is not the object of business, but rather a by-product of a firm's competencies operating in a free-market economy.[44]

With each rise and fall of the financial markets, there is a sudden need for society to seek out those who could be labelled as the cause or guilty persons whose greed ultimately hastened the collapse. It is during these times of sudden morality that we forget the words of Thomas Jefferson: 'Money, not morality, is the principal commerce of civilized nations.' The ever-virulent media exacerbates the degree of loss by reporting, almost sensationally, the totality of the financial losses instead of placing them into a broader economic context. Today's new scrutinized CEOs with executive pay packets have similarly replaced the early twentieth-century robber barons. The rise and backlash of corporate morality by the public and investors must be viewed as a natural reaction by people who were willing partners in the overvaluation of the market. Investors placed a premium on rising share prices, which acted in part to stimulate executive teams to adopt behaviours that were designed to increase the value of shares almost to the exclusion of all other activity. Warren Buffet steadfastly cautioned that this behaviour was not sustainable in the long term, but in many cases his words of wisdom were dampened by the deafening roar of market exuberance. Once again, we can see that the sin of corporate greed is a two-party system in which investors are uninformed but willing partners.

Reactionary behaviour following an economic downturn leads to over-regulation, which in many cases dampens business activity when it seeks to regulate activities by imposing additional bureaucracies. Two issues in business discussions are those of a social obligation between businesses and the society with which they interact and the existence of a 'moral economy' and the rise of an environmental consciousness. Corporations must demonstrate a value-based recognition (that is, qualitative and quantitative community involvement) of the principles held by the societies in which they operate.[45] Although most corporate business development initiatives begin with good intentions for the communities in which they operate or intend to operate, few are viewed within the context of the long-term effects on the local workforce and social structure. Bapat's enlightening research on the effects of the construction of an amusement park on local people in India points out that during the process of regional economic development by the government and the corporation, no group accounted for the interest of the indigenous people. The development was primarily justified by its job creation and development of the local economy potentials. Unfortunately, few local people were ever hired because of their lack of directly applicable skills. Exacerbating the situation even further, the amusement park was built on a part of common land that was shared by the local population, providing them with subsistence. Bapat's account of the Indian amusement park clearly demonstrates the need for corporations to develop proactively a moral and economic accountability.

As corporations endeavour to become participants in a global economy, they must also develop into organizations that are responsive to the needs of the communities in which they operate. This responsibility is one that weighs the profitability of the firm with the ability to execute business in the business environment offered by the geographic location. Continuous investor pressures often intimidate firms into simply taking a course of action that centres on short-term profit objectives versus long-term community responsibilities. McIntosh et al. indicate that participating in a global moral economy requires that organizations subscribe to the ideal of responsible corporate citizenship by addressing five management imperatives:[46]

1. Accountability, adopting a transparent operating philosophy implementing controls and measures that reflect honest and accurate reporting of financial activities and other business dealings;

2. Think interdependence by looking at products in an ecological life cycle, not simply at the point of sale to a customer. Customers dispose of products improperly because of a lack of proper disposal knowledge, inconvenience because they must incur additional time or cost and/or they are unaware that a product can be recycled or reused in some way;

3. Have clear principles reflecting a global set of values and guidelines which enable operating groups to integrate, not segregate, the rich diversity that multicultural operations have to offer;

4. Embrace change and complexity by proactively addressing change as a continual process, not as a periodic disruptive event. Complexity can be reduced by increasing communications and leveraging technology as often complexity is a result of miscommunications and a lack of clear guidelines on corporate behaviour;

5. Be educated and knowledgeable, cultivating human capital by investing in the education and training of individuals.

Corporate reporting must reflect the true nature of the activities of the company, just as a firm's social, civic and moral obligations must not be compromised under the guise of profitability. The traditionally practised, Machiavellian approach (the ends justify the means) of large multinational corporations will over time be rewarded less by more socially conscious investors. As information technology continues to make corporate value propositions more transparent to customers, technology also facilitates the need to report accurate, timely and meaningful information to the management team, partners, investors and other interested parties. Organizations engaged in tightly coupled partnerships soon realize that the quality and validity of information is paramount to reducing costly errors and miscommunications during the production process. The influence of structure, culture, customer preferences, and other factors such as taxation, politics, social consciousness and corporate morality will all contribute to remoulding the nature of what we do and determine the skills that firms must employ to meet the new competitive demands. The next chapter discusses the influence of cultures and national identity on the formation of global partnerships, and looks at the misconception of business evolution leading to a corporate nation state.

Notes

1 R. Reich, *The Work of Nations: Preparing Ourselves for 21st-century Capitalism*, New York: Alfred A. Knopf, 1991.

2 P. C. Mackay, 'Extraordinary popular delusions and the madness of crowds', in M. Fridson, (ed.), *Extraordinary Popular Delusions and the Madness of Crowds & Confusión de Confusiones*, New York: John Wiley & Sons, 1996, p. vii.

3 The Local Futures Group, London, available at www.localfutures.com, November 2002.

4 A. Pike, 'Regions miss out on new economy', *Financial Times*, 12 March 2001, p. 14.

5 The Local Futures Group.

6 C. Handy, *The Elephant and the Flea: Looking Backwards to the Future*, London: Hutchinson, 2001, p. 148.

7 'Central Information Management Unit. White Paper on the Vision and Strategy for the Attainment of E-Government', Blata: Government of Malta, 2000, available at www.cimu.gov.mt/documents/egovwhitepaper_for_cimu_website.pdf.

8 J. M. Keynes, *The General Theory of Employment, Interest and Money*, London: Macmillan – now Palgrave Macmillan, 1971, p. 316.

9 Eastern Caribbean Securities Exchange (ECSE) available at www.ecseonline.com/ecse.asp.

10 R. Buckminster Fuller, *The World Game: Integrative Resource Utilization Planning Tool*, Carbondale: Southern Illinois University, 1971, p. 14.

11 W. Mead, 'Roller-coaster capitalism', *Foreign Affairs*, January/February 1997, **76**(1): 150.

12 M. Moschandreas, *Business Economics*, London: Routledge, 1994, pp. 149–50.

13 K. Tateisi, 'Treating "big business syndrome"', in D. Dayao (ed.), *Asian Business Wisdom: Lessons from the Region's Best and Brightest Business Leaders*, Singapore: John Wiley, 2000, p. 102.

14 Tateisi, 'Treating "big business syndrome"', pp. 101–6.

15 A. Chattell, *Creating Value in the Digital Era*, Basingstoke: Macmillan – now Palgrave Macmillan, 1998, p. 241. According to Kaplan and Norton, the 'balanced scorecard' is a measurement tool for senior management that provides a comprehensive, four-point framework, consisting of financial, customer, internal business processes and learning and growth, to translate the company's vision and strategy into a coherent set of performance measures (see R. Kaplan and D. Norton, *The Balanced Scorecard: Translating Strategy into Action*, Boston: Harvard Business School Press, 1996).

16 G. Probst, S. Raub and K. Romhardt, *Managing Knowledge: Building Blocks for Success*, Chichester: John Wiley, 2000, p. 252.

17 P. S. Mills and J. R. Presley, *Islamic Finance: Theory and Practice*, Basingstoke: Macmillan – now Palgrave Macmillan, 1999, p. 5.

18 I. Warde, *Islamic Finance in the Global Economy*, Edinburgh: Edinburgh University Press, 2000, p. 46.

19 Mills and Presley, *Islamic Finance: Theory and Practice*, p. 5.

20 S. R. Khandker, *Fighting Poverty with Microcredit: Experience in Bangladesh*, Oxford: Oxford University Press, 1998, p. 3.

21 Khandker, *Fighting Poverty with Microcredit*, p. 3.

22 P. Underhill, *Why We Buy: The Science of Shopping*, London: Orion Business Books, 1999, p. 32.

23 G. Schröder, 'Shaping industry on the anvil of Europe', *Financial Times*, 29 April 2002, p. 21.

24 *Opportunity for All in a World of Change*, a White Paper on enterprise, skills and innovation, Department of Trade and Industry, available at www.dti.gov.uk/opportunityforall/pages/contents.html, December, 2002.

25 'Central Information Management Unit, White Paper on the Vision and Strategy for the Attainment of E-Government', p. 4.

26 'Office of the Prime Minister: Central Information Management Unit, e-Government Interoperability Framework', Blata: Government of Malta, version 1.0, July 2002, available at www.cimu.gov.mt/documents/cimu_t_0001_2002.pdf.

27 'eEurope 2003: A cooperative effort to implement the information society in Europe', Action plan prepared by the candidate countries with the assistance of the European Commission, June 2001, p. 1., available www.map.es/csi/pdf/eEurope_2003.pdf.

28 D. West, *Assessing E-Government: The Internet, Democracy, and Service Delivery by State and Federal Governments*, Providence: Brown University, 2000, available at www1.worldbank.org/publicsector/egov/EGovReportUS00.html.

29 West, *Assessing E-Government*, pp. 6–7.

30 Office of the e-Envoy, www.e-envoy.gov.uk/oee/oee.nsf/sections/briefings-top/$file/eeconomy.html.

31 Government Gateway, www.gateway.gov.uk/.

32 European Commission, *Towards a Knowledge-based Europe: The European Union and the Information Society*, Brussels: Directorate General for Press and Communications, October 2002, p. 4. available at europa.eu.int/information_society/newsroom/documents/catalogue_en.pdf.

33 European Commission, p. 12.

34 The Scottish Office; *Scotland: Towards the Knowledge Economy*, available at www.scotland.gov.uk/library/documents-w9/knec-02.htm.

35 See The Scottish Office, www.scotland.gov.uk/library/documents-w9/knec-02.htm.

36 See H. H. Sheikh Mohammed Bin Rashid Al Maktoum's website at www.sheikhmohammed.co.ae/, November 2002.

37 See the Dubai e-Government website, available at www.dubai.ae, November 2002.

38 See the Dubai e-Government website at www.dubai.ae/, December 2002.

39 See the Dubai IT Project website at www.itep.ae/itportal/english/main.asp, October 2002.

40 See the Dubai Internet City, available at www.dubaiinternetcity.com/, November 2002.

41 See the Dubai Media City, available at www.dubaimediacity.com/, November 2002.

42 See the Dubai Strategy Forum, available at www.dubaistrategyforum.ae, November 2002.

43 K. Phillips, 'The cycle of financial scandal', *The New York Times on the Web*, 17 July 2002, available at www.nytimes.com/2002/07/17/opinion/17Phil.html.

44 J. Kay, 'Profits without honour', *Financial Times*, 29/30 June 2002, p. 13.

45 M. McIntosh, D. Leipziger, K. Jones, and G. Coleman, *Corporate Citizenship: Successful Strategies for Responsible Companies*, London: Financial Times Management, 1998, p. 275.

46 McIntosh et al., *Corporate Citizenship*, pp. 278–9.

CHAPTER 4

The Redefinition of the Corporation and the Nation State

The emerging corporate structure of an organization operating in a network of value is significant because it is a prelude to an organizational shift towards a more transnational approach to business. A similar adaptation can be observed to some degree in a shift in the traditional structure of nation states. As stated in previous chapters, any company can now participate in some aspect of global commerce. In fact, it can be argued that all corporations now possess a global potential and must balance

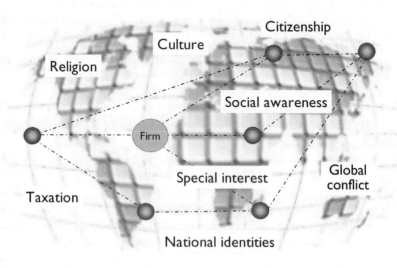

Figure 4.1 Factors that influence a network of value

factors such as culture, religion, citizenship, social awareness, special interest and other external forces, as illustrated in Figure 4.1. Like national governments, businesses operating in a global network of value must integrate these globally focused aspects of business into strategic thinking; this is especially true when the firm must strike partnerships that span national boundaries. Keeping this in mind, it is clear that in a synconomy two or more firms can partner, affiliate or form an alliance in which a mutually beneficial set of products can be offered to a global audience, in effect creating a virtual transnational company. In the past, small firms were typically prevented from entering remote markets due to the massive investment needed to facilitate international commerce. Today, however, services which were offered exclusively to and by multinational firms such as IBM, Philips, General Motors and other large organizations can now be obtained and to some degree offered by much smaller firms.

It could be argued that globalization is also changing the role of the nation state, enabling local governments to play a more significant role in forming interlocking networks, economic alliances and public–private partnerships.[1] The rise in power of more local government activity is not due to technology; however, technology plays a key role in providing the necessary economic and environmental incentives for the shift to occur. This significance in the new role of local government such as in cities within the EU is due to three factors, as observed by Shearman:

1. it is the combination of local experiences that make up the national economic, social and technical infrastructures and competitive capabilities;

2. cities have long been recognized as the foremost driver of regional development;

3. national policy resolutions to problems of competitiveness very often prove to be unsuccessful if not backed up/driven by local areas.[2]

One could argue that the economic power base within a nation state has already begun a migration to more regional sources such as sub-regions, states, or cities as global economies engage business at previously unknown levels of commerce. We are seeing the beginning of the fourth technological revolution, in which technologically enabled commerce permits regions to act synergistically with corporate entities and other forms of commerce. Wriston reflects on the historical aspects of technoeconomic transitions in his description of the third technological revolution:

In the three pillars of the order that resulted from the Industrial Revolution – national sovereignty, national economies, and military power – the information revolution has increased the power of individuals and outmoded old hierarchies.[3]

One could argue that in a synconomy, global economic activities define three new pillars of global social order: individual sovereignty, trans-national economies, and corporate economic power. Each of these is a recipient of the technological progress and new interconnectedness of business, society and government.

There is little doubt that corporations are undergoing a fundamental change that goes beyond a simple technological alteration, completely redefining a firm's structure, its people and skills, its approach to business and even the onset of a new array of social responsibilities. The need to stimulate economic growth fosters a parallel change within the nation state in which traditional government structures are streamlined to reduce cost and increase service, with a renewed focus on education, as Naisbitt observes:

> Where there is economic growth, there are also emerging more free-market form of governance – an acceptance of the fact that people, not political fiat, create economic opportunity.[4]

As McIntosh et al. point out, economic development in the new economy requires that governments and corporations work in closer harmony, not just within the region but with other regions to work towards increasingly achievable levels of economic interchange:

> Markets are not enough; capitalism cannot provide for all of society's needs and business has to work hand in hand with good government to address environmental issues, distribute wealth more fairly, fight corruption, oppression and human-rights abuses. If business is the principle engine of society, it has a clear responsibility not to abuse its new freedom and global role.[5]

However, as the role, power and importance of the large nation states reduce over time, the rise of smaller nations and regions within larger nations plays an increasingly greater role in facilitating commerce. As we discussed earlier, Naisbitt's predictions of smaller, easier to govern nation states seems more plausible in the not so distant future: 'As the importance of the nation-state recedes, more of them are being created.'[6] This economically driven phenomenon could continue to lead to larger countries dissolving into smaller governments (such as the former Yugoslavia and the Soviet Union) and smaller countries capitalizing on their ability to act quickly as integrated members of a single global economic environment.[7]

Economic interdependence acknowledges the fact that all national economies are now intertwined by government policies, technology and growing transnational business activity to the point where economic isolationist policies may no longer be an effective strategy to reduce any perceived threat that globalization presents to special interest groups. It is doubtful that the world's social structure will ever embrace a single form of government or a single set of regulatory statutes to control commerce. However, ever-increasing numbers of multidimensional economic agreements forge new relationships between nation states. Regrettably, the majority of these agreements are mainly structured to safeguard the traditional job protecting and import/export tariff schema which hinder a nation's overall competitiveness. Lipnack and Stamps make an important observation in the post-cold-war environment that corporations operating in a synconomy must incorporate into their strategic thinking:

> With the little noticed death of the internationalist dream of a One World Government in the past few decades, there is a pregnant vacuum waiting to birth a new vision of global governance. The emergence of *networks of nations* is upon us. This vision of the future sees multiple international networks where the members are sovereign nations. Each nation integrates into the global whole and yet remains an independent entity with its own integrity and substantial self-reliance.[8]

Like their corporate counterparts, nation states are evolving into a political, economic and cultural network that will be defined by agreements which, over time, simplify transnational business activities. One could argue that smaller nation states have the most to gain and are in the best position to lead this transformation of global commerce, because their inter-government structures contain less layers of bureaucracy and they have fewer special interest groups to pacify. However, in numerous smaller states, the special interest groups are indeed powerful and often sources of corruption.

As the synconomy continues to emerge, mirroring this multinational economic change is the renovation of small, medium-sized and large corporations that are engaging in transnational commercial activity, embracing new levels of customer service, offering greater ranges of products and demanding employees with higher levels of skills. The demand for skills and a greater ability to put business into a global context also alters the services that businesses provide to employees, as individuals are exposed to compensation plans that vary widely between organizations with a transnational corporate structure and across globally competing companies. To retain talent, corporations reinvent compensation offerings to supply benefits that more closely match the needs of a global workforce. There is growing speculation that corporations will evolve to encompass additional benefits and services which will ultimately perform many of the services traditionally performed by governments, creating a corporate state which crosses transnational borders. It would be naive to think that corporations will evolve to take on the responsibilities of running a nation state. Let us face facts: governments are not profitable ventures and although companies may provide benefits that resemble government functions, they are only a by-product of profit-making activities. As corporations take on more employee benefits such as at-work childcare, flexible hours, distance working, comprehensive retirement plans and insurance, they are underwriting one of the roles previously played by government, that of long-term security. However, as employment is now short term, these perceived effects are fleeting. It is possible for individuals to retire even more dependent on the government because of the lack of continuity in benefits between employers during an individual's lifetime, which brings us to the subject of taxation, to be discussed in the next section.

Taxation and the Redistribution of Wealth

The *Oxford Advanced Learner's Dictionary* defines 'tax' as 'money to be paid by people or businesses to a government for public purposes'.[9] Taxation is the system of collection used to acquire money from the taxpayer and redistribute funds to government agencies that use it for public purposes. Traditionally, this has been an unwritten social contract between the governing and the governed. All societies evolve, and it was during each evolutionary change that the social contract between government and citizens was restructured to keep pace (although often lagging behind) with the needs of people.

As businesses, people and economics become more tightly coupled internationally, corporations must become far more cognizant of the idiosyncrasies of the social contracts of each one of the geographies in which they operate. Although it could be argued that most corporations view themselves as being contained within a continual set of adjacent geographies, technology has now started an irreversible process of making international commerce easier, thus transcending geographic boundaries that were previously enjoyed only by multinational corporations. These factors are now so intermingled that corporations large and small must develop a greater understanding of the global, regional, and local socio-economic systems in which they operate.

A growing concern for governments is the application of taxes both within the nation state and to the transnational economic activities of the corporations operating across their borders. Another growing concern for governments across the globe is the issue of whether the current tax systems accurately reflect the needs of the people and, more importantly, whether the current tax structures are still viable public mechanisms for the redistribution of wealth. Corporations in a global synconomy must keep a strategic eye on the rising discourse on how globalization is increasing the gap between the 'have' and 'have nots', which seems to ignore completely the fundamental actions of a free-market system (which is rarely a fair or even distribution of wealth), as James and Nobes points out:

> A distribution of income and wealth that is solely determined by the market is unlikely to be the distribution most desired by society. In the market system, an individual's income is determined by the factors of production he or she owns and the price which those factors will fetch on the market. Society may not consider this to be a proper way of distributing its resources among its members. In an extreme case, for example, where an individual did not own any factors of production (that is, he had no capital or land and was unable to work), the individual would receive no income. If the community decides to influence the distribution of income and wealth, it is likely that the tax system will be one of the main methods employed.[10]

Given that the basic actions of free-market capitalism are based on the uneven or unfair distribution of wealth, how could globalization, which is an extension of free-market capitalism into a marketplace no longer bounded by geography, do anything but increase the gap? If anything, globalization should exacerbate the process until the economies of each nation state become so intertwined that world governments will be required to negotiate trade and tax policies which treat all citizens as equal partners in a single economic environment. Here again, governments and businesses must work together to identify how to improve the overall condition of the world by examining the global flow of capital and goods in a synconomy.

A more comprehensive debate would be to address the apparently growing dichotomy in society of those who 'can' and 'cannot'. Within each nation, growing numbers of individuals are re-examining their abilities and financial resources as determining factors of where they will live and to what extent they will contribute to the betterment of society. Within the US, individuals are assessing taxes such as state income taxes, sales taxes and property taxes to determine their overall tax obligation to ask where they should live. This is not a task to be taken lightly; taxation is a growing concern among people of all age groups and income levels. For example, a middle-class family living in New Hampshire enjoys almost no taxes on income, but a high property tax; when the children grow up and the couple reach retirement age, their income level drops but they are still burdened with a high cost of property tax. It would be better economically to move to a state with higher income tax (as long as their income remains lower than before) and lower property tax, such as Maryland, to preserve long-term financial resources. Corporations operating within a synconomy must consider these factors and their impact on employees as they develop strategies to locate operations and outsource work. The rising concern with taxation coupled with the strain on the current social security system in the US lead us to the conclusion that a fundamental redesign of the taxation system will have to occur in the near future. How will taxation change? Will state and federal governments adopt more simplistic mechanisms such as Pennsylvania's flat-rate income tax? Will the US government progress towards a consumption tax versus an income tax to shift from a nation of spenders and debtors to savers and investors?

As said above, these issues are important to companies operating in a synconomy because they reflect the changes in social structure, financial stability and buying behaviour of large customer segments and they have a direct impact on the local workforce. In the US and across Europe there is mounting anxiety over whether social security, pensions and other long-term retirement subsistence mechanisms will survive the changing social conditions of people living longer than the intended lifespan of these legacy social programmes. Systems such as the US social security system were founded on the premise that the government was in a better position to facilitate a minimum level of long-term financial security as the administrator of funds earmarked for social services and ultimately future retirement payments. Unfortunately, during the latter two-thirds of the twentieth century, the average lifespan increased and the birth rate slowed. These two factors combined with a plethora of economic anomalies – such as a the higher rate of divorces – have stretched the resources of the system to the point where budget problems can no longer be ignored. In the past, financial retirement planning and investment opportunities were reserved for the well-educated, financially secure, affluent American families whose savings opportunities were limited only by their imaginations. The average American was unaware, uninformed or did not have the means to participate in these investment vehicles to safeguard adequately his or her financial future. Today's average American family is no longer fettered by the boundaries of yesterday and has many investment opportunities to become less dependent on the government providing a subsidy in their golden years. Adjustments to the current system such as removing the limits on pre-tax retirement savings in a tax year, providing greater flexibility and access to directing pre-tax contributions to 401(k) and IRA plans, and educating young people about the fundamentals of financial responsibility to start them saving early, reduces the need for bureaucratic administration and sets the stage to reform, rethink and redesign the social security concept. Siems puts the matter concisely:

> Specifically, the current pay-as-you-go (PAYGO) Social Security system is structurally flawed and produces a declining rate of return that is far lower than the return that workers could earn through investing their taxes in private capital markets.[11]

If social programmes such as social security were to be privatized, it would release a citizen from the confines of a single country. Simply, if your retirement assets were managed independently, it would enable you to live anywhere in the world. Therefore, privatization of programmes such as social security could be linked to the idea of the globalization of citizens, in which an individual could select a place to live and work, irrespective of national boundaries. This may lead ultimately to an individual choice in nationality in lieu of nationality as a product of geographic allegiance, which is discussed later in this chapter.

So the question remains: are we taxing the right things to promote an improvement in the world's condition, or are we moving towards global taxation policies that merely serve a collection of nation states' self-interests and not those of their citizens?

Tax fairness is clearly a matter relative to the local or national values expressed in terms of legislation, which in turn varies considerably between countries and even within a country (such as the US, where each state imposes its own taxes). If this diversity in taxation is put into a global context, it is clear that achieving a standard global tax mechanism is just wishful thinking. Organizations such as the Organization for Economic Co-operation and Development (OECD) have been addressing how to adapt international tax arrangements to a new facilitated commerce in the emerging global environment. Their central questions are 'How should enterprises that operate in different countries be taxed? Can tax systems be simple, fair and effectively administered?'[12] In April 2002, the OECD's Global Forum

Working Group on Effective Exchange of Information released a model agreement for effective exchange of information in tax matters.[13]

Developing a means to interoperate within a diverse world of taxation is both a challenge to business and a new set of opportunities. For companies operating within a synconomy, global taxation presents opportunities that in many cases require a fundamental re-education of the business model. One small example is financial services companies operating in the US. Banks report to the Internal Revenue Service (IRS) the payment of interest on savings and mortgages; this data is used by the IRS to validate information provided by the taxpayer. Since there is a direct link on behalf of the taxpayer between the financial institution and the IRS, why not simply pay the bank any tax due and have them centrally reconcile it with the IRS? The reverse would be true for overpayment of any tax.

Taxation is a complex issue which has been debated for decades and will continue to be a source of contention for many decades to come. There is a healthy tension between the types and role of taxation and its effects on work and society. Specifically, does the imposition of a tax diminish the activities of people by providing a disincentive that curbs the actions of those who are taxed?

One group addressing the topic of Internet taxation across the US is the Internet Tax Fairness Coalition (ITFC), which is an alliance of businesses and industry groups such as AOL, Apple Computer, Cisco Systems, EDS, First Data, Information Technology Industry Council, Microsoft and Oracle, to name a few members. The ITFC favours a clear and simple set of tax rules for the borderless marketplace of interstate commerce in the US. Replacing the inconsistent state tax regulations, which add costs to businesses operating under multiple state authorities, the ITFC supports a radical streamlining of taxation schemes to facilitate the rise in electronic commerce, and, as a by-product, these changes would reduce the cost of traditional interstate commerce:[14]

- Establish simple and uniform sales and use tax rules which reduce compliance burdens for all taxpayers.

- Enact nexus standards for business activity taxes which eliminate uncertainty and the potential for double taxation.

- Promote availability of the Internet to all by prohibiting taxes on access fees.

- Prevent multiple and discriminatory taxation by extending the application of traditional tax rules to electronic commerce.

This taxation scheme was created by the US Congress after the passage of the Internet Tax Freedom Act in 1998 by the Advisory Commission on Electronic Commerce (ACEC), consisting of nineteen members including three state governors, representatives from technology corporations and other leading government officials and business leaders. The scheme was created specifically to study federal, state, local and international taxation and tariffs on transactions using the Internet and Internet access.[15] Although many nations, regional authorities and local officials have all been considering various levels of Internet and eCommerce taxation, no global agreements have been implemented. This does bring forth the question of an eventual global value added tax (GVAT), illustrated in Figure 4.2, which may simply be a network interchange fee in lieu of a direct tax.

In the emerging economy, government agencies will continue to provide traditional social services, acting as intermediaries between citizens who may or may not have the long-term means to support their lifestyles. As employment becomes increasingly temporary in nature, individuals will periodically require services, especially during times of personal tragedy and employment change or additional family support, such as daycare in the case of single-parent families. Government agencies also supply the necessary social infrastructure to citizens who do not have the means to participate in the economy and society successfully during the cyclical changes in the economy. Public service providers face the same challenge as corporate intermediaries in a synconomy, as they begin to form a network of government-based services, the value added by each agency becomes transparent as technological innovations continue to influence changes in society. Like their corporate counterparts, in many cases, social service providers must develop a clear value of their contribution to a network of interconnected social services. Ingresoll-Dayton and Jayaratne

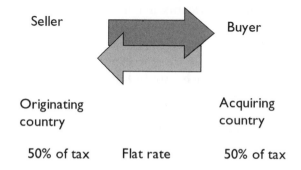

Seller   Buyer

Originating   Acquiring
country   country

50% of tax   Flat rate   50% of tax

Figure 4.2 Global taxation model

identify the rising awareness of social programme providers to be more accountable in the cost, quality and total services rendered:

> Federal and State funding for social services can no longer be taken for granted. Instead, social workers will need to advocated for and demonstrate the effectiveness of their programs. Insurance companies that provide third-party payment for social work treatment will increase their emphasis on cost containment and are likely to link reimbursement to demonstrated improvement.[16]

As government agencies form a network of interoperative services, they will assess the viability of performing these services in-house versus outsourcing them to private sector providers. Cost containment and value to the taxpayer will be the primary measurement criteria that will only be achievable by the continued application of technology and the establishment of a public–private social services infrastructure. The impact of technology on social programmes is threefold:

1. Technology enables more self-service and promises to reduce administrative data gathering.
2. It provides social workers with instruments to aggregate personal, public and private data into information which will effectively tailor programmes to the needs of the individual.
3. Technology provides social services management with the means to assess the effectiveness of service delivery to increasingly multicultural groups within a given geography.

As government agencies and private companies engage each other in the emerging network of partnerships, technology must also be used to ensure some level of privacy and security in citizen data, which is the subject of the next section.

Privacy: We Want to Reach out but not be Reached Ourselves

The technological revolution of the information age has been met with bittersweet results as the physical technologies offer us new ways to interact with the world and yet the same technologies are often resisted because they bring the world a little too close to us. The Internet was heralded as the single greatest invention for cross-cultural communication since the printing press. This new communication technology theoretically eliminated geopolitical boundaries and other socioeconomic barriers which were the product of previous generations of self-imposed nationalism. However, in reality, the Internet brought the idiosyncratic nature of geographically bounded cultural values into sharp contrast with each other, in many cases magnifying the differences and disparities for better or worse. Not as part of any conscious preconceived national plan, the Internet quickly became a mechanism for the wholesale distribution of western ideals, values and business practices, which has been regarded by many highly focused special interest groups, often harbouring significant political agendas, as a direct threat to local values. In extreme cases, this mass proliferation of business activity enshrined in American-centric ideologies has been interpreted as a direct assault on non-western local values and commerce and an undermining of the indigenous culture.

Synconomy makes clear that the new generation of technologies brings into the limelight a new set of corporate responsibilities to secure customer data and personal information. The consolidated identity card, which would act as a passport, driver's licence, entitlement card and link to other social services, presents an opportunity for governments to streamline operations by standardizing on an intergovernmental mechanism of exchange and would save tax money by reducing redundant information. Tasks such as a change of address could be reduced to a single transaction, which could be broadcast through a network of information interchanges to all government agencies, or even to selected private sector companies elected by the citizen, such as banks, employers or utilities. However, this consolidated identity scheme is shunned by many people because it appears too intrusive and conjures up images of Orwell's 'big brother' watching every movement of a citizen.

Although privacy legislation varies greatly between countries such as the UK, the US and nations in the EU, there is an even greater difference between countries across the digital divide. One could argue that the single common thread between all nations is that privacy between a corporation, government agency or charity and the citizen or consumer is based on a fundamental understanding of trust. In all cases, trust is either expressed or implied, a written or unwritten agreement between company and customer, or government and citizens, which perceives that each party having been granted access to information will use it discretely and act responsibly with the other party's personal information and/or sensitive data. The value of privacy can be expressed in the overall value proposition of a firm as a component of the relationship between the firm and the customer and as an element of brand identity, as depicted in Figure 4.3.

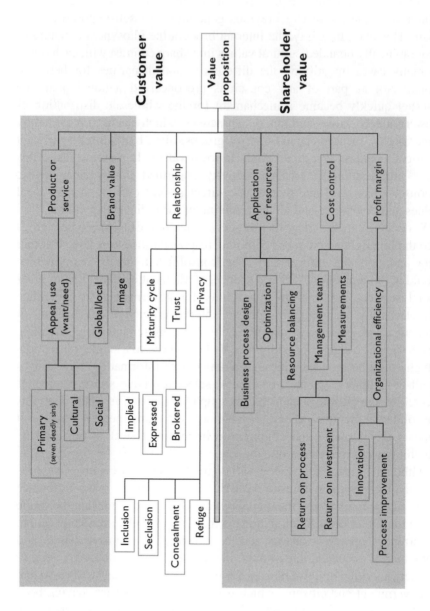

Figure 4.3 Privacy in the value equation

It is assumed that people desiring privacy have something to hide. Consumers today are beginning to realize that they are providing value information to firms freely, and that the same firms use the information mainly to promote corporate interest, returning little or no value back to the consumer. Consumers are thus beginning to ask themselves if information is indeed the new currency of the knowledge economy, and if so, should companies get customer information free?

Privacy can be considered a competitive asset rarely exploited as a marketing tool and often limited to the non-disclosure statement at the bottom of a firm's website. Corporations in a synconomy must be proactive in their approach to privacy by creating services which permit customers to preselect various elements of information that can be shared with associated members in a network of partnerships or cannot be shared outside the confines of the corporation. For many companies, the flow of detailed customer data across organizational boundaries and transnational borders is unexplored territory. Securing the integrity of customer information as it is transmitted through a network of business relationships typically falls outside the jurisdiction of the technology department or IT group, whose concerns are centred on physical data security. The passing of this information also falls outside the purview of the business unit because privacy is linked to both security and technology, so it is assumed to be an information systems problem. Corporate investments in technological security are substantial; however, establishing several simple non-technology privacy policies yield returns relatively quickly because many of the safeguards can be incorporated into the business agreements which span the corporations involved in the exchange.

If information is the currency of the knowledge economy, then customer knowledge must be the competitive weapon in the information age. Corporations offering transnational products and services must proactively educate customers on their policies concerning security and privacy, clearly stating how customer data will be used within the firm and by connected value chain partners. Elsewhere it was argued that privacy and security have a four-level topology: inclusion, seclusion, concealment and refuge.[17] Inclusion permits a customer to choose the information that can be made public about him or herself. Information seclusion is information that can be exchanged with retailers and suppliers detailing product preferences. Concealed information is exchanged between trusted sources, retaining a higher degree of privacy and/or anonymity as the transaction is in process. The final level is refuge, in which data privacy is guaranteed by the organization handling the transaction, often taking place only within the firm and in many cases requiring a comprehensive authentication scheme to preserve identity.

Corporations that establish synergistic electronic partnerships with external organizations and transnational entities must develop strategic initiatives which address the complexity of the issues in data collection, retention and dissemination at each level. Corporations operating in a synconomy are faced with the conundrum of securing information and maintaining privacy across all four levels while trying to engage with an ever-increasing network of partnerships. Corporate morals and ethics are also part of the value equation because each level of privacy contains greater amounts of personal data, customer behaviours and purchasing habits, making privacy increasingly complex. The technological paradox that corporate customers face in the new connected global economy is that the more one uses the Internet to gather information, make purchases, engage in eMail, and other collaborative activities, the more information is generated about the individual, and the less control individuals have over its dissemination.

The key lesson for companies engaged in global partnerships is that privacy, the systems to secure information and the policies to control data must be designed from the perspective of the customer and must allow for a variety of international regulations regarding how information is treated during its transmission and use within a firm. Corporations have an implied trust that customers view as part of their value proposition; they must show that they can act responsibly with the personal data entrusted to their care. What customers or global citizens fear most is that technology will be used maliciously – even if not by design – to restrict the liberty of individuals, such as in the following scenario which is possible with today's technology. A baby is born and then subjected to several genetic tests which indicate a higher than average probability of having a number of health problems. This data is sent to health and life insurance companies indicating the baby's potential high cost as a patient, resulting in him or her being blacklisted from medical and/or life insurance. This data could also be provided to potential employers and other sources who could use it when an individual applies for a job, a loan or other basic life activities. The new global connectedness of business raises a number of questions on information privacy, with enormous implications for security and access to personal data as it flows between organizations and across national borders. Corporations must address proactively their approach to the fair handling of information between members in a network of value, if only to allay the fears of customers.

Privacy of data and information about an individual citizen is made more complex as individuals become more global, potentially living in many nations at various times in their lives. As corporations develop more intimate customer relations, the national regulations controlling customer data may change as he or she migrates from country to country. This condition is especially true in the new EU, as people can now take up residence more easily in any member country. Additionally, individuals from the US who establish foreign residences for all or part of a year in anticipation of retirement compound the aggregation of customer information as it flows across international borders. This brings forth a new question: does data follow the customer across international boundaries and what constitutes citizenship? It is to these issues that we now turn.

Who is a Citizen and What is a Nation State?

One can argue that nationalism is a product of modernity, reflecting an individual's need to belong to an associated group of people in order to feel a sense of security in the environment in which he or she lives. Nationalism, although less than 300 years old, became a powerful force as the initiator of wars, the instigator of internal sociopolitical conflicts and an instrument for bigotry and other social unrests. However, citizenship allows the individual to establish an identity within the increasingly fragmented, traditional social structures, although the conventional social systems still reinforce notions of territorial identity and national heritage which seem to conflict with the growing discourse on global citizenship.[18]

Citizenship in a global environment must go beyond twentieth-century perceptions of acquiring rights; citizenship now must carry social obligations and responsibilities. Global responsibilities are not limited to individuals. As discussed in Chapter 3, corporations, too, must rise to the emerging economic conditions, acting as benevolent opportunists to make the most of global resources in an effort to improve the human condition globally. Just as national prosperity and corporations rise and fall on waves of economic activity, so to do the fortunes of nation states. The growing transnationality of business is vital in moving global economies towards synergistic parity, establishing a framework for the redefinition of governments, business and capitalism. Shillito and Marle relate this transition to an underlying realization by citizens/ customers that the generation of value is a product of both government and business:

Just as value has governed the evolution of products and services, so too has it governed the evolution of society. An examination of human history shows that nations grow, prosper, and frequently die. Civilization is evolving societies in which all people can grow and share basic human freedoms. Value governs this evolution, because governments are aggregations of services that exist to serve the needs of people.[19]

Value generation in business attracts highly skilled individuals who want to be part of an organization in which their work gives them a feeling of accomplishment and contribution to society. There is a substantial difference between the emerging global citizen and the feared rise of a homogeneous global culture. A global citizen is an individual who initiates global business transactions and takes part in national social functions, often living in many countries in his or her lifetime. Global citizens are often highly skilled knowledge workers, making them an important asset to regional economic growth. Global citizens seek out cultures and locations which offer lifestyles consistent with how they want to live. It is not too far-fetched to say that in the future, global citizens will ask nations to supply a prospectus to entice them to come. Just as corporations recruit talent today, nations will need to work with businesses to attract highly skilled talent to prime, money-generating activities such as start-up businesses, SMEs, research and international trade.

The latest advances in telecommunications technologies such as the Internet, mobile telephones and a host of other devices featuring bio-mechanical interfaces are indeed redefining the process of business on a global scale. These same technologies give individuals from all parts of the world an increased opportunity to exchange ideas, beliefs and morals, leading to a greater appreciation of different cultural values. Technology and globalization are linked, as a predominant force redefining social structures, as Archibugi and Michie point out:

> It is generally assumed that globalization will reduce the role and scope of nations, and it is not uncommon, including among technology analysts, for the terms 'national' and 'global' to be seen as opposites. In this case, globalization reduces the effectiveness of policies at the national level for promoting and organizing technological advance.[20]

As with previous technologies that increased the amount of communications, such as the printing press, telegraph, telephone and television, the new generation of technologies present the same implications to the socioeconomic structure. The most influential previous technology is that of the television. Television as a communications medium has adapted to the needs of most global cultures and has been an effective transmission device for seeding western ideals throughout the world. Each community has the ability to generate their own television programming but often elect to redistribute American programmes because they are often more cost-effective than producing programmes locally and they fulfil the local audience demand. However, it is not simply the accelerated rate at which these technologies foster changes within business and society that matters in a synconomy. Indeed, the bi-directionality of these devices is reshaping the social order:

> The new technologies encourage noninstitutional, shifting networks over the fixed bureaucratic hierarchies that are the hallmark of the single-voiced sovereign state. They dissolve issues' and institutions' ties to a fixed place. And by greatly empowering individuals, they weaken the relative attachment to community, of which the pre-eminent one in modern society is the nation-state.[21]

The advent of a higher frequency of interchange between the peoples of the world presents most individuals with a complex set of choices between local social behaviour and a more homogenized westernized lifestyle. It is because of the pervasiveness of new technology that it can be conceived as threatening to many special-interest groups seeking to preserve a local culture to the exclusion of western ideals. This tendency to preservation was identified by Naisbitt and Aburdene in 1990:

> In the face of growing homogenization, we shall all seek to preserve our identities, be they religious, cultural, national, linguistic, or racial.[22]

Accordingly, one could argue that in previous centuries, the process of globalization was an external, often-conquering faction that imposed its cultural rules on the local conquered population to maintain order and propagate a more homogeneous social behaviour. The legacy of the conquest-driven globalization process was that of economic, military, social and, to some extent, cultural and religious control to promote the expansion of a dominate country or ideology, such as British imperialism in the nineteenth century, Spanish and Portuguese expansionism in the sixteenth century and, looking further back, the Roman Empire during the turn of the first millennium. There has always been a perceived direct link between technology and control. As Wriston points out, the mechanisms of control are the perceived essence of the nation state:

The control of territory remains one of the most important elements of sovereignty. But as the information revolution makes the assertion of territorial control more difficult in certain ways and less relevant in others, the nature and significance of sovereignty are bound to change.[23]

In a synconomy, however, many of the mechanisms of control are redefined as technology alters our ability to reshape the functions and form of the nation state. Therefore, a historical oversimplification of the globalization process could be that prior to the latter half of the twentieth century, globalization was an external force that directly changed the commerce, culture and societal structure of a nation state. Today's globalization process is not based on one geographical group conquering another; rather, it is evolving into a process of progressive awareness of the interconnected global structure. As the ideals, values and attributes of society are more freely exchanged, globalization becomes localized by people who elect to adopt various aspects of culture from other peoples. This in effect shifts the globalizing process from an external process of cultural imposition to an internal process of individuals who, by personal choice, seek to copy the lifestyles or values of distant cultures. This is a complex problem for groups who prefer to preserve their national culture and values. It is because of changes within society that this new generation of globalization brings such violent reactions from incumbent social organizations and special interest groups. Simply, people have a greater awareness of world affairs, cultures and beliefs, made possible by advances in telecommunications technologies such as television and the Internet. Roche reminds us that it is the commonality of culture that binds together contemporary societies and its attributes are not simply linked to a specific social behaviour such as religion, but to many social attributes that are intertwined to form an effective common culture:

> Culture covers a variety of relevant factors including: the existence of a common language, and writing system; widely distributed and accessible electronic communications systems; and common or mutually comprehensible socialization, education and value systems.[24]

To cater to the needs of the relevant factors of culture, thus customizing products and services to deliver maximum appeal to significant market segments within specific geographies, is, as seen above, essential to twenty-first-century corporate value propositions. As social structures reconfigure themselves and economic markets pass through a cycle of breakdown and consolidation, businesses are presented with a plethora of opportunities centred on the renegotiation of the express and implicit social contract between citizens, business and government. Hoffman codifies globalization as taking three forms: economic, cultural and political, each presenting corporations with an additional set of variables to factor into a competitive strategy.[25] Organizations in a synconomy must design strategies that focus on optimizing economic conditions (such as access to lower cost labour, the establishment of a new market channel) while leveraging cultural aspects (such as product preferences) and becoming politically engaged in supporting socially responsible community activities. All these actions help to reinforce the fundamental social contract between the transnational corporation, the government, the local community and the global/local employees of the firm.

However, Micklethwait and Wooldridge indicate that the fleeting nature of the social contract and its lack of definition for the average citizen can be perceived as an element of freedom, but also its inherent weakness:

> Classical liberalism relies on the notion that there is an implicit contract between a government and its citizens, one which individuals enter into freely and may leave freely. In practical terms, that proposal has been (and still largely remains) a farce.[26]

The opportunity for corporations operating in a global network of value is to redefine the basic elements in the traditional social contract between employer and employee or between corporation and community. Micklethwait and Wooldridge's argument reveals that the long-term effect of globalization is that immigration occurs in two distinct forms, categorized by socioeconomic means: despair and choice. Immigration by despair, or poor people seeking a better life, has been the primary motivation for people for many centuries. Secondly, rich people immigrated to achieve a desired lifestyle. However, in today's synconomy, people are reconsidering their geographic loyalties, either when they reach a successful point in their career or they are newly educated young people, searching for regions that offer a lifestyle that is more representative of their tastes. The surprising reality of immigration is that it is not mainly destitute people seeking relief. It is a growing number of professionals searching for a country with a national value proposition that appeals to their lifestyle and social and environmental needs, providing conditions for individuals to achieve their goals.

This new movement of selecting a community by knowledge workers and other specialists does not invalidate nationhood or nationality; it does, however, raise the question of multinational citizenship or transnationality.

As the nation state is redefined by technological and economic factors, nationality and citizenship must also be readdressed. Roche rightly identifies the heart of the issue of nationhood and the structure of the nation state:

> From these structural changes and challenges we can now turn to consider some of the main ideological challenges to the dominate paradigm of social citizenship. Here the issues are less about the structural context of social citizenship and more about its definition and nature and the kind of moral community it involves.[27]

Individual citizens must develop a greater awareness of global commerce, cultural values and the causes and effects of transnational corporate policies in order to have the necessary skills required in a synconomy. Individuals must be vigilant for the single factor that restricts the process of synergistic economic prosperity: the seductive notion of socioeconomic isolationism. The essential understanding that individuals and corporations must have to operate successfully in a synconomy is that of the relationship between local business activities, generated by a member of a network of transnational partners, and the direct and indirect effects on their distant partners. Moreover, the interconnection between business activities of network partners must be understood in their socioeconomic context. For example, a reduction in local orders triggers a partner to lay off personnel in a distant location. If a firm is acting synergistically, the intensity of product demands and reductions can be minimized by sharing production-forecasting data so that one partner can proactively reroute activities to other partners. In effect, a reduction in orders from one partner should initiate a signal to other partners that there is unused capacity available. This type of synchronized business activity presupposes that as corporations form networks of value, they are indeed establishing linked communities of organizations operating in an extended value chain. Simultaneously, people are mimicking corporate behaviour and forming formal and informal communities inside a firm and with external business entities such as when they form communities of practice.

In *The Work of Nations*, Reich discusses the emergence of new American communities and the accompanying social attitudes that are transforming the way people view other social groups within America. Corporations operating in a synconomy must understand this social change because it focuses attention on an acute problem that is also happening across the globe and, more importantly, within the structures of internal multicultural organizations. In this sense, Reich noted the behaviour of people within a mid-to-upper economic class of people living in suburban America, which is bounded in communities of common property values. These people, labelled 'symbolic analysts', are pondering their social responsibility for people in an adjacent community:

> Since almost everyone in their 'community' is by definition as well off as they are, there is no cause for a stricken conscience. If inhabitants of another neighbourhood are poorer, let them look to one another. Why should *we* pay for *their* schools? So the argument goes, without acknowledging that the critical assumption has already been made: 'we' and 'they' belong to fundamentally different communities. Through such reasoning it has become possible to maintain a preferred self-image of generosity toward, and solidarity with, one's 'community' without owing any responsibility to 'them,' in another 'community.' Symbolic analysts – firmly connected to the global economy – thus are made to feel increasingly justified in withdrawing into enclaves bounded by their symbolic analysts, paying only what is necessary to ensure that everyone within the enclave is sufficiently well educated and has access to the infrastructure he or she needs in order to succeed in the global economy.[28]

Reich's observation of isolationist tendencies in the new economy is significant because it identifies the single, most important factor that ultimately leads to individuals and companies working unconsciously against global competitive forces: the tendency to promote self-interest to the exclusion of all others. In a synconomy, economic prosperity is directly connected to collaboration and social well-being. When one socio-economic group makes a determined effort to isolate itself from other groups, in effect it restricts its own long-term ability to grow. It may realize short-term gains, but as the world continues to behave as a collaborative network of economic relationships, economic isolationism replaces the boundaries of a physical geography with that of an invisible economic fence. For businesses worldwide, Reich's observations on social isolationism are a double-edged sword: they provide us with the insight to avoid the situation within a firm and take preventive measures to balance the interest of all individuals. They also present an opportunity to exploit social groups that demonstrate this behaviour, as can be seen in Houston, Texas where communities have been erected with high walls, surveillance cameras and home security systems, and in Miami where houses are encased with steel bars covering the windows.

One can speculate that the result of the shift towards regionalization will ultimately lead to the economic consolidation of smaller nation states. Nations will not lose their identity, but will spread economic risk by seeking partners and working towards economic integration. A prime example of this success can be seen in the rise of regional economic units such as the EU. In the Middle East, the Gulf Cooperation Council (GCC) Customs Union recently announced the move towards monetary union by 2010.[29] Understanding this pattern of economic behaviour is important for companies operating in a synconomy because it identifies tax, regulatory, customs and other logistical implications to how products will be distributed. Additionally, consumer behaviour will also change, while geographic borders are invisibly redrawn around economic activities.[30]

The initial progression of this phenomenon will be to forge economic links across cultural bonds. However, it could be argued that this economic linking behaviour could easily be developed beyond regional boundaries, centring on a shared common culture, such as Portugal and Brazil. The Massachusetts Institute of Technology's Digital Nations consortium aspires to address major social challenges (improving education, enhancing health care, supporting community development) through the innovative design and use of new technologies. The consortium's ultimate goal is to empower people in all occupations and lifestyles to invent new opportunities for themselves and their societies.[31]

Nation states as we know them today will not simply disappear. In fact, they are still a necessary device needed to protect justice, defence and other human values. However, many of the functions that are currently a part of the nation state will, over time, migrate in three directions:

1. a more regionalized approach to economic and trade activities

2. corporations taking on the provision of select services as part of compensation

3. citizens taking a more proactive role in long-term social security and retirement benefits.

These issues are important for corporations because although they appear to add to operating costs, they represent new opportunities. Let us now turn to another aspect of nation states operating in a synconomy, that of disintermediation.

Disintermediated Regional People of a Global Corporate Nation

As the global economy gets larger, the component nation players get smaller and smaller.[32]

How people act, react and change the definition of nationhood over time has a direct implication on the next evolution in the structures of corporations and the development of their value propositions. There is a distinct difference between national feeling and nationalism. National feeling, which can be traced back to the Middle Ages, is the sense of belonging to a geography, community or group of culturally like-minded people. This is represented by expressions such as the 'motherland' or 'fatherland', reflecting a sense of attachment to a region and sovereign. The concept of nation – or nation state – actually has its roots in medieval Europe. However, 'nationalism' is a much more recent term, used during the latter part of the eighteenth century to describe unity, autonomy and identity between an individual and a more formalized recognition of a nation state. Naturally, there are several types of nationalism and manifestations of national feelings throughout history. Although some of them happen within a state (such as Italian and German nationalisms in the nineteenth century), there are other types, such as nineteenth-century French nationalism, which tends to happen between neighbour states, or religious nationalism, such as that of Islam, which crosses geopolitical boundaries.

In the context of business and commercial evolution, national feeling and nationalism can be equated to the state of corporations during the twentieth century. Operating paternalistically, companies during the 1950s and 60s offered lifetime employment, security and a sense of stability. These factors motivated most employees to exhibit a sense of corporate feeling, the corporate equivalent of nationalism, today called 'corporate loyalty'. During the 1980s – and much more evident, in the 1990s – there was a shift from corporate loyalty to free agency. This was because of the erosion of the traditional social contract between employer and employee – loyalty in exchange for security. Knowledge workers have been the chief proponents of this shift, as they realized that technological advances in telecommunications gave them the ability to work from home as effectively (or in many cases more effectively because of the lack of traditional interruptions such as meetings and casual co-worker interruptions) as in a fixed office space. In the landmark issue of *Fast Company* in early 1998 entitled *Free Agent Nation*,[33] Pink et al. and other industry thinkers put forth not just the notion of free agency for knowledge workers and specialists, but the means, sources and tools required to achieve free agency.

This transfer of loyalty from large familiar corporate entities to loyalty to oneself, or allegiance to a small group of interconnected service providers and associates, resembles the intrinsic shift in the power of nations when viewed in the context of globalization. Although nationhood and corporations are not interchangeable social constructs, both do represent hierarchies that are decomposing as a direct result of the new capabilities brought about by technology. The change comes from the combined forces of disintermediation, globalization and a new awareness of being attached to a more local social group. Likewise, the implications of changes in the overall delineation of nation states; their associated power and provision of social services should not concern corporations, other than the possibility of changes in tax laws, but this macro-socioeconomic shift presents businesses operating in a synconomy with new opportunities for collaboration and profit.

For manufacturers, retailers and other entities engaged in international trade, Naisbitt's observation on the relationship between capitalistic homogenization and cultural heterogeneity provides an insight into how organizations operating in a synergic economy can differentiate a component of their value proposition: 'The more universal we become, the more tribal we act.'[34] Therefore, one could argue that global firms must offer two distinct types of product: global homogeneous products that apply to consumers' lifestyles independent of the geography in which they are consumed, and products that have a specific cultural appeal. This balance of global singularity and cultural specificity describes McDonald's behaviour, as discussed in Chapter 1.

For other business entities such as financial institutions, multinational companies and service organizations, the balancing act between globally applicable services and locally applied activities follows much the same lines as their manufacturing and retail counterparts. However, one could argue that firms customizing a product are in effect providing a service which presents an additional opportunity to firms offering services. Few firms will be able to adapt and customize their products to all local markets and this opens opportunities for firms that have in-depth local knowledge to offer cultural customization as a product in its own right. For example, an organization such as Sinometrics International offers services that are sensitive to local cultures and show a deep understanding of local social idiosyncrasies, beyond the simple translation of language, such as use of graphic metaphors, product iconography and other usability issues, thus increasing a product's cultural awareness.[35]

The ability to provide services globally and locally also applies to individuals who have subscribed to the concept of the free agent nation. However, the smaller, more agile corporate structure of free agents allows them to create partnerships, affiliations and associations that easily cross transnational boundaries and ultimately arrive at synergistic behaviour in a network of value.

Nations may continue to evolve into smaller sovereign states as projected by thinkers and futurists like Naisbitt, mirroring the same decoupling of larger corporate entities. Therefore, one can see how these two dissociated but similar phenomena can be interpreted as a social revolution towards a corporate nation. There is a rising discourse on the role of corporations and the perceived decline in the nation state. One could argue that transnational corporations today are evolving into entities reflecting combinations of cultural ideals and values, but that they will not exist as a means to govern society. Culture is a critical element in creating a working business environment that transcends geopolitical borders, as Mills notes:

> Culture is about values, not so much the values of the firm, an error of emphasis that executives often make, as of those within it. Executives who identify, codify, and promote the values of their firms forget that it is people, not companies, who do things. The values that matter most are those that are embraced by, and guide the actions of, the people of the firm.[36]

The cultural aspects of a corporation have traditionally been overlooked in favour of a generic, standardized or homogenized culture that mimics the company's directors or the headquarters. This is primarily because, in the traditional command and control hierarchy, the corporate policies emanate from a small core of corporate senior managers. In a synergistic global economy, firms must work from a transnational perspective in which a centralized group offers homogeneity and regional operations offer local functions. When approaching geographic markets outside their internal expertise, firms operating in a network of value will often partner with organizations that are existing market portals such as the international versions of AOL or companies which offer localization services such as SDL International in the UK, or Transco, a Chinese localization service.[37] Localization firms offer not just local language translation services, but they also provide in-depth knowledge on specific market and technical requirements, such as cultural icons that only apply within a single marketplace, as noted by SDL International:

> As part of the Web site design, it is necessary to avoid culture-dependent symbols that are not clear to an international audience. A classic example would be an American mailbox with a little flag to indicate that there is new mail. This symbol is used on many sites to indicate e-mail but people outside of North America don't necessarily recognize the mailbox. For a Web site, a better symbol would be an envelope, which is universally understood.[38]

Just as most businesses cannot be all things to all people, transnational firms will partner with a network of localization firms, using them either as a gateway to an existing market or as a resource for local corporate groups to be more intelligent in their approach to a local market. Localization services are also found in conjunction with universities such as Ireland's University of Limerick's Localization Research Centre, which provides not only local market and industry information within Europe but also provides consultative services.[39]

Corporations are at a crossroads between the globalization of business and the localization of the workforce. As organizations depend more on external entities to operate globally, they must also turn towards providing services to employees and, in some cases, partners. Traditionally, these services have not been part of the corporate set of acknowledged responsibilities, and can be exemplified by corporate morality, social awareness, environmental concerns and extended services such as daycare and retirement planning. At first glance, there is evidence of an erosion in the services that nation states have provided traditionally and a rise in the benefits that larger employers supply, such as local benefits, daycare, telecommuting and expanding coverage in medical, dental and optical insurances. However, although government agencies are beginning to outsource human services to corporate providers, corporations are not intending to replace government services, only to act as a mechanism for the delivery of services.

Walsh makes a critical observation that is a key motivation for corporations and governments to address cooperatively the role of the nation state and its subsequent boundaries:

> All other things being equal (such as the probability of success), there is a stronger incentive to commit resources to an innovation where the market is large than where it is small. The greater the resources for any innovation, the greater the number of design alterations that may be explored at once; consequently, the shorter the time taken to find the best solution, the quicker the innovation may be launched and the longer the period for the innovation form to earn monopoly profits.[40]

This creates a compelling opportunity for smaller market countries to combine limited government and business resources to establish a shared technological infrastructure, trade negotiation functions, market aggregation services, and research and development activities. The co-opetition of shared infrastructures must transcend international boundaries so groups of cooperating nations can act as economic entities enabling global competition on a level playing field. This is not to advocate cartel-like behaviour; it is however, a direct mechanism for SMEs to develop synergistic parity with their multinational counterparts.

The need to construct the essence of a corporate nation state has led to the establishment of globalization consultant organizations such as the Web of Culture, which provides professional guidance and certification to US corporations seeking to globalize their presence on the Internet.[41] The first implementation of the Internet was centred on corporations establishing a single point of contact using the World Wide Web as a mechanism for information centralization. Now that the Internet is maturing, companies are realizing that staying connected to customers is more than just having a website. Making Internet sites more sensitive to cultural needs and establishing a corporate presence in local markets effectively extends the reach of a firm by localizing product and service offerings to highly specialized social market segments. Firms such as the Web of Culture provide established companies with a transition plan and strategy that factors in cultural needs, which are traditionally overlooked during product design.

One can argue that globalization is a long-running phenomenon and cultural expansion has traditionally been a product of an external power or conquest – a clearly defined enemy usurps local power and imposes rules, regulations and customs that alter the cultural value of the indigenous people. Over time, the culture of the conqueror is absorbed and, for better or worse, is reflected in the local customs. However, the new form of globalization observed in today's society reflects an irreversible internal transformation caused by four key factors: the media; advances in telecommunications technology; travel; and the acquisition of a western education by (non-western) young people. Corporations operating in a synconomy must incorporate these four factors into their global strategies because they play pivotal roles in formulating various aspects of strategic thinking, such as brand awareness, human resource development and the creation of a local corporate image. The media, the technology industry and other sources of news have reported a continued adoption of western values or elements of a western lifestyle by literally every nation on earth. In most recent times, this export of American-centric values, products and lifestyles has met cultural, political and social barriers, as special interest groups register their disapproval of the adoption or adaptation of a western lifestyle into the fabric of local culture. Here again, this can be seen not only at the level of nations, but in corporations and other organizations, as indicated by Naisbitt and Aburdene:

But even as our lifestyles grow more similar, there are unmistakable signs of backlash: a trend against uniformity, a desire to assert the uniqueness of one's culture and language, a repudiation of foreign influence.[42]

Therefore, businesses large and small operating as participants in a network of value must consider the factors of culture, the changing socialization of national power and the impact of these factors on their workforce, while developing a globally focused value proposition. Operational synergy can be achieved when organizations engaged in transnational business forge relationships based on the assessment of the goals, aspirations and value propositions of collaborating organizations. These factors and those that reflect new social attitudes such as child labour, ecology and other local values shape the definition of a firm's corporate citizenship. As we will see in Chapter 5, the individual plays an integral part in how a firm embraces the new globalization of business and acts as a mechanism to monitor and regulate the effectiveness of a company's value proposition.

Notes

1 M. Castells and P. Hall, *Technopoles of the World: The Making of Twenty-first-Century Industrial Complexes*, London: Routledge, 1994, p. 23.

2 C. Shearman, 'Localisation within globalization', in M. Talalay, C. Farrands and R. Tooze (eds), *Technology, Culture and Competitiveness: Change and the World Political Economy*, London: Routledge, 1997, p. 111.

3 W. Wriston, 'Bits, bytes and diplomacy', *Foreign Affairs*, January/February 1997, **76**(1): 173–4.

4 J. Naisbitt, *Global Paradox*, London: Nicholas Brealey, 1994, p. 229.

5 M. McIntosh, D. Leipziger, K. Jones and G. Coleman, *Corporate Citizenship: Successful Strategies for Responsible Companies*, London: Financial Times Management, 1998, p. 6.

6 Naisbitt, *Global Paradox*, p. 30.

7 J. Naisbitt and P. Aburdene, *Megatrends 2000. The Next Ten Years ... Major Changes in Your Life and World*, London: Sidgwick & Jackson, 1990, p. 12.

8 J. Lipnack and J. Stamps, *The TeamNet Factor: Bringing the Power of Boundary Crossing Into the Heart of Your Business*, Essex Junction: Oliver Wight Publications, 1993, p. 355.

9 A. S. Hornsby, *Oxford Advanced Learner's Dictionary of Current English*, Oxford: OUP, 1991, p. 1317.

10 S. James and C. Nobes, *The Economics of Taxation: Principles, Policy and Practice*, Hertfordshire: Prentice Hall Europe, 1996, p. 10.

11 T. Siems, 'Reengineering social security in the new economy', *Social Security Privatization*, (22), 23 January 2001.

12 Organization for Economic Co-operation and Development, available at www.oecd.org, November 2002.

13 Organization for Economic Co-operation and Development, available at www.oecd.org/pdf/M00028000/M00028528.pdf, December 2002.

14 The Internet Tax Fairness Coalition available at www.salestaxsimplification.org/, November 2002.

15 The Advisory Commission on Electronic Commerce (ACEC) available at www.ecom-mercecommission.org/, November 2002.

16 B. Ingresoll-Dayton and S. Jayaratne, 'Measuring effectiveness of social work practice: beyond the year 2002', in P. Raffoul and C. Aaron McNeece (eds), *Future Issues for Social Work Practice*, Boston: Allyn & Bacon, 1996, pp. 29–30.

17 J. DiVanna, *Redefining Financial Services: The New Renaissance in Value Propositions*, Basingstoke: Palgrave Macmillan, 2002, p. 183.

18 M. Roche, *Rethinking Citizenship: Welfare, Ideology and Change in Modern Society*, Cambridge: Polity Press, 1992, p. 245.

19 M. Shillito and D. Marle, *Value: its Measurement, Design and Management*, Chichester: John Wiley & Sons, 1992, pp. 41–2.

20 D. Archibugi and J. Michie, 'The globalization of technology: a new taxonomy', in D. Archibugi and J. Michie (eds), *Technology, Globalization and Economic Performance*, Cambridge: Cambridge University Press, 1997, p. 172.

21 J. Mathews, 'Power shift', *Foreign Affairs*, January/February 1997, **76**(1): 66.

22 Naisbitt and Aburdene, *Megatrends 2000*, p. 126.

23 W. Wriston, *The Twilight of Sovereignty*, New York: Charles Scribner, 1992, p. 7.

24 Roche, *Rethinking Citizenship*, p. 41.

25 S. Hoffman, 'Clash of Globalizations' *Foreign Affairs*, July/August 2002, **81**(4): 107.

26 J. Micklethwait and A. Wooldridge, *A Future Perfect*, London: William Heinemann, 2000, p. xxvi.

27 Roche, *Rethinking Citizenship*, pp. 47–8.

28 R. Reich, *The Work of Nations: Preparing Ourselves for 21st-century Capitalism*, New York: Alfred A. Knopf, 1991, p. 278.

29 *Gulf Business*, Dubai: Motivate Publishing, November 2002, **7**(7): 101.

30 J. Newhouse, 'Europe's rising regionalism', *Foreign Affairs*, January/February 1997, **76**(1): 71.

31 *Digital Nations*, Massachusetts Institute of Technology, available at www.dn.media.mit.edu/, December, 2002.

32 Naisbitt, *Global Paradox*, p. 40.

33 D. Pink, M. Warshaw, S. Davis et al., 'Free agent nation & free-agent almanac', *Fast Company*, December/January 1998, **12**, pp. 131–60.

34 Naisbitt, *Global Paradox*, p. 26.

35 SinoMetrics International, Inc, available at www.sinomet.com/, October 2002.

36 D. Mills, *e-Leadership: Guiding Your Business to Success in the New Economy*, Paramas: Prentice Hall, 2001, p. 140.

37 Transco, Beijing, available at www.transco.com.cn/, December 2002.

38 SDL International, available at www.sdlintl.com/white-papers-articles/premium-white-papers/premium-white-papers-how-to-internationalize.html, December 2002.

39 University of Limerick: Localization Research Centre, available at www.lrc.csis.ul.ie/index.html, December 2002.

40 V. Walsh, 'Technology and the competitiveness of small nations: review', in C. Freeman and B.-A. Lundval (eds) *Small Countries Facing the Technological Revolution*, London: Pinter Publishers, 1988, p. 41.

41 The Web of Culture, available at www.webofculture.com/, September 2002.

42 Naisbitt and Aburdene, *Megatrends 2000*, p. 103.

CHAPTER 5

National Allegiance, Corporate Loyalty and Religious Complexity

How corporations and individuals are influenced by nationality, culture, collaboration and transnational business processes is the subject of this chapter, which seeks to examine the need for individuals to assess their value proposition to an organization. As the world enters into a cultural mêlée between product/lifestyle homogeneity and social/cultural hetero-geneity, one issue is clear: as individuals experience more homogeneous products and experiences, the greater the need to feel connected to something. World travellers are beginning to see the influence of the same products and groups of brands at every airport, changing the travel experience within airports from a previously enjoyable experience of different cultures into continuous shopping for western products, only interrupted by the destination. Synconomy is not about the westernization of global commerce; as said above, corporations operating in a synergistic economy work best when they leverage cultural diversity and bring the greatest range of products to the largest groups of people at the lowest possible cost. To accomplish this, individuals must endeavour to do two things simultaneously:

1. they must learn a set of specialized skills, such as communications, international relations, distance leadership and a deeper understanding of cultures;

2. they must unlearn preconceived notions and cultural stereotypes in order to embrace diversity and blend social differences into the value proposition of the firm.

Now our attention is turned towards how these forces influence individuals and their view of a firm, as illustrated in Figure 5.1.

In a synconomy, firms will seek to form partnerships, strategic alliances and corporate associations simply to gain access to markets beyond their current markets and avoid risks in making large investments in local infrastructure without specific local knowledge, as observed by Blaine:

> The strategic alliance provides the firm with a non-equity vehicle for conducting certain international activities and represents a specific agreement between two or more firms to achieve a limited strategic objective.[1]

Three key factors facing business today are nationality, employee loyalty and the influence of cultural factors such as religious doctrine and social norms. To the individual, nationality, as we discussed in Chapter 4, is changing in two respects: corporations are beginning to offer benefits usually perceived as nation states' duties, thereby becoming more transnational in structure; and individuals are more globally oriented and question the importance of nationality as technology erodes the traditional geopolitical boundaries of nation states.

However, for many people, nationality still provides a sense of stability, permanence and the unexplainable desire to belong to a group sharing a common set of values. In times of economic or political instability, nationalism is offered as a mechanism that binds society into a social network of togetherness. For corporations operating in a synconomy, the increased importance of national allegiance is represented and reinforced by economic agreements, such as locating the headquarters of the firm in the country of incorporation. Employees naturally want to be loyal to a firm or organization. Individuals believe that they enter into a social contract with an employer which will capitalize on their intellect and channel their productivity to add value to a product or service. This social contract extends to include a further belief that a firm acts in the best interest of its stockholders, with a sensitive eye towards a greater responsibility to the environment, morality, ethical behaviour, community awareness and a reciprocating loyalty back to the individual. However, much business activity during the past 20 years has been interpreted by employees as a relentless process to commoditize their skills and abilities, reducing their relationship with the firm to a temporary condition demonstrated by downsizing, outsourcing, right sizing, organic growth and so on.

Two other factors, for the most part ignored by corporation strategies over the past 50 years, are religion and cultural values in two contexts: firstly, as a means to add value to the mix of products and services and,

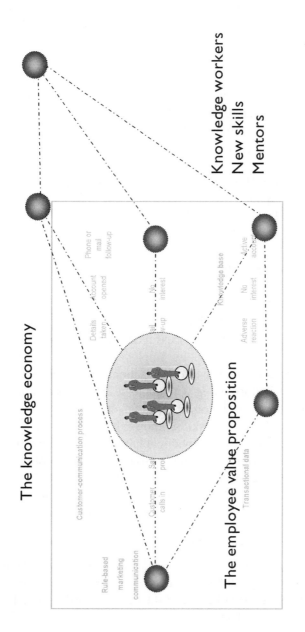

The knowledge economy

Customer-communication process

Rule-based marketing communication

Customer calls in

Sales proposal

Details taken

Account opened

Phone or mail follow-up

No interest

Knowledge base

No interest

Adverse reaction

Active account

Transactional data

The employee value proposition

Knowledge workers
New skills
Mentors

Figure 5.1 A look inside a firm

secondly, as an effective means of leveraging multinational knowledge within an expanding employee base. Consequently, multinational companies and their associated business processes to some degree have embraced the value of culture. In doing so, they also realized that culture is often influenced by religious practices that necessitate the development of specialized products such as Islamic banking, kosher foods and other niche products. These factors are an increasingly important element to corporate strategic agendas which facilitate the evolution of a firm to more of a transnational structure. As this migration occurs, individuals will play a vital role in the transformation, because the rate at which an organization can change is directly proportional to its ability to incorporate these factors into mainstream business activities and its skill in adapting to ever-changing conditions. Having dealt with these issues from a corporate point of view, in this chapter, we will take a closer look at how synconomy affects the individual.

Synconomy and the Individual

In the ever-accelerating business climate, the role of the individual is continually commoditized by rates of pay, threatened by advancing technology, minimized by business process redesigns, and often de-emphasized by a lack of long-term loyalty by employers. However, people are the essence of a synconomy because the actions of consumers, producers, suppliers and distributors acting within a cohesive socioeconomic structure enable business to meet its objectives and deliver customer/shareholder value. Moreover, the ability, skills, knowledge, wisdom and insight that individuals possess act as a metaphorical lubricant to the continuity of business and the continuation of economic growth, as Naisbitt observes:

> The more economies of the world integrate, the less important are the economies of countries and the more important are the economic contributions of individuals and individual companies.[2]

In a synergistic business environment, individuals need to think differently about how they add value, conceive products, sell to customers, acquire materials, service clients and interact with colleagues. This change in thinking is not due to any one new factor found in today's business climate; rather it is a product of the aggregated effects of the evolving technological advances of the later part of the twentieth century. Technology's silent, steadfast and inescapable influence has shaped and reshaped both the process of business and the societies in which it operates. From the individual, this requires a continuous re-evaluation of personal goals and objectives at both home and at work, prompting everyday decisions such as: do I want that new car with the automatic everything despite the fact that my current automobile is still capable of providing me with transport? Buckminster Fuller begins to address the early stages of the change individuals are undergoing in his *Untitled Epic Poem on the History of Industrialization*, published in 1962, which is quoted at length because of its eloquence:

> The inherent
> the **social** meaning of **Industrialization**
> is not well understood
> not because it is difficult –
> only because it is so comprehensive.
>
> The form of its ultimate
> design and behavior pattern
> has probably been clearly envisaged by few
> even amongst those
> who have served it most willingly.
>
> It seems least of all understood
> by the professional
> painters, architects, novelists, and clergy,
> who have seen the price
> that men have paid for it,
> without understanding what they were paying for.
> Wherefore sometimes
> painting Industrialization with AWE
> mostly have the artists painted it with PAIN.
> The **economic** meaning of Industrialization is simple.
> It is the augmentation
> of the integrally born power
> and mechanical effectiveness of the individual
> in the struggle to conquer and derive satisfaction
> out of his precast, involuntary environment.
>
> This augmentation is achieved
> by industrialized man
> in many ways, and

of the mechanics of the augmentation, more later,
but economically analyzing, it may be said that: –

man achieves it **as a worker**
because the tools of modern industry
enormously increase his power of doing work.

(And one of the problems of our time
is that the worker
gets insufficiently paid
for this increase in power.)

He achieves it as a **capitalist or owner**
because of the endless opportunities
offered for the development of new tools
in the competition of tools.
(But also one of the problems of our times
is that individual owners' opportunities
are being curtailed.)

And he achieves it **as consumer**
because he can buy, for the dollars
gained by a limited number of hours of work,
any number of tools ...[3]

Buckminster Fuller identifies a fundamental change in work as individuals shifted from craft skills to informed skills as a by-product of the process of post-industrialization. Synconomy, with its pervasive connectedness, is ushering in the next evolutionary step in business, a shift from *informed skills* to *interpretive* ones. Interpretive skills give the ability to adopt and adapt causal relationships and comprehend complex phenomenon. These interpretive skills are essential, because as business continues to reduce operating cost by enabling business processes to operate beyond the confines of the traditional corporate entity, individuals within a firm will have to interoperate within a framework of integrated, seemingly autonomic cells of competencies. To coordinate dispersed activities, synchronize complex transnational production schedules, assess cultural values against performance criteria in remote workforces and other multifaceted tasks requires a high degree of knowledge and experience. These factors will contribute to the well-known idea that top-rate corporations always seek out top-notch talent. The struggle to attract and retain talent, sometimes characterized as a 'talent war', is only just beginning as the new business environment emerges.

Moving Human Capital to the Balance Sheet

Corporations embracing the new business environment profess that people are their greatest asset, and yet it is interesting that the firm's key asset is noticeably absent from corporate balance sheets. What is more baffling is that human capital assets are surprisingly difficult to assign a meaningful value. It could be argued that the non-disclosure of the quality and significance of these assets in firms engaging in work that is directly dependent on intellectual output (such as research firms, consulting companies and universities) is misleading to investors. Karl Erik Sveiby, who developed the TANGO simulator and formed Celemi International, is an advocate of recognizing 'organizational and individual talent' as 'intangible assets' on corporate balance sheets, reflecting people as corporate assets of the knowledge economy.[4] As organizations shift from hierarchical management into a networked structure, they must establish a process of continuous learning to remain competitive. Alternatively, they can recruit talent as changing conditions demand. However, if other firms also require the same skilled individuals, a firm will find itself always acquiring talent at a premium price, thereby raising operating cost over time.

Developing a mechanism for measuring the value of human capital assets and, more importantly, establishing a metric that monitors the effectiveness of human capital employed is a subject that could fill an entire book. Therefore, to capture the essence of the concept, the following example is used to demonstrate just one of the many approaches to the problem. Table 5.1 represents a small research and advisory firm in Cambridge, England, whose objective was to develop an understanding of the relative value of each employee, not to assess individual performance, but to quantitatively measure the performance of the group in order to identify where to invest in additional skills.

The framework of Table 5.1 combines a qualitative instrument with a quantitative measurement, allowing the firm to understand the relative contribution of each employee to the total team output. The firm realized that to execute their value proposition to customers, they must have two essential competencies: a set of corporate capabilities (consisting of management skills and industry experience) and highly skilled talent (capable of performing research and advisory activities). The top half of the spreadsheet allows each individual to rate his or her own abilities in four key areas of expertise. In this example, the employee asset value – the product of the total equity of the firm – is multiplied by the employee's relatively ranked potential skills contribution, which is calculated by dividing the employee's relative ranking (found in employee total) with the

Table 5.1 Employee balance sheet calculations

Have each employee rate themselves on the following team attributes

Scoring (1 = novice, 2 = general, 3 = knowledgeable, 4 = highly skilled, 5 = expert)

Employee names ==>		John	Mary	Fiona	Stephen	Richard	John	Michael	Blaine	Heather	Lisa	Claire	Phillip	John	David
Capabilities															
Management															
Marketing		2	3	2	4	1	1	3	5	3	2	1	1	4	5
Sales ability		4	1	2	5	4	2	3	4	4	3	1	3	3	3
Mentoring ability		1	3	4	2	5	2	2	2	2	3	3	2	2	4
	Total	7	7	8	11	10	5	8	11	9	8	5	6	9	12
Experience															
Network of people		2	3	3	3	3	3	3	4	1	2	4	2	3	3
Structure vs ambiguity		2	3	4	3	2	3	3	3	3	3	4	2	3	2
Administrative ability		1	2	4	3	3	2	3	4	3	2	4	3	3	3
	Total	5	8	11	9	8	8	9	11	7	7	12	7	9	8
Talent															
Research															
Research ability		2	3	4	3	2	3	3	3	3	4	3	4	3	4
Ability to summarize		3	3	2	3	2	2	2	2	2	2	3	4	3	3
Technology fluency		2	3	4	2	3	3	3	2	3	4	3	5	2	2
	Total	7	9	10	8	7	8	8	7	8	10	9	13	8	9
Advisory															
Relationship building		4	2	1	2	3	4	2	3	3	3	2	3	2	3
Speaking ability		1	5	2	4	2	5	3	1	1	2	3	3	3	3
Facilitation skills		2	1	1	4	1	1	2	3	5	1	1	3	3	4
	Total	7	8	4	10	6	10	7	7	9	6	6	9	8	10
Employee total		26	32	33	38	31	31	32	36	33	31	32	35	34	39
Employee asset value		£96,961	£119,337	£123,066	£141,712	£115,607	£115,607	£119,337	£134,254	£123,066	£115,607	£119,337	£130,525	£126,795	£145,442
Employee realised value		£7,325	£9,016	£9,298	£10,706	£8,734	£8,734	£9,016	£10,143	£9,298	£8,734	£9,016	£9,861	£9,579	£10,988

% area effectiveness

Management	55.24
Experience	56.67
Research	57.62
Advisory	50.95

Total team scores

		% by area
Management	116	25.05
Experience	119	25.70
Research	121	26.13
Advisory	107	23.11

Total team score 463
Total team members 14

55.12%	Total team rating	
70.00%	Rating goal	

Team effectiveness – return on equity 7.56%

Revenues	£3,076,088
Earnings	£130,450
Equity	£1,726,653

total team score. Additionally, the employee's realized value is the total earnings of the firm multiplied by the employee's relatively ranked potential skills contribution. This indicates the contribution of the employees' relatively ranked skills to the total ability of the firm to generate a profit; it is not an indication of an individual's performance. In this example, one can see that the firm needs to invest in upgrading the skills required for advisory, which had the low score of 107. The firm also realized that employees with a total score of less than 33 required additional investment to make them interchangeable within the firm. This spreadsheet is also used to identify gaps in overall team skills, which is then applied to the firm's strategic plans to generate the specifications for new hires.

In this sense, companies need to rethink how they hire. Organizations should not hire for specific jobs because this is just too narrow and rigid in an ever-changing workplace. Instead, organizations must rethink the way they organize and accomplish work. The best way to accomplish this goal is to use behavioural interviews, which identify and discuss the interviewee's cognitive and associative skills, that is, their ability to think and apply knowledge gathered from experience.

It is clear that within a corporation individuals and their knowledge of process, product and customer are the key to adding value while operating an interconnected set of synergistic business processes. The combined know-how or knowledge capital of a firm gives it the ability to make dynamic adjustments to the product mix, production process or in the relationships with suppliers, partners and distributors. To achieve this process dynamism, individuals within a firm must develop a more proactive and almost entrepreneurial approach in their execution and monitoring of the business processes. Information technology, which is often seen as an enhancer of productivity, is indeed a double-edged sword. It generates previously unheard of levels of information to augment the process of business, but, at the same time, these voluminous amounts of information clutter an individual's ability to place issues into a greater context in which knowledge is the product. If indeed one subscribes to the notion that information and knowledge are the baseline of the emerging global economy, then internal organizations must never be complacent with the current operating state of a firm, no matter how efficient it appears to be. In fact, internal organizations should continually challenge their cost structures to assess every process that is outsourced and determine why they cannot offer the same service inside the corporate structure. If the goal of a firm is to reduce transaction costs continually, then the responsibility for continual process improvement is set squarely with the levels of the organization that are close to the process, not with senior management. Senior management must adopt a policy of being a resource that operating groups can use to secure funding and other resources in their pursuit of process optimization. Organizations that strive to lower costs continually must remember that cost reduction is a tactic, not a strategic manoeuvre to produce more value for the customer. More importantly, when the cost reduction is simply reducing the workforce to adjust to changes in the demand cycle, firms may be losing key intangible assets such as product knowledge and other operational expertise which is held by their previously espoused greatest asset, people. Therefore, to avoid this mistake, one could argue that individuals, as an asset, should have a value proposition reflecting their potential to contribute to both the long- and short-term goals of a firm, as we shall see in the next section.

The Employee Value Proposition

Corporations recognize that the combination of skills and experience represented by employees is a valued asset. Recently, industry gurus and scholars in human sciences have relabelled the administration of people, careers and their associated output as 'human capital management'. Although contemporary organizations across the globe recognize that technology's advance and the increasingly interconnectedness of global labour market businesses are changing the social nature of employment, people realize that they too have a value proposition not only to a corporation, but also to themselves. It therefore seems logical that people should develop an inwardly focused value proposition, and that corporations must develop a corresponding value proposition for employees. Unfortunately, even with the new social realization of human capital's value, no comprehensive mechanism has emerged to either measure the overall effectiveness of the application of employee knowledge or reflect its overall value as it constitutes itself as an asset to the corporation. Donkin observes that corporate attempts at measuring the qualitative and quantitative aspects of human capital have traditionally failed because of the complex and often interpretive task of assessing a mixture of multifaceted variables. In his words: 'There is a simple reason for this. People are complicated. They act in different, often unpredictable ways. Their contribution in the workplace differs too.'[5] Donkin notes that a consistent corporate behaviour in all firms making headway in this area was to drop the term 'human capital' in favour of the term perceived as less dehumanizing, 'competency'.

However, what individuals today are seeing, as in the aftermath of the Black Death of the mid-fourteenth century, is a dramatic alteration in the relationship between labourers' worth and their role in society.[6] In the years that followed the great plague of medieval Europe, all demographic groups of society experienced a catastrophic reduction in population. Surviving artisans suddenly realized that they could command higher wages due to the shortage of available workers. This change in attitude, which triggered a rapid rise in wages, moved many governments to set limits on wages. Even with this intervention, the change in attitude was irreversible and eventually led to the capitalistic behaviour we have today. The change in medieval workers' attitudes was thus brought on by a rapidly changing socioeconomic structure due to the sudden loss in population. Today, technology has advanced to the point where information is now the currency of business and is no longer restricted to the traditional confines of any one organization. Workers realize that knowledge means the ability to place information into a context in which a firm can realize a profit. The result is an increasing awareness that knowledge is becoming the more valued commodity, and a change in worker attitude is being realized today just as quickly as in the late Middle Ages.

Chattell describes human capital as a two-way interchange that dynamically seeks to add value, continuously balancing the goals of the firm with the needs of the individual:

> Human capital is the capacity to create value at all times – not just under the known conditions of the day. For people to grow, they must be presented with meaningful challenges, and given room to turn them into possibility-expanding outcomes.[7]

Corporations are finding that employees are not satisfied with jobs that simply strive to cut costs continually; their activities need to add value in three dimensions; to the firm; the customer; and the employee. For example, David Sutherland, of the Business Innovation Consortium, claims that global employers must present an employee value proposition to attract and retain the best talent in order to remain competitive. Sutherland describes the employee value proposition as comprising a balance between four key areas of employee concerns: home and family, work to live, work-oriented and reward-oriented. 'Home and family' issues and the concerns of 'work to live' centre on the physical impact of the job on the commitments of the family such as location, flexibility in the work schedule, level of business travel, childcare and clarity in the role itself.[8] Individuals with a balanced work and reward orientation are more focused on the attributes of the job, such as how challenging is the work, is the work cutting edge, the level of internal mobility, internal equity, performance measurements, and less focused on just compensation. The point Sutherland makes is clear:

regardless of the difficulties in economic conditions, corporations must have a continuous influx of talent to remain competitive. One could argue that it is during a time of economic downturn that a firm needs to take action along two lines: the retention of existing, highly talented personnel, and the recruitment of new talents. The issue of human capital, its retention and acquisition, is paramount for corporations operating in a global synconomy because, in many cases, people are the differentiating force within a firm, and when they leave it, a company's ability to remain competitive becomes a complex matter. This situation is exacerbated when the employee goes to work for another global competitor.

Corporations operating synergistically within a network of value-added partners can reduce the loss of employee knowledge by acting as brokers on behalf of the employee in an outplacement capacity, relocating the individual within the associated network. This is helpful during corporate downsizing because it keeps the talent within the extended network still indirectly accessible to the company. Correspondingly, individuals must periodically assess their skills relative to the business and proactively acquire additional skills to adapt as the business environment changes. Individuals in a synergistic business process must develop an inward-facing, employee value proposition which consists of a portfolio of skills and experiences. Using the contextual framework of a personal balance sheet, skills and experience are considered assets that have value and when viewed together are equated to competency. Competency is both an appreciating and depreciating asset which requires regular periodic investment in the form of skills acquisition. One could argue that the changing nature of business in a global environment makes a strong case for corporations and individuals to be continually adding and refreshing skills.

From a corporate perspective, continuous learning increases a firm's ability to do productive, profitable work, and provides a ready source of applied knowledge to adapt to changes in the competitive environment. Therefore, every investment in additional training and education yields a higher return than a simple investment in technology or other capital expenditure, because of individuals' abilities to reapply knowledge to many conditions, often without additional investments. However, the highly skilled worker is more valuable and can easily be lost to a competitor if not properly challenged, as noted by Handy: 'Education sets you free, but erodes your commitment to a place, a country or even an organization.'[9] Highly skilled individuals in a synconomy are no longer bound by geography or corporate affiliation, and they often value quality of life, economic, social and environmental factors at a higher priority, which is connected to their choice of company and location.

Senior management teams in global corporations must meet this challenge by managing human capital assets proactively. This requires a shift in thinking from viewing people as a ready commodity to actively managing personnel as a portfolio of skills, as Mills notes:

> Globalization often underachieves its value-creation potential in part because firms fail to leverage existing assets effectively. A key underleveraged asset is personnel, a tangible entity that embodies intangibles such as knowledge, effort, initiative, and intelligence. To leverage its human assets, a firm needs a program of motivation that transforms individual elements (such as compensation, selection, and personal development) into a mutually supportive coherent whole.[10]

Motivation comes in many forms. Different benefits or advantages appeal to different individuals. For example, younger employees find value in transferring to foreign locations, whereas married employees with children traditionally tend to want a less mobile position in order to maintain a more stable home environment. However, one could argue that since the new world of business is moving towards a greater propensity for transnational work, moving the family may provide necessary skills to children which would become more valuable later when their careers begin. The need to balance family and business lives is fundamental in the new business environment. Individuals realize that personal enjoyment of work is no longer a fantasy but an attainable goal, when an organization values the individual not simply as an employee, but a performing asset in the portfolio of corporate competency, as observed by the Conference Board:

> Many CEOs observe that people want to feel a passion for the company's work, to become part of a higher purpose than business results alone, and to balance their work and family lives more effectively.[11]

Achieving a sense of corporate loyalty is indeed difficult if employees think that their jobs are in jeopardy because of sudden changes in business activity. Employee loyalty is eroding rapidly because of a perceived lack of loyalty from the employer to the employee. Corporations have long identified that training new employees is a significant cost, yet this investment is quickly discounted when the size of the organization must be reduced. In fact, the aggregate loss of value in the human assets of the company needs to be reflected in the balance sheet. Karl Erik Sveiby contends that if the knowledge, skills and expertise that people possess are indeed an asset to the firm, their combined value should be reflected on corporate balance sheets.[12] Venture capitalists have long identified the value of knowledge and skills when they assess the founders of a firm, which is why they demand to know a great deal about the founders before they make an investment. Often the venture capitalist's objective during the early stages of analysis is to get to know the founders individually, to understand how they think and, most importantly, to perceive how they work as a team. Like a start-up company, established firms must also get to know their people better. Senior managers in a synconomy experience a shift in roles, becoming more of a resource to internal and external entities and less of a control point.

Chattell identifies two key roles for senior management teams in leveraging the employee value proposition, as the progenitors of meaningful challenges and the resources that reduce the limits and barriers which are generally established by the structure of the organization. Chattell further identifies that the key to capitalizing on knowledge assets is to organize knowledge by its relevance.[13] Knowledge is exploited when it is incorporated into the process of the business and it reaches its highest value when the assimilation of knowledge becomes a daily activity of each individual in the firm. A major challenge for today's corporations is that people are becoming increasingly mobile in their careers, often taking with them their experience in process, product and customer knowledge when leaving the firm. If employees do indeed have a value proposition to a firm and it recognizes knowledge as a corporate asset, then leveraging knowledge assets must be a discernible plan. Exploiting knowledge is a complex activity with no simple, universally accepted method, which is evidenced by the increasing number of books on the subject. However, if one considers that each employee, affiliate or partner of a company is an asset with an intrinsic value proposition, one can achieve leverage by dividing knowledge into three categories, as described by Lipnack and Stamps:

> Cross-boundary groups also generate knowledge capital that exists in all three forms: *inside* people in memory and internal cognitive models; *outside* people in commonly accessible information such as databases; and *between* people as they connect parts and pools of knowledge together and develop enduring understandings.[14]

Organizations operating in a synconomy must embrace this three-category understanding in order to develop strategic initiatives that leverage individual knowledge. This is of paramount importance the moment an organization begins to use more and more external relationships to support core and non-core processes. Knowledge that falls into the first category –

that of '*inside* people' – is best exploited by putting into place a programme that encourages active mentoring in three ways:

1. senior management and highly experienced professionals to junior staff

2. junior staff or specialized people to senior executives (better known as reverse mentoring)

3. peer-to-peer mentoring, typically accomplished within specialized areas or line organizations at all levels.

Corporations operating in a synconomy must excel in engaging individuals in such as way that they mentor across organizational and functional hierarchies.

Mentoring does not need to be a complex process. Each person should establish a specific topic, skill, technique or method in which he or she holds particular expertise. The goal should be to develop mechanisms that will transfer this knowledge to another person within a three-month period, if possible, using a variety of meetings, coaching sessions, technologies, conference calls or any communications medium. This mentoring should be incorporated into the normal work schedule as a pure investment in advancing a firm's competency. The minimum requirement should be that each person mentors four people a year, more, obviously, being better.

For example, in a large multinational chemical company, there are five departments organized to produce product lines of similar chemical compounds. Each department has international production centres. If an individual receives mentoring from a senior executive four times a year and from a peer located in another functional department, in less than two years he or she will have acquired not only skills that enhance his or her ability to work within the functional discipline, but also a comprehensive view of the inner workings of the firm, thereby increasing the depth of knowledge on how the firm works holistically. This cross-organizational exchange is vital because it enables an individual to observe the processes, methods, procedures and operating policies of departments external to his or her line management, enabling him or her to identify potential intra-company operating synergies.

Companies operating in a synconomy's network of partners have discovered that the second category of knowledge exploitation, '*outside* people', is much more difficult to accomplish. This is because distance, technology and operating procedures often require that this knowledge should be made explicit and easily accessible. In a synconomy, knowledge technology becomes the mechanism for collaboration and bi-directional activities, competency and corporate know-how become the means. Although technologies such as databases, chat rooms, newsgroups and other collaborative media and software components make possible the collection and rapid dissemination of knowledge, organizations have discovered that when knowledge is formalized by technology, individuals often fail to use it optimally or, in some cases, become intimidated by the formal procedure. For example, an individual may become self-conscious about his or her writing skills which can be viewed and judged by the entire company. Additionally, the capture, consolidation, summation and distribution of explicit knowledge all require organization, which in many firms is left, by default, to the information technology department. When organizations formalize knowledge as simply an administrative function removed from the core business process which it supports, knowledge that is used in conjunction with the process remains underleveraged.

For example, a large consulting organization used a collaboration technology to establish databases on vertical industry knowledge, practitioner knowledge, consulting techniques, methodologies, general discussions, client information and almost any other topic that consultants would benefit from sharing. The first round of implementation was not considered a success because of the lack of input by consultants and the low amount of utilization. When the project was reviewed, managers discovered that consultants were not willing to participate actively because it was a non-revenue-generating activity at odds with their compensation scheme. Financial and career incentives were put in place and the second round of implementation was more successful. However, it also fell short of expectations. A second project review revealed that although the large majority of consultants were now participating and exchanging knowledge at unprecedented levels, the plethora of databases located across the entire enterprise made finding specific knowledge difficult. In the third wave of implementation, a comprehensive catalogue was developed and a knowledge oversight group was established, with representatives from all departments periodically reviewing how the databases were being used, where they were located, how easy was it to find them, and so on. In the final wave of implementation, knowledge databases were organized around navigation, which came in three forms: a hierarchical structure similar to the organization's structure; a catalogue by topic area; and an internal search engine posted on the Internet to aggregate all internal databases. Obviously, the third means became the method of choice. Although this story may scare companies into not creating methods and mechanisms to share knowledge, it must be said that firms operating in a network of value partnership must create mechanisms for the employees to share knowledge smartly and efficiently.

The third category of knowledge capital generation is '*between* people', and it is closely linked to the preceeding discussion on outside people. This category is more complex, as companies in a synconomy enter into operating agreements with external entities supplying specialized value. This raises questions about how to deal with issues such as cultural biases and languages, and whether you can really expect consultants, partners or affiliates to part with the knowledge which they consider their own intellectual property or an asset of their firm.

Intellectual property and its ownership in whatever form must be an integral part of the employee value proposition. However, the management of intellectual property is now more complex when knowledge workers and partners bring to the organization expertise which will influence the design, efficiency and utilization of interconnected business processes, without having a clear mechanism to transfer knowledge formally to the corporation. Knowledge workers realized in the 1990s that mobility was a key factor in the advancement of salary and position, as corporations scrambled to acquire talent. Traditional restrictive geographic employment contracts became ineffective because technology allowed workers to create consulting and contract relationships with distant employers. One issue that has yet to be fully understood by organizations is the ownership or usage rights to the knowledge of an individual as a member of a network of value, which can be transitory. As argued elsewhere, this issue raises a number of questions which organizations adopting transnational behaviours, employing knowledge workers and, more importantly, engaging in partnership will need to address:

- Is the knowledge, experience and wisdom of employees a possession of the employer or is it rented, or perhaps licensed from the employee?
- To what degree is the total knowledge of the employee the property of the employer?
- To what extent can employers claim ownership of employee-generated knowledge that is only remotely connected with the employer's business?
- When knowledge workers provide their own office infrastructure (computers, backup systems, filing cabinets), to what extent do employers have access to search or claim ownership to the knowledge contained within the devices?
- What is the level of ownership between the consultant and the new knowledge he or she acquires while engaged in transient activities within a firm?[15]

Sidestepping a debate on the complex, international legal issues that suddenly arise from the new levels of transnational collaboration and integrated business processes, organizations must consider circumventing these issues in an effort to encourage collaboration and not thwart a firm's ability to compete. One could argue that as business process activities become more transparent, the need to guard corporate secrets becomes less important because the process is no longer the differentiating factor. If a firm is outsourcing a process to a partner, it is because they already know how the process works, performs and functions. In most cases, they will already be doing it for someone else, hence it is not really a corporate secret.

To operate in a synconomy, organizations must address the issues of human capital management on a never before imagined scale, crossing cultures, social values and nation states. Human capital assets are no longer contained within a hierarchical corporate structure, but are evolving into a network of highly refined skills, forming cells of corporate competencies, as illustrated in Figure 5.2.

The single skill that corporations and individuals must develop to embrace the change in business conditions is the adoption of a process orientation, placing the customer at the centre of the process. This customer focus is necessary for the corporate value proposition because it dynamically drives changes in the underlying business processes in tune with changes in customer demand. From an individual perspective, a process focus is the key to establishing an employee value proposition because it gives relevance to an individual's skills in generating value which matches corporate goals and objectives. Additionally, corporations that are becoming transnational must create an environment of continuous education and mentoring to improve product quality and reduce the cost of continually attracting talent.

Therefore, in a synconomy, the value of the individual becomes a key element in extending the global reach of a firm because it is a resource that can be leveraged and an asset that can be measured against corporate objectives. Individuals, however, are influenced by their environment, being a product of the social structure in which they reside. How individuals integrate into society, especially when they achieve transnational mobility and elect to relocate to areas that are more attractive to the lifestyle to which they aspire, will be an issue that corporations will need to factor into strategic initiatives and global capability plans. In the next chapter, we turn to a few of the crucial aspects of knowledge workers' environment, namely taxation and social programmes, which play an increasing part in influencing their decisions on where to live and work.

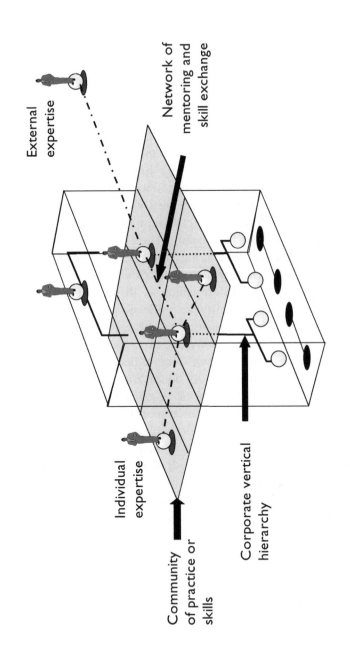

Figure 5.2 The network of human capital assets

External
expertise

Network of
mentoring and
skill exchange

Individual
expertise

Corporate vertical
hierarchy

Community
of practice or
skills

Embracing the Changing Lifestyles in a Corporate Synconomy

Concepts such as re-engineering, empowerment, globalization, disinter-mediation and the digital revolution have created a condition in which businesses are reconsidering the structure of their activities and individuals are examining the nature of work itself. The first consequence of this reassessment of value-adding activities has given rise to individuals rediscovering their true value to a company, resulting in the birth of what is now called the 'knowledge economy'. As individuals in the global workforce transform into knowledge workers and obtain other highly specific skills, they invariably reach continually improving levels of economic security. This process of increasing economic prosperity continues until an individual reaches a level of financial security that enables him or her to realize a personal shift from working because he or she has to meet financial obligations, to working as a means of self-fulfilment. Today's knowledge workers are discovering that they must strike a balance between the demands of work and the needs of personal time. They are realigning their business and personal priorities, which is driving changes within the corporation, altering human resource policies, product designs and the direct application of labour to business processes.

This self-realization of the knowledge class has enormous implications for corporations operating in a synconomy, because knowledge workers are the most likely candidates to adopt transnational behaviours by acquiring the necessary skill sets, such as advanced communications, negotiation, cultural empathy, social responsibility, cross-cultural sensitivity and multi-language skills. Knowledge workers and, to some extent, all workers will need to incorporate into their daily lives a new process of continuous learning, spanning the length of a career. As technical skills are enhanced by the acquisition of social, managerial and collaborative skills, individuals must be able to put external factors and shifts in the business and economic climate into a greater context in order to spot trends on which the firm can capitalize. For example, globalization is considered by many to be a process in which consumers from all nations desire a specific type or style of product, in many cases objectifying a western or American ideal. This process has been described as suppressing local culture in favour of adopting a homogeneous lifestyle. However, as Naisbitt and Aburdene point out, this phenomenon contains two trends:

> The more homogeneous our lifestyles become, the more steadfastly we shall cling to deeper values – religion, language, art, and literature. As our outer

worlds grow more similar, we will increasingly treasure the traditions that spring from within.[16]

One could argue that the perception of globalization by consumers creates two distinct opportunities: the creation of generic homogeneous products which cater to one customer segment, and the development of highly specific cultural products which are valued by another customer segment. Kugler rightly identifies that selling to global citizens is not about the features and functions of product. It consists of a deep understanding of attitudes and behaviours, influenced by religion, culture and patterns of consumption.[17] Developing skills that sense market demands by regional and local populations is critical for corporations engaged in transnational business. Kugler's observation is critical in developing an understanding of consumers in a global synconomy – there is no such thing as a homogeneous nation:

> Behaviours and attitudes reflect income and social class more than nationality. For example, there may be more similarities between the urban populations of Malaysia, Thailand and Taiwan than within each country alone.[18]

It would be naive to think that the world would embrace a single, generic suite of products and jettison the rich diversity of cultural, ethnic and religious products simply to have a common lifestyle. In fact, the chances of this ever happening seem remote and could, in a very broad sense, be considered anti-capitalistic, because such a scenario would reduce the number of consumer choices. Cultural behaviour, according to Jim Blythe, is a set of beliefs and values that are not only shared by a large group of people but must be learned, making the attributes of culture both subjective and arbitrary, influenced by religion, language, class and other more localized idiosyncrasies.[19] Kugler, again from an Asian perspective, pinpoints an often overlooked issue: that although consumers in the affluent class of Asian society are seeking western-style products, they have a deep-seated cultural awareness of collectivism which is distinctly different from their western, individualistic counterparts. As one would expect, Kugler dispels a common misconception that although Asians within several market subsegments adopt western products, they do not abandon their social roots, they simply use the products within a cultural context.[20] One thing is clear: in a synconomy, corporations must develop the competency to sense global market demands through several lenses – fashion, price, profitability, cultural appeal, religious conformity, social acceptability and other customer-centric characteristics.

Another aspect of the new corporate global reach is the changing composition of the workforce and the influence of local, cultural preferences. Firms must now contend with issues such as compensation, benefits and corporate citizenship on a global scale. Small companies are not immune to this condition, as they must often address the differences that exist between the headquarters location and satellite offices in all corners of the world. The organization Meridian Resources has identified global diversity as a mechanism to increase productivity, making a company more responsive to the changing needs of more regionalized customers:

> Meridian broadly defines diversity to include national and regional cultures, race, ethnicity, age, gender, the interpersonal dimensions of work and communication styles, and many other dimensions of diversity. We create a strong linkage between diversity and business results with a specific focus on business issues such as collaboration, innovation, globalization, multicultural teams, global projects and leadership.[21]

The key issue Meridian identifies is that organizations must develop solutions that leverage global diversity by employing technology to facilitate the development of corporate knowledge in which no one tool or method is used. Organizations must have a broad pallet of mechanisms such as face-to-face learning, self-paced materials, Internet-enhanced distance learning tools and a process for synthesizing these multiple communications into information that can be used by all parts of a global organization. The key learning for corporations engaged in the synconomy is to embrace the new global nature of business and the decentralized structure of the organization by assessing these changes as new opportunities. Corporations actively leveraging global diversity must avoid the temptation of developing inter-company policies that act in the same way as protectionist economics striving to preserve the past, which is the subject of the next chapter.

Notes

1   M. J. Blaine, *Co-operation in International Business*, Aldershot: Avebury, 1994, p. 95.

2   J. Naisbitt, *Global Paradox*, London: Nicholas Brealey, 1994.

3   R. Buckminster Fuller, *Untitled Epic Poem on the History of Industrialization*, Charlotte: Heritage Printers, 1962, pp. 55–61.

4   Celemi, available at www.celemi.com.

5   R. Donkin, 'Measuring the worth of human capital', *Financial Times*, 7 November 2002, p. x.

6   J. DiVanna, *Thinking Beyond Technology: Creating New Value in Business*, Basingstoke: Palgrave Macmillan, 2002.

7   A. Chattell, *Creating Value in the Digital Era*, Basingstoke: Macmillan – now Palgrave Macmillan, 1998.

8   D. Sutherland, 'Attracting and retaining world-class talent: the employee value proposition', Baltimore: Business Innovation Consortium, p. 4. available at www.bicnow.com/what/EVPPOV.pdf.

9   C. Handy, *The Elephant and the Flea: Looking Backwards to the Future*, London: Hutchinson, 2001.

10 D. Mills, *e-Leadership: Guiding Your Business to Success in the New Economy*, Paramas: Prentice Hall, 2001, p. 145.

11 The Conference Board, *The CEO Challenge: Top Marketplace and Management Issues 2001*, New York: The Conference Board, 2001, p. 17.

12 K. Sveiby, *The New Organizational Wealth: Managing and Measuring Knowledge-Based Assets*, San Francisco: Berret-Koehler Publishers, 1997, p. 163.

13 Chattell, *Creating Value in the Digital Era*, p. 154.

14 J. Lipnack and J. Stamps, *Virtual Teams*, New York: John Wiley, 1997, p. 237.

15 DiVanna, *Thinking Beyond Technology*, p. 94.

16 J. Naisbitt and P. Aburdene, *Megatrends 2000. The Next Ten Years … Major Changes in Your Life and World*, London: Sidgwick & Jackson, 1990, p. 104.

17 R. Kugler, 'Marketing in East Asia: the fallacies and the realities', in D. Dayao (ed.), *Asian Business Wisdom: Lessons from the Region's Best and Brightest Business Leaders*, Singapore: John Wiley, 2000, pp. 199–203.

18 Kugler, 'Marketing in East Asia', p. 200.

19 J. Blythe, *The Essence of Consumer Behaviour*, Harlow: Pearson Education, 1997, p. 90.

20 Kugler, 'Marketing in East Asia', p. 201.

21 Meridian Resources, available at www.meridianglobal.com/, October 2002.

CHAPTER 6

International Trade, Protectionism and Global Economic Impact

This chapter endeavours to bring all the aforementioned factors into a context which organizations can use to understand the relationship of their business processes to value generation in a global exchange of inter-operating business transactions. The increasing globalization of business during the last two decades of the twentieth century saw multinational firms becoming transnational entities operating across geographic boundaries. This change from local/international business to a transnational operating philosophy reflects how organizations must adapt structurally to approach business in a connected global marketplace.

The fundamental change, as Drucker points out, is migrating from an operating philosophy that views the firm's structure as a traditional, locally domiciled firm with remote international operations to a transnational approach in which the firm acts as one economic unit embracing a world marketplace.[1] Although the distinction seems to be a matter of semantics, the distinguishing aspect of this structural change is in the delineation and construction of the core business and non-core business processes. In the transnational firm, as Drucker claims, functional aspects of various business processes such as selling, servicing, public relations and legal affairs remain local, and functions such as parts, machines, planning, research, finance, marketing, pricing and management are centralized at headquarters, which can physically be anywhere.[2]

From a synergistic perspective, firms need to adopt and apply two operating philosophies that in themselves must act synergistically within the firm: centralized functions should be consolidated for economies of scale and scope, while localized activities should not simply be made autonomous but perhaps franchised in structure, as illustrated in Figure 6.1. That is,

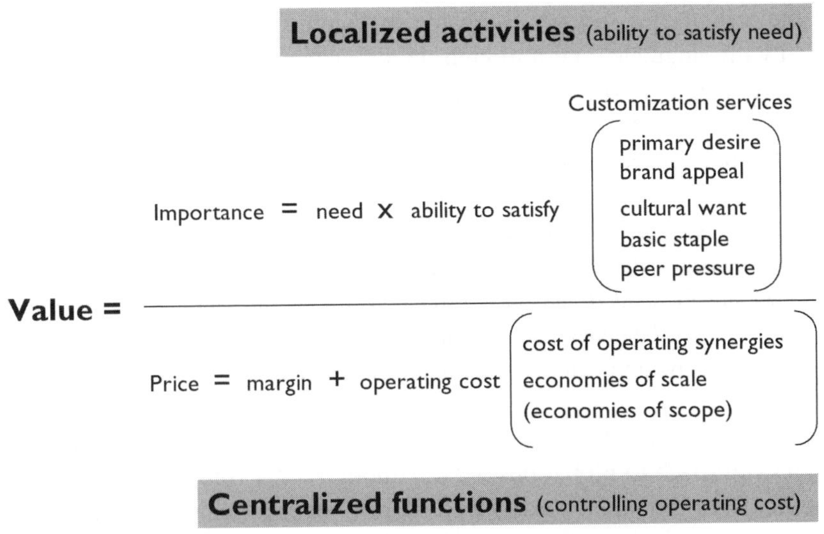

$$\text{Value} = \frac{\text{Importance} = \text{need} \times \text{ability to satisfy} \left\{ \begin{array}{l} \text{Customization services} \\ \text{primary desire} \\ \text{brand appeal} \\ \text{cultural want} \\ \text{basic staple} \\ \text{peer pressure} \end{array} \right. }{\text{Price} = \text{margin} + \text{operating cost} \left\{ \begin{array}{l} \text{cost of operating synergies} \\ \text{economies of scale} \\ \text{(economies of scope)} \end{array} \right.}$$

Centralized functions (controlling operating cost)

Figure 6.1 Values and synergies

locally facing functions – such as public relations – should be autonomous because of local knowledge. However, public relations activities in all parts of the firm should be coordinated using technology as part of a comprehensive, integrated approach in a global brand or corporate image.

The groups within an organization who have direct interactions with customers, suppliers, government agencies, the media and other external entities must develop skills of being aware of the attitudes of external sources towards a firm. In effect, they must become the sensing mechanism for a corporation's external policy-making processes, such as corporate identity, brand image, environmental policies, community interaction policies and other means which connect the firm to the operating environment. Corporations must be aware that as they engage in more transnational activities in a synconomy, their success in achieving operational synergies with other firms will depend, to some extent, on their ability to act as a mechanism for economic stability, in order to avoid being perceived as an exploitive predator. Therefore, firms engaged in global commerce must have the acuity and nous to use resources to reduce the perception of threatening the local economy. Corporations entering into a foreign market or developing a partnership with a distant firm must be wise and increasingly aware of religious preferences, cultural idiosyncrasies and social customs, using factors such as language to engage local customers, workers and special interest groups which may feel threatened by the arrival of a foreign company. Nationalism and culture are closely fused with language, and although many businesses regard English as the standard language of business, corporations truly attempting to achieve synergies with foreign partners must become competent in developing a multilingual approach to business, as Naisbitt and Aburdene discuss:

> language is the pathway to culture. If the inhabitants of a Third World country sense that an outside culture is gaining undue influence, they will feel their values are threatened and may respond with cultural nationalism, vigorously asserting their language and/or religion, just as they would counter a political or military invasion with renewed political nationalism.[3]

Corporations use technologies such as the Internet to develop a multilingual approach to global business. Although not a complete solution, the Internet does provide a ready mechanism to engage local people, partners and customers in ways that can reflect linguistic familiarity; websites can also include cultural imagery and other mechanisms to entice a customer into developing a closer relationship with the firm. Within Europe, language is not the unifying agent between nation states; economic activity provides the cohesive force that brings together firms operating in a multicultural environment. The single European market provides businesses operating in Europe with access to an economic structure that over time (the next two or three years) will reach an operating parity with the economy of the US, although we could argue that Europe will trail slightly behind in growth rate because of a smaller amount of investment in innovation by government and private sources. Participation in an aggregated European market means that as the market evolves and establishes reciprocal trade deals with other economic zones outside Europe, businesses operating within the market will lower their cost of operations simply because of the reduced level of government regulation. Therefore, the expectation is that the market will create an environment that facilitates inter-market trade and commerce within Europe which is easier, less bureaucratic and is sensitive to local needs, while making commerce outside Europe more convenient and less problematic.

Peter Sutherland, former director general of the World Trade Organization, makes an important point, placing trade functions within a local/global context:

> The real trade wars take place within countries, between consumers and special interest groups. Trade between countries brings mutual benefits. Those who genuinely wish to reduce barriers between rich and poor should

strongly espouse free-trade policies and expose those special interests (for example, steel, textiles and agriculture) that urge ultimately self-defeating protectionist measures.[4]

As Sutherland observed, when countries erect trade barriers to protect special interest groups they restrict their ability to participate in global commerce and often internalize the imbalance of factions within the nation state. Firms participating in a global synconomy must strive to strike a balance in trade without their country of origin erecting barriers to commerce. Understanding not only how to balance economic activity but also how to communicate the resulting benefits to local and national people is a core competency that many firms overlook.

One of the many roles of government is to facilitate the engine of commerce with a consistent level of economic stability or, at the very least, a predictable economic infrastructure. In other words, the mechanisms by which corporations can engage in international and domestic business activities must meet a predictable level of operability. The means of commerce, that is, the laws, regulations, tax rates, tariffs and other controlling instruments, must be focused not on protecting the interests of special groups, but on the free and unencumbered global exchange of goods and services. One could argue that protectionism and other restrictive trade practices are simply quick fixes, often leading to economic isolationism, and ultimately acting as tourniquets on the flow of international exchange which they were designed to protect. World governments should be looking towards new ways of engaging, collaborating and encouraging cross-border exchange, and less towards serving local self-interest. Local self-interest can best be served by government strategies designed to increase the flow of goods and services, thereby, over time, altering the long-term prosperity of society in general.

Countries erect barriers to commerce when their constituents perceive a threat to local commerce in the form of job losses and other actions considered to be draining on the local economic output. To illustrate this, consider two countries producing similar goods, say, cars. Country A has a long history of automotive prowess and country B is a relative newcomer. Over time, the newcomer can offer vehicles that rival the incumbent's and because country B delivers cars that customers want, the automotive output of country A is reduced. Suddenly, country B is perceived as a threat to the economic automotive output of country A. To correct this imbalance, the car-producing companies of country B offer to build manufacturing facilities in country A so that employment levels can, to a degree, be maintained. Several factions within country A still insist that country B is an economic threat because the profits associated with production are now being exported back to country B. In this scenario, two observations are obvious: firstly, the profits go to the firm with the best product, process and organization, regardless of where the firm is located, and secondly, the role of government should not be to erect barriers to restrict foreign competition, but to enable capital market mechanisms so that investors in country A can easily invest in the automotive corporations in country B, thereby sharing in and repatriating the profits. In fact, one could argue that the basic principle of free-market capitalism is to promote and reward organizations that meet consumer demand with a high-quality, fairly priced product, regardless of physical or geographic location. What individuals often forget is the relationship between an action in one industry and its influence on another, as Krugman noted:

> To observe that productivity growth in a *particular industry* reduces employment *in that same industry* tells us nothing about whether productivity growth *in the economy* as a *whole* reduces employment in the economy as a whole.[5]

This perception of the direct connection between productivity and job reduction is often a topic of protest by industry special interest groups, trade unions and citizen groups. If one considers applying the same basic economic premise to companies operating within a synconomy, the direct connections are not as clear, but equally valid. Therefore, in an environment in which business is continuously connected using technology and synergistically operating towards shared goals, an increase in productivity in one company may result in a decrease in total jobs within that region, but it may also bring about an increase in jobs or reduce costs in another firm in another region.

Another issue which corporations operating in a network of value must consider is how transnational transactions that occur within their network of value are recorded and reflected in their statements of operations. The influence of indirect sales via a transnational network is a little discussed phenomenon described as actions by a majority-owned foreign affiliate (MOFA) or a majority-owned US affiliate (MOUSA).[6] Harry Freeman, of the Mark Twain Institute, described the phenomenon thus: a traditional, cross-border export is one where a company such as IBM in the US sells goods or services directly (US export) to Bayer in Germany (German import). When IBM's UK subsidiary sells products (UK export) to Bayer in Germany (German import,) the sale is not a US export. However, this sale through the majority-owned IBM UK affiliate is a MOFA.[7] Similar to this macroeconomic measure, corporations utilizing a network of partners, affiliates and associations need to create the same multifaceted measurement to determine accurately the effectiveness of brands, sales campaigns, customer service levels and other, formerly internal, benchmarks.

As corporations strive to make their processes more externally focused by seeking lower cost alternatives to in-house resources, technology, coupled with economic infrastructure, makes it possible to establish these business alliances anywhere in the world. Therefore, it behoves governments to address proactively the longer term issue of an incremental rise in the overall standard of living versus the short-term myopia of local protectionism. No country is immune from this dilemma. This means that businesses operating in a synconomy must actively establish relationships with various government agencies as strategic partners to address issues of commerce, community and social responsibility. Similar to other external relationships, the interactions with government agencies must also be measured within a set of operating criteria such as reciprocity between services rendered to the community and tax incentives. Governments and corporations must act as socially responsible strategic partners to ensure long-term rises in the standard of living. More importantly, governments and corporations working in strategic partnerships must be measured and held accountable to both local people and world citizens. As corporations act more synergistically with businesses in a network of value and with a wider variety of government agencies, their ability to control and direct resources and apply corporate assets is critical to their long-term viability, which is the subject of the next section.

Conducting the Corporate Orchestra

An orchestra is a large group of highly skilled musicians, with varying degrees of competency, who come together to make music. A conductor acts as an instrument in his/her own right, carefully arranging the execution of talented output to bring about the desired result, music. Rarely, if ever, would a conductor approach this task without having a score (a manuscript showing what each instrument is to play) from which to conduct his/her efforts. Similarly, in order to conduct a corporation in a synconomy, management must have a plan. Recently, and often repeated in times of economic downturn, strategic planning has been jettisoned for the short-term goal of 'what can we do this quarter'. When management teams take on the posture of 'we haven't got time for strategy', they send a clear, perhaps unconscious message to individuals in the company that strategy is like philosophy; it is nice to know when you have time to spare. As corporations engage in synergistic activities with external global business partners, this 'strategy-free in times of turmoil' approach to business will no longer do, because, from the perspective of the partner, the firm will be perceived to be unreliable. If one recalls the definition of strategy as 'planning and directing an operation in a war or campaign',[8] it would be difficult to imagine a commander at the most intense moment of battle saying to his troops: 'all right lads, forget the strategic objective, just shoot anything you can see as you run backwards.'

Therefore, corporations in commerce with global partners, suppliers and customers need to have comprehensive strategic plans, which must be revisited frequently and modified, adapting to changes in the world's economic climate. Strategic plans are essential for directing the actions of a firm in a network of value, not by providing detailed, formulaic, planned activities, but by providing a set of guidelines in which empowered individuals can act within a framework of acceptable business expectations. The strategic orchestration of business processes and the competencies required in their execution demand that senior managers develop plans which cover a long planning horizon, incorporating the firm's vision, value proposition and best intelligence on future market conditions. This forward-looking strategy must not simply project today's business mathematically into an incrementally adjusted future operating rate; it should be the foundation for how the business will operate within the parameters of an unknown future. Strategies should inspire, not restrict, an organization's ability to do today's work while preparing for the future, as Lipnack and Stamps observed:

> Don't be afraid to raise expectations. People can do great things by themselves when they have a clear view of the whole. A long-term plan with four-, eight-, and twelve-year targets will help. This future-look provides the context for making short-term trade-offs and decisions.[9]

As corporations today begin to form globalized networks of value, they are quickly realizing that globalization must be addressed along five distinct fronts: the firm's supply chain; its distribution channels; its internalized functions; its leadership, and its collaborators. However, contemporary firms must face the new business landscape of global competition with the same three mechanisms to generate value that were used by their predecessors; either increase revenues; decrease costs; and/or leverage the existing internal assets or external partnerships to gain market reach.

A business entity comprises individuals organized traditionally in a hierarchical structure, or in the form of a matrix. In a synconomy, businesses are formed by a network of competencies. Traditionally, the internal structure of an organization works on the premise that people within the organization will orchestrate their activities in concert with the goals of the firm to achieve the output desired by customers. In previous manifestations of a firm, the coordination of resources in both domestic and multinational companies was part of a shared commitment of labour, capital and physical resources to work towards the output without the need of any legal agreements. The firm worked because it was based on an implicit trust in the relationship between the sub-organizations of the firm all pulling towards the same objective. During the last quarter of the twentieth century, in many cases organizations pushed profit and loss responsibilities down to the lowest operating level within the firm, effectively making each sub-organization a small company. In some cases, this has worked well, as in consulting organizations and other discrete function groups which can work interdependently and interchangeably without a large cost in the reallocation of working assets. However, in other organizations, this practice acted as a damper on cross-functional activities, primarily because it encouraged sub-organizations to commit only resources in which they could measure a direct profit from their activities. The informal nature of transactions between members of a firm enables it to engage in supporting a business process and adapting to change without the need for a contractual obligation, but acting in the best interest of the firm because of the common bond of the company.

The combination of organizational structure and measurements used to assess the output of a firm leads to an operating condition of authoritarianism or cooperation which can be either an asset or a liability to corporations embracing synergistic relationships. As firms decouple into more outsourced relationships with other firms, the implicit trust that was the primary basis of the relationship to harness resources must now be represented by more formal means, such as outsourcing contracts, bi-directional licensing agreements and other, more legally binding documents. This additional layer of complexity can be minimized as firms operating together learn, over time, to trust each other's actions as the relationships mature. Therefore, organizations operating synergistically must develop a hybrid approach that retains the flexibility of the informal organization's ability to harness resources while adopting a mechanism that measures the performance of each organization against their contractual obligations.

The uncertainty of market demand, coupled with the complexity of the decentralized business structures operating synergistically, creates the need for an increased level of communication to coordinate the efforts of all parties involved in bringing a product or service through a cross-border, multi-organizational business process. This new demand on business to be ever-vigilant on the quality and timeliness of information is only accomplished through the establishment of a technological infrastructure that supports a high level of collaboration, coordination and bi-directional communications. In a synconomy, the relationship between two organizations can decay rapidly in the face of changing business conditions, if one firm perceives that one of the partnering organizations is better informed on the changing factors and is not honestly disclosing information relevant for making business decisions.

Collaboration that leverages a technological infrastructure is an essential element in facilitating the exchange of information, guaranteeing the quality of data and ultimately synchronizing the business processes between each member in a network of value-driven relationships. Technology applied to the organization's value proposition presents new opportunities for corporations to increase their productivity and acquire new customers, but it is also the essential element in participating in a network of partnerships, as we will discuss in the next section.

The Value of Technology and Trade

> Merchants have no country. The mere spot they stand on does not constitute so strong an attachment as that from which they draw their gains.
>
> *Thomas Jefferson*

In the present business environment, organizations and the media are examining the true value of technology and the perception of benefits applied to the organization versus the overall cost of technology. It could be argued that the rise in technological scepticism found in the discourse of today's media may simply be a way to attribute to something tangible – or semi-tangible – the ill feeling that most businesses are experiencing after the technological euphoria of the 1990s. However, what many companies are overlooking is that technology, regardless of its perceived benefits or actual contributions to operating profits, is playing and will continue to play a decisive role in competing in a global market. Companies cannot compete without technology, and firms today must not simply use technology, but learn to leverage it in a rapidly interconnecting business environment. The full potential of collaborative technologies such as the Internet has yet to be realized, but also we could argue that its true potential has yet to be imagined. One must remember that at the birth of the electrification of industry in the early 1900s, no one prophesized the use of the computer or even conceived of today's telecommunications capabilities.

One could argue that at this juncture in business activity, it would be prudent for organizations engaging in global commerce or anticipating competing in a market of transnational activities to invest aggressively in technology in preparation for the next wave of competitive pressures. Corporations do not simply need to invest, they also must reassess their business model, the structure and functions of the firm, and the ways through which technology will facilitate a transition from the current state to a future state. Technological futurists and other industry experts are not merely prophesizing the capabilities that technology could bring; they are, in many cases, using a method of predictive theory to gain insights into how organizations can use technology to add value. Davis and Davidson state that predictive theory provides the means to conceptualize what can be done, and technology acts as a mechanism between scientific innovations and their application to business activities:

> Predictive theory is the bridge between science and economy, and technology is that travel across such bridges.[10]

One of the predictions and express intentions of the Internet was to eliminate effectively all companies that performed the services of a traditional middleman or intermediary. To some extent and within several industries, disintermediation occurred when companies failed to realize the influence that technology has on the value of primary customer attributes, such as convenience, savings, a broad selection and trust. However, many industries did not experience a complete abandonment of existing channels to market or supply chain relationship because their relationships with their partners was, in many cases, more valuable than the perceived benefits of the technological switch.

In 1991, Robert Reich described how few products are still the end result of domestic manufacturing output and, more importantly, how the international nature of products is not always apparent to the customer:

> When an American buys a Pontiac Le Mans from General Motors, for example, he or she engages unwittingly in an international transaction. Of the $20,000 paid to GM, about $6,000 goes to South Korea for routine labor and assembly operations, $3,500 to Japan for advanced components (engines, transaxles, and electronics), $1,500 to West Germany for styling and design engineering, $800 to Taiwan, Singapore, and Japan for small components, $500 to Britain for advertising and marketing services, and about $100 to Ireland and Barbados for data processing. The rest – less than $8,000 – goes to strategists in Detroit, lawyers and bankers in New York, lobbyists in Washington, insurance and

health-care workers all over the country, and General Motors shareholders – most of whom live in the United States, but an increasing number of whom are foreign nationals.[11]

In the years following Reich's observation, the Internet ushered in the dot-com boom, when every business contemplated its ability to sell in a world with no market borders, without strategically assessing its products' international appeal. The profound and yet barely explored change that the Internet and electronic commerce technologies have brought to business is simply to give small to medium-sized businesses the same international-ization capabilities to their products and services. Organizations competing in an international marketplace must seek global reach, not only of company and product but also of brand, service to the community and all facets of the firm. Technology's ability to connect, communicate, collaborate and cooperate is awakening corporations to the fact that not only are they now more globally focused, but their organization is adopting varying degrees of transnationality.

The real debate about technology centres on a fundamental re-evaluation of what is to be considered a foreign or domestic product and, more impor-tantly, does it really matter?

The True Value of Technology

Moschandreas reminds us that technological change can be applied to two key objectives of the corporation: the ability to change the business process thereby lowering costs or optimizing the process (as discussed in previous chapters); and as a mechanism to introduce new products, alter the type of product or simply enhance a portfolio of traditional products:

> Major product innovations are almost by definition characterized by a unique-ness which gives monopolistic power to the producer. Not all new products, however, are major new innovations. Many are simply variants of existing products forming additions to an existing range of available brands. Their introduction increases competition and reduces concentration.[12]

It can be argued that the true value of technology in a syncomomy is not simply to reduce the overall cost of business, but to make possible inno-vations that create new business opportunities. The emergence of a knowl-edge economy in which individuals leverage increasingly new levels of data and information makes it clear that technology's value is not based in its perceived application to current business challenges but in its ability to enhance innovation, as Wriston notes:

> Information technology has also produced a new source of wealth that is not material; it is information – knowledge applied to work to create value. When we apply knowledge to ongoing tasks, we increase productivity. When we apply it to new tasks, we create innovation.[13]

Technology provides corporations with the ability to take a holistic view of their internal business processes and place them into the context of a global, competitive marketplace. In essence, technology enables organizations to break down business processes into manageable components and then reassemble them into value-adding activities that span corporate entities and international boundaries. Chattel observes that technology gives companies the ability to view their operations as a component of an entire industry in which their value-adding contribution can be realized, relative to the output of a total customer value proposition encapsulated in a set of interoperating, value-based activities:

> Information systems providing end-to-end and holistic views of the business process and the industry value chain, are being used to ensure that all aspects of the performance-generating equation are considered.[14]

However, despite the elegance of integrated technological solutions, external factors such as culture, economic pressure, social awareness, changing corporate and social structures and other non-technical issues have a direct bearing on the benefits attained by a firm as it applies technology. Although the benefits of technology are directly linked to a firm's ability to apply technology to its business processes and indirectly linked to external factors, as Young observed, the continual advance of technology is setting the pace at which organizations must adopt and adapt:

> Culture may influence the degree to which technological goals may be successful or otherwise, but the technological imperative establishes the rules of the game.[15]

It could be argued that autonomic computing in a synergic business environment will be the next logical step in the computing environment because it will create higher reliability in the interoperable processes within the business. The value proposition for this technological migration will be in its ability to transform not only the process of business within a firm but a firm's ability to interoperate with business processes outside the firm.

As businesses continue to streamline business processes and outsource individual components of a process, they realize that the value of a firm is its ability to orchestrate the interactions of the process, not the execution of each process component. Therefore, if autonomic computing is taken in this context, it becomes a valuable mechanism for gathering and disseminating information on how the business is operating, recommending actions that should be taken to correct business interoperability and predicting the next set of actions that a senior management team should make. In this context, autonomic computing becomes a key technology for establishing a 'business intelligence', similar to a firm's central nervous system. This is important because business process components that are outsourced or any activity that is no longer within the firm's direct control must be supplied with comprehensive, timely data to ensure their optimal performance. The rapid facilitation of the business process feedback loop is a vital link between management and the act of directing the level at which business operates.

However, the heart of the problem for autonomic computing is getting the world to adopt a technological standard or single set of guidelines. World history has shown that this is often more difficult than the development of the technology itself, as evident with the electric power cable and the international standard, or metric system of measurement. Therefore, one can assume that since the chance of the entire world ever adopting one technological standard is very small, the key characteristic of autonomic computing will be to adopt several (not an infinite number) generic interface protocols. The ability of adaptation in autonomic computing is what sets it apart from traditional computing technologies, making it self-aware and similar to people who can speak several languages. Thus, the fundamental element of autonomic computing will be to simplify computing and shift the focus from processing power to the fidelity of interoperability between discrete functions of computing itself. Put simply, its value is in its ability to connect to others. It will be the connective aspect of autonomic computing that brings to business the global coordination of decentralized and complex activities. This is a value proposition that will appeal to many multinational firms.

If one considers that a small business incubator may enable start-up businesses to exhibit synergistic behaviour because they share a common infrastructure to minimize costs, then it becomes clear that technology organizations over time will adopt a similar model for some of their operations. This can be seen in outsourcing contracts and other externally focused technology activities. However, technology's effectiveness must be measured and periodically assessed in order to keep up continually with the competition. It is possible for technology organizations to provide a synergistic infrastructure by outsourcing and in-sourcing technology services. However, Renkema makes an important point when viewing the ability to achieve synergies in a hierarchical organization:

> Generally speaking, the higher an organizational level, the more difficult it will be to realize synergy, since both coordination efforts and the complexity of this infrastructure will increase.[16]

Renkema's observation is central to the future of technology organizations and their role in creating value within the firm, because it focuses on one issue that has invariably been a limiting factor for organizations and impedes their ability to reach an operating synergy with external entities: traditionally, organizations have struggled with technology's benefit to the whole firm versus a single saving or capability within individual operating groups such as departments, divisions or subgroupings. Does the acquisition of a technology and its maintenance directly benefit the decentralized organization, or does it provide a capability to all parts of the firm? If so, how is the cost distributed to the appropriate cost centre? This reflects the continual dilemma of centralization versus decentralization of the technology function within a firm, which has plagued technology organizations since the 1960s, as depicted in Figure 6.2.

The central control of technology for economies of scale pitted against the autonomous control by individual operating groups to achieve specific objectives is similar to reshuffling the deck chairs on the Titanic. This is even more true if the debate fails to consider one central concept: what is the best thing to do to support the company's value proposition in the current and future environments in which the firm operates and will operate? It also presents an opportunity for organizations to take a giant step forward. If one subscribes to the central argument of this book, that is, that business is being reshaped into an external network of technology-enhanced clusters of corporate competencies resembling traditional companies in function but not in structure, and that the role of technology is to coordinate a dynamic set of globally diverse business activities, then a proactive approach would be to practise technological synergy internally first in order to reduce the risk.

Therefore, as organizations continue to move away from traditional hierarchical structures towards a network of linked competencies, a company could reduce the risks of organizational trauma in the form of

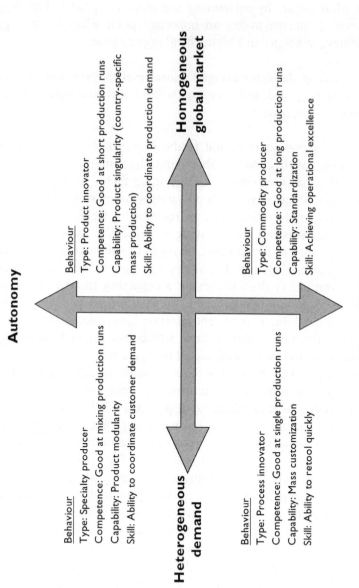

Autonomy

Behaviour
Type: Specialty producer
Competence: Good at mixing production runs
Capability: Product modularity
Skill: Ability to coordinate customer demand

Behaviour
Type: Product innovator
Competence: Good at short production runs
Capability: Product singularity (country-specific mass production)
Skill: Ability to coordinate production demand

Homogeneous global market

Behaviour
Type: Commodity producer
Competence: Good at long production runs
Capability: Standardization
Skill: Achieving operational excellence

Behaviour
Type: Process innovator
Competence: Good at single production runs
Capability: Mass customization
Skill: Ability to retool quickly

Heterogeneous demand

Centralization

Figure 6.2 The dilemmas of business

losses in productivity and other interruptions by employing technology as a means to experiment and transition from one state to the other. In Chattell's view, technology presents an organization with an opportunity to achieve a new level of operating performance. On the other hand, a firm's ability to achieve higher performance levels, restructure processes, rethink work and reform the organization rests squarely on a firm's ability to think beyond the traditional use of technology and approach to business:

> It is now widely accepted that the new technologies are not only wasted but positively harmful if they are used to automate the organizational approaches, structures and processes of the past. Most important of all, it has now become clear that the new technologies do not in themselves determine the organizational effectiveness. The effective company of the 21st century will have to be very different in all major aspects – it just happens that it will need the new technologies in some form to make it work.[17]

Technology must be viewed from the perspective of how it is applied to a firm within a global context, as Archibugi and Michie articulate: technology must have a place in the taxonomy of globalization – global exploitation of technology, global technological collaboration, and/or global generation of technology.[18] Archibugi and Michie postulate that the global exploitation of technology increases international trade because technology can be readily exported, enabling foreign companies to realize benefits quickly. However, its influence on international trade is a consequence, not a cause. Their second observation is that technology fosters an increased level of collaboration within government research agencies and the academic community. This results in a trend towards joint ventures between intra-country government agencies, internationally sponsored collaborations and cooperative ventures between the private and public sector.

One can consider that technology can be employed in the global generation of new technological capabilities to invent new technological advances. Aggregating technologies as a means to discover succeeding generations of technology requires the fundamental adoption of a structure that allows organizations to interact and collaborate dynamically. Government agencies and individual corporations may not be fashioned in a manner that can readily capitalize on new invention exploitation on a global scale. It seems that multinational and/or transnational corporations may be better suited to harvest the product of technological innovation, because their structure readily supports the speed required to participate dynamically. Therefore, because many businesses and governments will not be able to adapt quickly, they will enter into ever-increasing collaborative ventures between the public and private sector to be either technology-led initiatives focused on innovation, or technology-intensive activities centred on increasing productive output. Regardless of the structure which an organization adopts or the technologies it employs, companies must deliver value in a global environment, as we will explore in the next section.

Delivering Value in the New Global Framework

It is easy to say that corporations must become part of a global network of value. A more difficult task is to define the characteristic behaviour that all companies must adopt to liberate value from their organizations as a member of such a network. In this book, we have explored a variety of formulas for value, each presenting a variation of the same theme which places the customer at the centre of value and shareholders as the counterbalance to keep the utilization of resources within a reasonable margin of profitability. How corporations engage in networked business activity will occur in four stages:

1. developing interactive processes that create links to suppliers and customers;

2. identifying non-core processes that can be externalized and executed by other organizations under a defined relationship;

3. identifying core processes that can also be outsourced;

4. reaching a level of interconnection with partners so that they can achieve operational synergy.

Corporations must have a clear value proposition to communicate their mission and a means to convey that mission to employees and other members in a network of value-added relationships, as depicted in Figure 6.3.

In a network of partnerships, it is essential that a firm should not only establish core and non-core processes, but also identify core and non-core competencies which allow all partners to be active contributors in a network of value. Competencies must not be confused with primary process components or corporate functions; they are a fundamental concentration of key skills enabling a company to perform discrete activities. Core competencies such as the sharing of customer data for activities

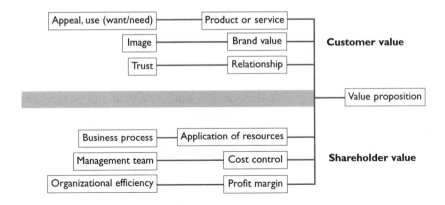

Figure 6.3 Components of the value proposition

such as product demand planning, customer segmentation and brand effectiveness are critical as the speed and volume of transactions continues to rise. Core competencies include:

- Sharing data (customer, inventory levels, replenishment levels)

- Exchanging information (customer trends, segmentation analysis, forecasting, logistics management, demand aggregation)

- Leveraging knowledge (collaborative product design, joint decision-making, process optimization)

while non-core competencies include:

- Human capital management

- Information technology and systems

- Benefits administration

- Training.

Apart from core and non-core competencies, organizations must make a conscientious effort to avoid the problem of process hesitation, which is the result of the combined effects of process repetition (when a process becomes second nature and transactions or events are often overlooked) and a lack of a process for handling process exceptions. Organizations engaged in global commerce often concentrate their negotiating powers on the definition and detailed specification of the terms and conditions of the relationship and the correct methods of processing transactions between the two firms. Unfortunately, business conditions are not static; changes in customer or supplier activities invariably occur, and exceptions arise. It is during the process exceptions, when customer issues, supplier problems or technical breakdowns occur outside the boundaries of the agreed-upon relationship, that organizations experience process hesitation, process disconnection and, sometimes, process failure.

It is not possible to predict all possible exceptions and/or changes which can occur to a global relationship in a network of value. Therefore, it is important that firms develop periodic assessments of the relationship and its operating parameters at the onset of the relationship. The dynamic nature of a network of value is its ability to adapt as the needs of global customers change. To deliver value in a global framework, the elements of the firm's value proposition must be considered with regard to how each relationship with external sources influences the component of value.

Each component of value faces a transformation in function as a product of technological advance, for example business processes extend beyond the confines of a firm – tightly integrated to other firms that provide discrete activities such as services to participate in collaborative commerce. One collaborative effort that demonstrates this principle is collaborative planning, forecasting and replenishment (CPFR). CPFR is conceptually a process in which vendors and customers provide supply-and-demand information that is aggregated, shared and processed in a jointly maintained database. The promotion of collaborative commercial services by organizations such as Voluntary Interindustry Commerce Standards Association (VICS)[19], whose mission is to improve the efficiency of supply chains, has set cross-industry standards designed to simplify the flow of information on products, materials and merchandise. One aspect of VICS is the Collaborative Planning, Forecasting and Replenishment Committee,[20] which has developed a set of integrated business processes that galvanizes a collaborative supply chain by providing a single source for information, transactions and business-to-business collaborative planning. Firms operating in a syncomy must develop corporate competency in collaborating with partnering entities, intimately sharing design, planning, production and a host of transactions that typically were rarely transmitted outside a firm. Another example of this emerging collaboration between companies can be found at the WorldWide Retail Exchange (WWRE),[21] which provides an environment and services to facilitate not just the aggregation of purchases, but a suite of options in which a firm can slowly move towards a highly integrated business model:

■ Services such as worldwide design planning and management allow firms to collaborate on product designs, exchange product ideas and create a set of technical assets including documents, digital images and other specifications across multiple projects.

■ Demand aggregation services permitting buyers to standardize items and aggregate item sourcing by participating in demand pools for volume purchasing, auctions or simply to streamline the process of request for information (RFI), request for quotation (RFQ) and request for proposals (RFP).

■ Worldwide item management allows a company centrally to manage product data across a synchronized global catalogue of direct and indirect goods.

■ A function of the worldwide trade logistics service is the 'global trade compliance' tool which acts as a comprehensive source for firms to access information on compliance with government regulations, determine licensing and documentation requirements, and assigning classification codes.

One core function that the WWRE offers is called 'the collaborative planner', which requires firms to rethink their traditional business process functions in order to collaborate effectively at the level of detail required to achieve operating synergies with external firms. Firms operating synergistically in an environment in which business processes are so highly integrated must have shared or similar goals, clearly defined objectives and, most importantly, adequate performance measurements. Sharing forecast, inventory, supplier, order and other basic but vital information introduces the firm to another core competency which they must develop, that of relationship management. Simply, the sensitivity of this information coupled with the need to achieve joint performance objectives makes assessing, selecting, evaluating and maintaining operating partnerships a skill that will be critical to long-term viability in a synconomy.

However, collaborating with suppliers, producers and other entities that enable the production of goods and services is only part of the new business equation. Developing a dialogue with customers, as Frimanson and Lind observe, can play a pivotal role in synergistic behaviour:

A customer may be more knowledgeable than a supplier may be concerning how to use the product sold by the supplier, whereas the supplier knows more about how to produce the product. As the business enterprise is not a coherent or monolithic subject, but rather an organizational system constituted of individuals and departments, we would expect to find a division of knowing within as well as between business enterprises.[22]

However, leveraging customer and supplier insight to achieve innovation is often difficult for organizations because, in many cases, they lack the skills to ignite the innovation spark and, more importantly, they fail to establish an environment that takes the innovation forward into commercialization. Organizations can accelerate the process of value creation when they use other organizations which act as a catalyst for innovation, such as the Business Innovation Consortium[23] in Baltimore, Maryland and the Thinking Studio in Aurora, Ohio.[24] To leverage innovation, economies of scale and scope, corporations will have to achieve operational synergies based on relationships within the networked community of value where technology is only a small part of the value equation.

Notes

1   P. Drucker, 'The global economy and the nation state', *Foreign Affairs*, January/February 1997, **76**(1): 167.

2   Drucker, 'The global economy and the nation state', p. 168.

3   J. Naisbitt and P. Aburdene, *Megatrends 2000. The Next Ten Years … Major Changes in Your Life and World*, London: Sidgwick & Jackson, 1990, p. 125.

4   See P. Sutherland, 'Why we should embrace globalization', *Finance & Development*, quarterly magazine of the International Monetary Fund, available at www.imf.org/external/pubs/ft/fandd/2002/09/sutherla.htm.September 2002.

5   P. Krugman, 'Is capitalism too productive?', *Foreign Affairs*, September/October 1997, **76**(5): 91–2.

6   A majority-owned foreign affiliate (MOFA) is a firm outside the US owned and controlled by one or more foreign firms and/or persons; a majority-owned US affiliate (MOUSA) is a firm established in the US, owned and controlled by one or more foreign firms and/or persons. *Globalization, Trade Liberalization and Benefits*, Chevy Chase: The Mark Twain Institute, July 2002, p. 2.

7   H. Freeman, 'Measuring globalization', *Globalization, Trade Liberalization and Benefits*, Chevy Chase: The Mark Twain Institute, July 2002, p. 4.

8   A.S. Hornsby, *Oxford Advanced Learner's Dictionary of Current English*, Oxford: Oxford University Press, 1991, p. 1270.

9   J. Lipnack and J. Stamps, *The TeamNet Factor: Bringing the Power of Boundary Crossing Into the Heart of Your Business*, Essex Junction: Oliver Wight, 1993, p. 341.

10 S. Davis and B. Davidson, *2020 Vision: Transform your Business Today to Succeed in Tomorrow's Economy*, London: Business Books, 1991, p. 187.

11 R. Reich, *The Work of Nations: Preparing Ourselves for 21st-century Capitalism*, New York: Alfred A. Knopf, 1991, p. 113.

12 M. Moschandreas, *Business Economics*, London: Routledge, 1994, p. 33.

13 W. Wriston, 'Bits, bytes and diplomacy', *Foreign Affairs*, January/February 1997, **76**(1): p. 176.

14 A. Chattell, *Creating Value in the Digital Era*, Basingstoke: Macmillan – now Palgrave Macmillan, 1998, p. 239.

15 G. Young, 'Culture and technological imperative', in M. Talalay, C. Farrands and R. Tooze (eds), *Technology, Culture and Competitiveness: Change and the World Political Economy*, London: Routledge, 1997, p. 30.

16 T. Renkema, *The IT Value Quest: How to Capture the Business Value of IT-Based Infrastructure*, Chichester: John Wiley, 2000, p. 195.

17 A. Chattell, *Creating Value in the Digital Era*, p. 45.

18 D. Archibugi and J. Michie, 'The globalization of technology: a new taxonomy', in D. Archibugi and J. Michie (eds), *Technology, Globalization and Economic Performance*, Cambridge: Cambridge University Press, 1997, p. 176.

19 Voluntary Interindustry Commerce Standards Association, available at www.vics.org, December 2002.

20 Collaborative Planning, Forecast and Replenishment Committee, available at www.cpfr.com, December 2002.

21 WorldWide Retail Exchange, available at www.worldwideretailexchange.org or www.wwre.org, December 2002.

22 L. Frimanson and J. Lind, 'The balanced scorecard and learning in business relationships', in H. Hakansson and J. Johanson (eds), *Business Network Learning*, Oxford: Elsevier Science, 2001, p. 59.

23 D. Sutherland, 'Business Innovation Consortium', Baltimore, Maryland, available at www.bicnow.com, November 2002.

24 Pine and Gilmore, 'Strategic Horizons, LLP, Thinking studio', Aurora, Ohio, available at www.customization.com/, December 2002.

CHAPTER 7

Conclusion: Synergistic Relationships

If world economies and businesses are moving towards the establishment of regional or national competitiveness, what is the prize? Will there simply be winner countries with winning economies, and, if so, what of the losers? Is it possible for governments and businesses to evolve into a more evenly distributed state of economic operating synergies? Can consumers help to level the dramatic shifts in the supply and demand cycle by developing more purposed buying habits such as advanced ordering or pre-committing stock to production? This conclusion focuses on putting all these factors into a framework of strategic thinking which enables a corporation to leverage existing business assets and proactively engage in global change. It was not the intention of this book to be a quick fix, corporate, self-help book; it is merely a text aiming to provide a collection of viewpoints, causing the reader to think differently when approaching strategies and solutions. Many of the factors that will influence and, more importantly, dictate changes in business will increasingly come from external forces, not as a result of previous methods of forecasting, so the number of prognostications and prophecies have been limited in order to focus on the fundamental aspects of the emerging business environment, here labelled the 'synconomy'.

The merger and acquisition activity of the last two decades of the twentieth century holds many lessons for companies about to embark on a journey to become synergistic transnational firms operating in a network of value. Corporations often undertake mergers and acquisitions to achieve operating synergies in the belief that bringing together two organizations will result in an output greater that the combined output of both firms. Companies fail to achieve synergistic behaviour because they dismantle their individual value propositions in pursuit of integration. Output is not the objective of an operating synergy; the goal is the increase in performance relative to the output. In a merger or acquisition, achieving an operational synergy is not about doing what both firms do today at a lower cost; synergy is creating value that only exists beyond the capabilities of either organization.[1] The objective of synergy in a network of value-added partners is the same: a level of performance that delivers a capability beyond the abilities of either partner. This is often made more challenging by distance, language, culture and other operating inconsistencies. Lindstrom argues that in order for corporations to achieve operational synergy, they must share comparable philosophies, goals, core values and practices in functional areas such as value gain for customers, brand handling, channel optimization, infrastructure, data exchange and consumer maintenance.[2]

The Synergistic Value Agenda

Participating in a network of value and achieving a high degree of operating synergy with global partners does not happen by accident, nor does it simply occur if the firm buys mountains of technology. Realizing synergistic value requires a strategy built on a series of successive business scenarios which move the corporation towards synergistic behaviour. Synergy is a mechanism to realize a higher return on investment than other means available in the emerging global competitive marketplace. We must remember the definition of synconomy as the process of interoperation between geographically distant entities in which the capabilities and productive output of the combined organizations act in synergy to produce a capability greater than the sum of its parts. To achieve any type of operational synergy, a company must establish a synergistic value agenda, which indicates not simply the goal of the relationship with external entities but the strategic intent of the value-added behaviour. To develop a synergistic value agenda, companies must first identify the type of synergy to be achieved, as noted by Ansoff:[3]

- *Sales synergy* – using common distribution channels, common sales administration of common warehousing, combining products to create a complete line, common advertising and combined reputations;

- *Operating synergy* – higher application of facilities and personnel, spreading of overhead, advantages of a common learning experience, and large-lot purchasing;

- *Investment synergy* – joint use of plant, common raw material inventories, transfer of research and development from one product to another, common tooling, common machinery, shared infrastructure;

- *Management synergy* – combined industry knowledge, or gaining cross-industry knowledge, and experience.

Once a firm identifies an opportunity for a synergistic relationship, it must subsequently define a series of business scenarios based on a value proposition in which synergy can be achieved. It would be rare to accomplish this under one single scenario. Although it might be possible, it would be more prudent for most organizations to develop several scenarios in which a number of alternative paths give the firm options once the process is underway. Each scenario identifies the competencies required to execute the business process and fulfil a value proposition. Once competencies and skills are identified, the firm must examine the external providers in a network of partners in order to determine their potential for achieving process synergy. Companies large and small that seek synergistic relationships develop business scenarios based on six steps:

1. A fundamental re-examination of their value proposition with periodic reassessments.

2. Deliberate decomposition of business processes to determine what activities are best performed internally or externally.

3. A regular realignment of skills, capabilities and competencies to fulfil the requirements of the business process.

4. Frequent appraisals of the technology infrastructure and its relativity to the business processes it serves.

5. A comprehensive method of communications applied to all parts of the organization.

6. A repurposing of management as a resource for operating groups within the firm.

To extend core business processes outside the traditional boundaries of a firm – or to outsource core and non-core process activities – demands that each external relationship must meet criteria establishing the extent of the relationship, as depicted in Figure 7.1.

Lindstrom makes a critical observation, noting that achieving operational synergy between two organizations depends, firstly, on an assess-

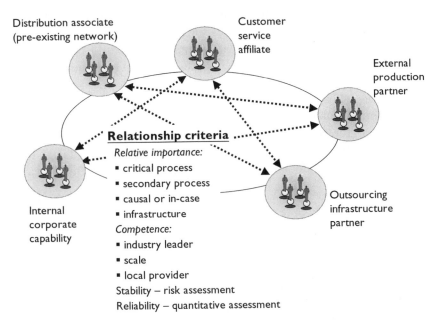

Figure 7.1 Relationship map

ment of the technological and communications infrastructures within each group, and, secondly, on a synchronization of the definitions and treatment of information, terms and data. After that, synergy depends on the establishment of which components of information captured at the point of control are the most accurate and reliable sources.[4] The key to establishing relationships that will sustain synergistic behaviour is having skilled workers who can place business issues into a global context. Senior managers, knowledge workers, practitioners and professionals should develop the skills that enable them to think strategically.

The Behaviour of Globally Skilled Workers

To compete in a global environment, an organization must leverage diversity by engaging a cross-cultural, multinational, highly talented workforce that starts at the boardroom, projecting a consistent vision throughout the organization. Leveraging knowledge assets, the ability to globalize, refining corporate competence, exploiting competitiveness, technological innovation and business transformation are all company-wide initiatives that require people within the firm to acquire new skills and develop competencies. A synconomy requires an organization to leverage technology and establish processes that aggregate skills into competencies which sense the market, prioritize opportunities, envision new business scenarios, adapt processes and adopt new ideas to deliver value to customers in increasingly new ways, as illustrated in Figure 7.2.

Developing globally focused skills is not restricted to middle-level managers and other professional staff. These new skills must be embraced by the entire organization while bringing together talent from many geographic and cultural sources. The Conference Board ascertained why:

> Globalization involves more than merely selling or producing abroad. Corporate strategy and performance, acquisitions and divestitures, risk management, accounting and reporting, increasing scrutiny of corporate legal and civil behaviour around the world, and many other factors result in a highly complex global perspective. To successfully handle such a complex mechanism, senior management should be culturally and nationally diverse.[5]

The Conference Board's working group noted issues which hold a significant learning for organizations trying to come to grips with increasing diversity. Its participants realized that the quality of the corporate board members experiences at meetings increases when board meetings are few per year and longer in duration. More surprisingly, members placed a high value on the conversational exchange during and after dinner, a result of having to arrive the day before and spend the night. The higher touch factor, coupled with moving the location of the meetings and structuring a more intensive orientation for new board members, was rated as providing a higher overall value than simply supplementing meeting with technologies such as video teleconferencing and conference

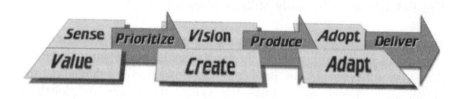

Figure 7.2 Map of corporate competencies

calls.[6] The value of a face-to-face human exchange is that it creates a shared tactile experience which establishes an informal bond between individuals in an organization. This physical meeting humanizes the relationship that often becomes sterile, albeit speedy, in the increasing volley of daily eMails. The personalization of management is similar to the higher touch relationships with customers. Leaders separated by distance in a transnational firm must work harder at regular, predictable intervals of communications between subordinates and peers.

The significant learning that the Conference Board's research indicates is that at board level, conferencing technology is most effective when used in narrowly defined, highly specific topics. The insight that is most applicable to all firms engaged in meetings requiring a creative interchange on complex issues is that face-to-face meetings and technology-enhanced meetings both have value, but not to the exclusion of each other.[7] Technology has its place in the value equation; when used effectively, it can be leveraged to facilitate highly focused meetings with face-to-face meetings, providing organizations with sufficient sensing mechanisms to stay abreast of customer, market and local community behaviours. It is also evident that a more culturally diverse organization at all levels is more agile in its ability to sense and interpret variations in customer requirements and competitive pressures. Overall, it can be argued that cultural diversity is a prerequisite for building the perspectives and thought leadership necessary to engage in the complex business environment that is emerging.

Cultivating Thought Leadership

Thought leadership is as much an art as a science. It is an essential ingredient for firms in a synconomy because, in the process of cultivating thought leadership, the organization discovers new solutions and becomes more adept at adapting resources to meet the challenges described in business scenarios. From a practical point of view, cultivating thought leaders makes every employee involved smarter by association. The materials produced by thought leaders are most often a by-product, not a direct solution to a problem. Mainly, thought leadership comes from aggregating many solutions to which one has been exposed over time into applied solutions for various business scenarios. By connecting similar processes, products, technologies or organizational structures to a current problem, the thought leader brings a viewpoint that satisfies one of four basic levels of perspectives: cross-industry insight; industry intelligence; industry best

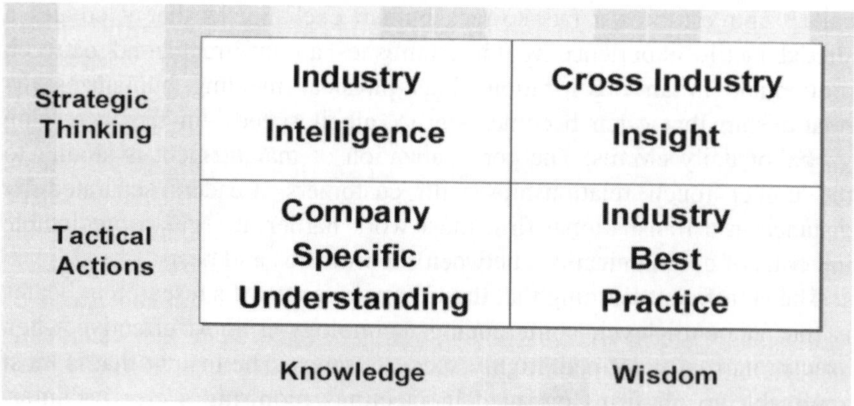

Strategic Thinking	**Industry Intelligence**	**Cross Industry Insight**
Tactical Actions	**Company Specific Understanding**	**Industry Best Practice**
	Knowledge	Wisdom

Figure 7.3 The thought leadership model

practice; or company-specific understanding. These perspectives can be organized into four areas of applicability to a set of business conditions or problems, as illustrated in Figure 7.3.

Many ideas come from one or all four of these domains and are combined, matched or synthesized to meet similar circumstances. For example, a consultant who is engaged in redesigning the mortgage process may have consulted with several financial institutions; the new process design reflects a combination of ideas from many firms. Additionally, a technologist many see the potential of newer technology and anticipate the next generation of capabilities even before they are available. This foresight can be used to design new business processes and procedures which can be rapidly moved into place when the technology becomes available. Thought leadership ideas and innovations originate from a variety of unrelated sources, and often coalesce together at a time when a new challenge presents the right conditions. Establishing a mechanism to acquire thought leadership and a process to cultivate it within a firm is necessary for companies in a synconomy because many of their potential partners may not have an understanding of how to achieve a synergistic relationship, and as a consequence a firm may play a leadership role in the relationship.

Generating Cross-organizational and Transnational Value

Every organization has a realized and unrealized potential to add value in a network of global businesses. However, many organizations struggle with assessing their potential and directing resources to achieve new levels of productivity and profitability. This problem is acutely true in organizations that now appreciate that they too are engaged in a single global marketplace. Therefore, companies must proactively address the implications of globalization, disintermediation, culture, religion and other social factors to devise new value propositions to customers and deliver reasonable returns to shareholders. To help to measure and refine their global potential, Figure 7.4 provides a framework for thinking about how to link goals and objectives to the establishment of corporate competencies.

Organizations can hedge their bets on how to embrace the new global reach of business by establishing external relationships and slowly externalizing portions of business processes in an effort to free internal resources to focus on capitalizing on the organization's core competencies. Mixing internal and external resources between core and non-core process execution demands that corporations should develop a new competency of coordinating resources under complex business conditions. However, establishing external relationships and participating in a global network of value is indeed the clearest path towards long-term viability in the emerging competitive marketplace.

In summary, businesses today are embracing an emerging, complex, global marketplace where logistics and distribution become critical mechanisms that can either, and with equal swiftness, propel a firm to profitability or push it to the brink of insolvency. Technology reduces time and space to commodities that are easily traded for capabilities. Thus it is heartbreaking as a global citizen to realize how easily corporations and nations such as the US can mobilize and distribute military power to almost any corner of the globe in a few days, and yet the world still struggles to distribute foodstuffs to all people on a daily basis. One can only hope that when all nations are truly global in a synconomy, some of the world's most dreadful problems will indeed be solved as quickly and efficiently as technology and the cleverness of individuals allows it.

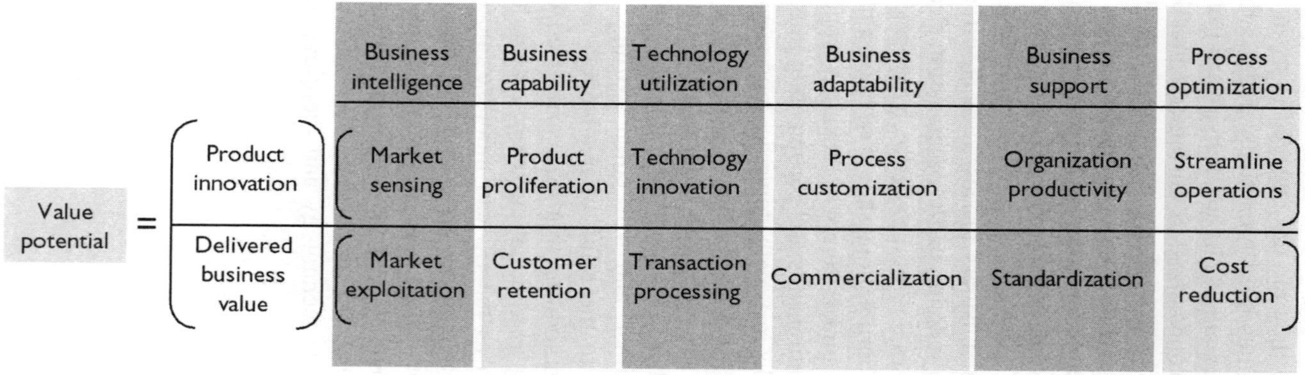

Figure 7.4 Value potential model

Notes

1 M. Sirower, *The Synergy Trap: How Companies Lose the Acquisition Game*, London: Free Press, 1997, p. 21.

2 M. Lindstrom, *Clicks, Bricks & Brands*, London: Kogan Page, 2001, p. 122.

3 H. Igor Ansoff, 'Synergy and capabilities', in A. Campbell and K. S. Luchs (eds), *Strategic Synergy*, London: International Thompson Business Press, 1998, p. 25.

4 Lindstrom, *Clicks, Bricks & Brands*, p. 131.

5 The Conference Board, *Globalizing the Board of Directors: Trends and Strategies*, New York: The Conference Board, Inc., 1999, Research Report 1242-99-RR, p. 5.

6 The Conference Board, *Globalizing the Board of Directors*, p. 28.

7 The Conference Board, *Globalizing the Board of Directors*, p. 28.

BIBLIOGRAPHY

H. Igor Ansoff, 'Synergy and capabilities', in A. Campbell and K. S. Luchs (eds), *Strategic Synergy*, London: International Thompson Business Press, 1998.

D. Archibugi and J. Michie, 'The globalization of technology: a new taxonomy', in D. Archibugi and J. Michie (eds), *Technology, Globalization and Economic Performance*, Cambridge: Cambridge University Press, 1997.

B. Benoit, 'Wal-Mart finds German failures hard to swallow', *Financial Times*, 12 October 2000.

M. J. Blaine, *Co-operation in International Business*, Aldershot: Avebury, 1994.

T. Blair, 'Keynote address', Labour Party Conference, October 1 2002, source: www.itv.com/news.

J. Blythe, *The Essence of Consumer Behaviour*, Harlow: Pearson Education, 1997.

R. Bruce and R. Ireland, *Migration to Value Chain. Collaboration through CPFR*, VCC Associates, available at www.vccassociates.com.

R. Buckminster Fuller, *Untitled Epic Poem on the History of Industrialization*, Charlotte: Heritage Printers, 1962.

R. Buckminster Fuller, *The World Game: Integrative Resource Utilization Planning Tool*, Carbondale: Southern Illinois University, 1971.

R. Buckminster Fuller, *Synergistics: Explorations in the Geometry of Thinking*, New York: Macmillan Publishing, 1975.

R. Buckminster Fuller, *Operating Manual for Spaceship Earth*, New York: Arkana-Penguin Group, 1991.

R. Camrass and M, Farncombe, *The Atomic Corporation: A Rational Proposal for Uncertain Times*, Oxford: Capstone Publishing, 2001.

M. Castells and P. Hall, *Technopoles of the World: The Making of Twenty-first-century Industrial Complexes*, London: Routledge, 1994.

'Central Information Management Unit. White Paper on the Vision and Strategy for the Attainment of E-Government', Blata: Government of Malta, 2000, Available at www.cimu.gov.mt/documents/egovhitepaper_for_cimu_website.pdf.

J. Champy, *X-Engineering the Corporation. Reinvent your Business in the Digital Age*, London: Hodder & Stoughton, 2002.

A. Chattell, *Creating Value in the Digital Era*, Basingstoke: Macmillan – now Palgrave Macmillan, 1998.

Y. Chen and C. Shahabi, 'Improving user profiles for E-commerce by genetic algorithms', Los Angeles: Integrated Media Systems Centre and Computer Sciences Department, University of Southern California, available at www.imsc.usc.edu/research/, November 2002.

C. Christensen, *The Innovator's Dilemma: How Disruptive Technologies can Destroy Established Market*, Cambridge, MA: Harvard University Press, 1997.

T. Davenport and L. Prusak, *Working Knowledge: How Organizations Manage What They Know*, Boston: Harvard Business School Press, 1998.

W. H. Davidow and M. S. Malone, *The Virtual Corporation. Structuring and Revitalizing the Corporation for the 21st Century*, London: Harper Business, 1993.

S. Davis and B. Davidson, *2020 Vision: Transform your Business Today to Succeed in Tomorrow's Economy*, London: Business Books, 1991.

J. DiVanna, *Redefining Financial Services: The New Renaissance in Value Propositions*, Basingstoke: Palgrave Macmillan, 2002.

J. DiVanna, *Thinking Beyond Technology: Creating New Value in Business*, Basingstoke: Palgrave Macmillan, 2002.

R. Donkin, 'Measuring the worth of human capital', *Financial Times*, 7 November 2002.

P. Drucker, 'The global economy and the nation state', *Foreign Affairs*, January/February 1997, **76**(1).

Dubai Strategy Forum, available at www.dubaistrategyforum.ae, November 2002.

eCommerce Times, Sherman Oaks: Triad Commerce Group, 17 May 2001, available at www.ecommercetimes.com/perl/story/9804.html.

'eEurope 2003: A cooperative effort to implement the Information Society in Europe', Action plan prepared by the candidate countries with the assistance of the European Commission, June 2001, available at www.map.es/csi/pdf/eEurope_2003.pdf.

H. Eisenberg, 'Reengineering and dumbsizing', *Quality Progress*, May 1997.

European Commission, *Towards a Knowledge-based Europe: The European Union and the Information Society*, Brussels: Directorate General for Press and Communications, October 2002, available at europa.eu.int/information_society/newsroom/documents/catalogue_en.pdf.

P. Evans and T. Wurster, 'Strategy and the new economics of information' in D. Tapscott (ed.), *Creating Value in the Network Economy*, Boston: Harvard Business School Press, 1999.

Financial Services Hybrid Products: Marketing the Second Wave, London: IBM Corporation White Paper, 2001, available at www.ibm.com/industries/financialservices/, September 2002.

P. Franczak, 'Value is in the eye of the beholder', *Consumer Markets*, KPMG LLP, August 1999, available online at usserve.us.kpmg.com/cm/article-archives/actual-articles/value.html, November 2002.

H. Freeman, 'Measuring globalization', *Globalization, Trade Liberalization and Benefits*, Chevy Chase: The Mark Twain Institute, July 2002.

M. S. Fridson (ed.) *Extraordinary Popular Delusions and the Madness of Crowds & Confusion de Confusiones*, New York: John Wiley, 1996.

L. Frimanson and J. Lind, 'The balanced scorecard and learning in business relationships', in H. Hakansson and J. Johanson (eds), *Business Network Learning*, Oxford: Elsevier Science, 2001.

D. Gardner, 'Slim pickings for the global brand in India', *Financial Times*, 11 October 2000.

N. Goldmann, 'The caring extranet: implementing extranet business communities', *Journal of Internet Banking and Commerce*, October 1999, **4**(1).

J. Hagel III and M. Singer, 'Unbundling the corporation', *Harvard Business Review*, March–April 1999, Reprint 99205.

R. Hagstrom, *The Warren Buffet Portfolio: Mastering the Power of the Focus Investment Strategy*, New York: John Wiley, 1999.

M. Hammer and J. Champy, *Reengineering the Corporation: A Manifesto for Business Revolution*, London: Nicholas Brealey, 2001.

C. Hampden-Turner and F. Trompenaars, *Building Cross-cultural Competence: How to Create Wealth from Conflicting Values*, Chichester: John Wiley, 2000.

C. Handy, 'Trust and the virtual organization', in D. Tapscott (ed.) *Creating Value in the Network Economy*, Boston: Harvard Business School Press, 1999.

C. Handy, *The Elephant and the Flea: Looking Backwards to the Future*, London: Hutchinson, 2001.

P. Hines, R. Lamming, D. Jones, P. Cousins and N. Rich, *Value Stream Management: Strategy and Excellence in the Supply Chain*, Harlow: Pearson Education, 2000.

S. Hoffman, 'Clash of globalizations' *Foreign Affairs*, July/August 2002, **81**(4).

A. S. Hornsby, *Oxford Advanced Learner's Dictionary of Current English*, Oxford: Oxford University Press, 1991.

B. Ingresoll-Dayton and S. Jayaratne, 'Measuring effectiveness of social work practice: beyond the year 2002', in P. Raffoul and C. Aaron McNeece (eds), *Future Issues for Social Work Practice*, Boston: Allyn & Bacon, 1996.

S. James and C. Nobes, *The Economics of Taxation: Principles, Policy and Practice*, Hertfordshire: Prentice Hall Europe, 1996.

J. C. Jarillo, *Strategic Networks: Creating the Borderless Organization*, Oxford: Butterworth-Heinemann, 1993.

G. Junne, 'The end of the dinosaurs? Do technologies lead to the decline of multinations', in M. Talalay, C. Farrands and R. Tooze (eds), *Technology, Culture and Competitiveness: Change and the World Political Economy*, London: Routledge, 1997.

J. Kay, 'Profits without honour', *Financial Times*, 29/30 June 2002, p. 13.

S. R. Khandker, *Fighting Poverty with Microcredit: Experience in Bangladesh*, Oxford: Oxford University Press, 1998.

R. Kaplan and D. Norton, *The Strategy Focused Organization*, Boston: Harvard Business School Press, 2001.

J. M. Keynes, *The General Theory of Employment, Interest and Money*. London: Macmillan – now Palgrave Macmillan, 1946.

J. M. Keynes, *A Treatise on Money (1930). The Collected Writings of J. M. Keynes*, vol. V, London: Macmillan – now Palgrave Macmillan, 1971.

P. Krugman, 'Is capitalism too productive?', *Foreign Affairs*, September/October 1997, **76**(5).

R. Kugler, 'Marketing in East Asia: the fallacies and the realities', in D. Dayao (ed.), *Asian Business Wisdom: Lessons from the Region's Best and Brightest Business Leaders*, Singapore: John Wiley, 2000.

P. Lau, 'The seven deadly sins of service management', in D. Dayao (ed.), *Asian Business Wisdom: Lessons from the Region's Best and Brightest Business Leaders*, Singapore: John Wiley, 2000.

D. Li, 'Chinese family values in transition', in D. Dayao (ed.), *Asian Business Wisdom: Lessons from the Region's Best and Brightest Business Leaders*, Singapore: John Wiley, 2000.

M. Lindstrom, *Clicks, Bricks & Brands*, London: Kogan Page, 2001.

J. Lipnack and J. Stamps, *The TeamNet Factor: Bringing the Power of Boundary Crossing Into the Heart of Your Business*, Essex Junction: Oliver Wight, 1993.

J. Lipnack and J. Stamps, *Virtual Teams*, New York: John Wiley, 1997.

E. Luce, 'Hard sell to a billion consumers', *Financial Times*, 25 April 2002.

N. Machiavelli, *Discourses on Livy*, Oxford: Oxford University Press, 1997.

P. C. Mackay, 'Extraordinary popular delusions and the madness of crowds', in M. Fridson, (ed.), *Extraordinary Popular Delusions and the Madness of Crowds & Confusión de Confusiones*, New York: John Wiley, 1996, p. vii.

T. Malone and R. Laubacher, 'The dawn of the e-lance economy', in D. Tapscott (ed.), *Creating Value in the Network Economy*, Boston: Harvard Business School Press, 1999.

J. Mathews, 'Power shift', *Foreign Affairs*, January/February 1997, **76**(1).

M. McIntosh, D. Leipziger, K. Jones and G. Coleman, *Corporate Citizenship: Successful Strategies for Responsible Companies*, London: Financial Times Management, 1998.

W. Mead, 'Roller-coaster capitalism', *Foreign Affairs*, January/February 1997, **76**(1).

J. Micklethwait and A. Wooldridge, *A Future Perfect*, London: William Heinemann, 2000.

D. Mills, *e-Leadership: Guiding Your Business to Success in the New Economy*, Paramas: Prentice Hall, 2001.

P. S. Mills and J. R. Presley, *Islamic Finance: Theory and Practice*, Basingstoke: Macmillan – now Palgrave Macmillan, 1999.

M. Moschandreas, *Business Economics*, London: Routledge, 1994.

J. Naisbitt, *Global Paradox*, London: Nicholas Brealey, 1994.

J. Naisbitt and P. Aburdene, *Megatrends 2000. The Next Ten Years … Major Changes in Your Life and World*, London: Sidgwick & Jackson, 1990.

B. Nalebuff and A. Brandenburger, *Co-opetition*, New York: Doubleday, 1996.

J. Newhouse, 'Europe's rising regionalism', *Foreign Affairs*, January/February 1997, **76**(1).

K. Nordström and J. Ridderstråle, *Funky Business: Talent Makes Capital Dance*, London: Pearson Education, 2000.

'Office of the Prime Minister: Central Information Management Unit, e-Government Interoperability Framework', Blata: Government of Malta, version 1.0, July 2002, available at www.cimu.gov.mt/documents/cimu_t_0001_2002.pdf.

V. Packard, *The Waste Makers*, London: Longmans, Green, 1960.

J. Parikh, 'Managing by detached involvement', in D. Dayao (ed.) *Asian Business Wisdom: Lessons from the Region's Best and Brightest Business Leaders*, Singapore: John Wiley, 2000.

C. Pass and B. Lowes, *Dictionary of Economics*, Leicester: Unwin Hyman, 1999.

K. Phillips, 'The cycle of financial scandal', *The New York Times on the Web*, 17 July 2002, available at www.nytimes.com/2002/07/17/opinion/17Phil.html.

A. Pike, 'Regions miss out on new economy', *Financial Times*, 12 March 2001.

J. Pine and J. Gilmore, *The Experience Economy: Work is Theatre & Every Business a Stage*, Boston: Harvard Business School Press, 1999.

D. Pink, M. Warshaw, S. Davis et al., 'Free agent nation & free-agent almanac', *Fast Company*, December/ January, **12**, 1998.

M. Porter, *Competitive Advantage*, New York: Free Press, 1985.

M. Porter, 'Strategy and the Internet', *Harvard Business Review*, March 2001.

M. Porter and M. Skapinker, 'Death of the net threat', *Financial Times*, 21 March 2001.

G. Probst, S. Raub and K. Romhardt, *Managing Knowledge: Building Blocks for Success*, Chichester: John Wiley, 2000.

J. Rayport and J. Sviokla, 'Exploiting the virtual value chain', in D. Tapscott (ed.), *Creating Value in the Network Economy*, Boston: Harvard Business School Press, 1999.

R. Reich, *The Work of Nations: Preparing Ourselves for 21st-century Capitalism*, New York: Alfred A. Knopf, 1991.

T. Renkema, *The IT Value Quest: How to Capture the Business Value of IT-Based Infrastructure*, Chichester: John Wiley, 2000.

M. Roche, *Rethinking Citizenship: Welfare, Ideology and Change in Modern Society*, Cambridge: Polity Press, 1992.

G. Schröder, 'Shaping industry on the anvil of Europe', *Financial Times*, 29 April 2002.

C. Shearman, 'Localisation within globalization', in M. Talalay, C. Farrands and R. Tooze (eds), *Technology, Culture and Competitiveness: Change and the World Political Economy*, London: Routledge, 1997.

M. Shillito and D. Marle, *Value: Its Measurement, Design, and Management*, Chichester: John Wiley, 1992.

T. Siems, 'Reengineering social security in the new economy', *Social Security Privatization*, (22), 23 January, 2001.

M. Sirower, *The Synergy Trap: How Companies Lose the Acquisition Game*, London: Free Press, 1997.

W. Sombart, *Luxury and Capitalism*, Ann Arbor: University of Michigan Press, 1967.

C. Stabell and Ø. Fjeldstad 'On value chains and other value configurations', Working Paper 1995/20, Sandvika, Norway: Norwegian School of Management, 1995.

C. Stabell and Ø. Fjeldstad 'Configuring value for competitive advantage: On chains, shops and networks', *Strategic Management Journal*, 1998, **19**(5).

T. Stewart, *The Wealth of Knowledge: Intellectual Capital and the Twenty-first Century Organization*, London, Nicholas Brealey, 2001.

D. Sutherland, 'Attracting and retaining world-class talent: the employee value proposition', Baltimore: Business Innovation Consortium, available at www.bicnow.com/what/EVPPOV.pdf.

P. Sutherland, 'Why we should embrace globalization', *Finance & Development*, quarterly magazine of the International Monetary Fund, September 2002, **39**(3).

K. Sveiby, *The New Organizational Wealth: Managing and Measuring Knowledge-based Assets*, San Francisco: Berret-Koehler, 1997.

K. Tateisi, 'Treating "big business syndrome"', in D. Dayao (ed.), *Asian Business Wisdom: Lessons from the Region's Best and Brightest Business Leaders*, Singapore: John Wiley, 2000.

The Conference Board, *The CEO Challenge: Top Marketplace and Management Issues 2001*, New York: The Conference Board, 2001.

The Conference Board, *Globalizing the Board of Directors: Trends and Strategies*, New York: The Conference Board, 1999, Research Report 1242-99-RR.

The Scottish Office, *Scotland: Towards the Knowledge Economy*, available at www.scotland.gov.uk/library/documents-w9/knec-02.html.

ThinkCycle, *Open Collaborative Design*, available at www.thinkcycle.org/.

M. Treacy and F. Wiersema, *The Discipline of Market Leaders*, Reading, MA, Perseus Books, 1997.

P. Underhill, *Why we Buy: The Science of Shopping*, London: Orion, 1999.

V. Walsh, 'Technology and competitiveness of small countries: review,' in C. Freeman and B.-A. Lundval (eds), *Small Countries Facing the Technological Revolution*, London: Pinter, 1988.

I. Warde, *Islamic Finance in the Global Economy*, Edinburgh: Edinburgh University Press, 2000.

D. West, *Assessing E-Government: The Internet, Democracy, and Service Delivery by State and Federal Governments*, Providence: Brown University, 2000, available at www1.worldbank.org/publicsector/egov/EGovReportUS00.html.

'A White Paper on Enterprise, Skills and Innovation: Opportunity for all in a World of Change', United Kingdom: Department of Trade and Industry, available at www.dti.gov.uk/opportunityforall/pages/contents.html, December, 2002.

F. Wiersema, *Customer Intimacy*, London: HarperCollins, 1998.

W. Wriston, *The Twilight of Sovereignty*, New York: Charles Scribner & Sons, 1992.

W. Wriston, 'Bits, bytes and diplomacy', *Foreign Affairs*, January/February 1997, **76**(1): 173: 4.

G. Young, 'Culture and technological imperative', in M. Talalay, C. Farrands and R. Tooze (eds), *Technology, Culture and Competitiveness: Change and the World Political Economy*, London: Routledge, 1997.

INDEX

A

ADRs 101
Advisory Commission on Electronic
  Commerce 143
Alliances 27
Amazon.com 95
America On Line 94, 142
  AOL Brazil 94
American Depository Receipts *see* ADRs
Apple Computer 142
Asian Business 85
Assets 25
ATMs 41
Automated Teller Machines *see* ATMs

B

Balanced Scorecard 113
Bangladesh 117–8
Banking Industry 93–4
Bayer 192
Big Brother 145
Big Business Syndrome 112–13
Biometric Recognition 4
Black Death 174
Brand Image 46, 106, 119, 189, 198
Branding 118–20
  Co-branding 120
  Cultural branding 120
  Niche-branding 120
  Religious branding 120
Brown University 124, 125
Buckminster Fuller, Richard 12, 67–8,
  110, 169–70
Buffet, Warren 130
Bureaucracy 22, 137
Business-to-business 206

Business Change 15–16
Business Competency 23
Business Cycles 3, 9, 13
Business Innovation Consortium 175
Business Intelligence 111–12, 200
Business Models 5
  Creating customer value model 35, 37–8
  Product-selling business model 35–7
Business Processes 4, 6, 12, 22, 26

C

Capability 25
Capital 100–1, 104, 107
  Flow of 100–1, 103, 139
Capital Market 11, 101, 107–8
Capitalism 110
Celemi International 171
Chat-rooms 62
China 85
Cisco Systems 142
Client–server Computing 4
Coca-Cola 36–7
Cold War 137
Collaboration 20, 24, 58, 61, 63–4, 84,
  89–91, 119, 121, 165
  Collaborative commerce 23, 62–3
  Collaborative skills 50
  Cross-cultural collaboration 60
  Multi-organizational collaborations 60
  and Nation states 58–9
Collaborative Planning, Forecasting and
  Replenishing Committee 206
Communications 82, 90–1
Community of Practice 62
Competency 25, 114, 204
Competition 3, 11, 13, 18, 20, 34, 54, 76,
  94, 104, 194, 199